MORAL

An Introduction to Ethics and Critical Thinking

REVISED EDITION

Charles K. Fink

Hamilton Books
An Imprint of
Rowman & Littlefield
Lanham • Boulder • New York • Toronto • Plymouth, UK

Library of Congress Control Number: 2016950980
ISBN: 978-0-7618-6842-2 (pbk : alk. paper)
eISBN: 978-0-7618-6843-9

⊖™ The paper used in this publication meets the minimum
requirements of American National Standard for Information
Sciences—Permanence of Paper for Printed Library Materials,
ANSI Z39.48-1992

For Chrissy,
Kedric, Michael, Andy, Andrea,
and Kaia

Contents

Preface

Morality sometimes conflicts with self-interest. Suppose you are in a position to cheat on an important test. You realize that cheating is wrong, but why should this matter to you? Why be honest? Or suppose you find a wallet—containing a large sum of money—lying on a sidewalk. You might keep it, or you might return it to its owner. Of course, the right thing to do would be to return the wallet. But why do the right thing? Generally stated, the question raised here is this: Given the choice between morality and self-interest, why be moral? You may be tempted to say, "Well, because it's the right thing to do." But the question is why this sort of answer—an appeal to morality—should matter to you at all. Maybe you should care about being moral, but why? And why should you care more about morality than about your own self-interest in those cases in which they conflict?

You might claim that morality and self-interest only seem to conflict. In reality, it is in everyone's best interest to be moral. One argument that might be given for this is the following:

(1) God rewards people for being moral and punishes people for being immoral, if not in the present life, then in the afterlife.
(2) It is in everyone's best interest to receive God's rewards and to avoid God's punishments.

Therefore:

(3) It is in everyone's best interest to be moral.

There is another version of this argument that rests on the doctrine of *karma* rather than on the existence of God. According to this doctrine—accepted by

Buddhism, Hinduism, and other Indian religions—the good that we do invariably has good consequences for us, and the evil that we do invariably has bad consequences for us. We reap what we sow, if not in this lifetime, then in future lifetimes. If this is true, then, of course, it is in our own best interest to be moral.

Many people would find this argument convincing, but not all. How do we know that God exists? How do we know that there is an afterlife? Even if God does exist, why should we believe that God rewards good behavior and punishes bad behavior? Similar questions can be raised about the alternative version of the argument. Why should we accept the doctrine of *karma*? Why should we believe in reincarnation?

Another argument that might be advanced for the claim that it is in everyone's best interest to be moral is the following:

(1) People tend to treat us as we treat them: if we treat others well, they tend to treat us well in return; if we treat others badly, they tend to treat us badly in return.

(2) It is in everyone's best interest to be treated well by others.

Therefore:

(3) It is in everyone's best interest to treat others well. (Insofar as behaving morally involves treating other people well, it is in everyone's best interest to behave morally.)

This argument, unlike the previous one, does not rest on controversial assumptions. But what about the reasoning? It may be true that people *tend* to treat us as we treat them, but there are exceptions. Sometimes people treat us badly even when we treat them well. Sometimes people are simply not in a position to reciprocate or retaliate. Why should you help someone who can never return the favor? If you can lie, or cheat, or steal without anyone knowing about it, why shouldn't you? The premises of the above argument may be true, but the conclusion does not follow from them; what follows is that it *tends* to be in everyone's best interest to treat others morally.

It may be rational to be moral, but neither of the two arguments we have considered establishes this. It is significant, though, that most people do not recognize this as a problem. Most people care about morality even if they are unable to explain why. This may be, as some research suggests, ingrained in human nature. (For a thorough discussion of this possibility, see Marc Hauser's *Moral Minds*. In *Taking Darwin Seriously*, Michael Ruse argues that evolution has engineered human beings to be moral.) It is also worth noting that people care about having reasons for the things they believe. The question "Why be moral?" poses a problem for us only because it is not immediately apparent what rational grounds there might be for living a moral life. Despite the professions of faith people sometimes make, people like to have reasons for the things they believe. This may also be ingrained in human nature. According to a long-standing tradition, dating back to Aristotle, what distinguishes human beings from other animals is our rationality.

This is a book about moral reasoning, or "ethics and critical thinking." Ethics is a branch of philosophy concerned with the analysis of moral ideas. It tries to explain, not only why morality should matter to us, but what morality is all about. Is morality entirely conventional, or does it have an objective status? What is the relationship between morality and religion? Do we have moral knowledge, or only moral opinions? What is the right thing to do? What should we say about tough moral issues—such as the problem of abortion, euthanasia, or war? Ethics is a discipline which tries to answer such questions. Critical thinking, on the other hand, is not a discipline but a skill. It is the ability to analyze ideas and evaluate reasons for belief, among other skills in reasoning. A book on ethics and critical thinking, therefore, seeks to provide rational grounds for moral belief, or at least to provide students with the skills needed to rationally formulate such beliefs for themselves.

This book covers issues within the three main divisions of moral philosophy—meta-ethics, normative ethics, and applied ethics—with careful attention to the role of argumentation in the study of ethics. The first chapter introduces ideas from elementary logic, distinguishes between two types of moral arguments, and discusses fallacies that commonly occur in moral reasoning. It contains numerous examples and exercises to provoke discussion and to help students develop their critical-thinking skills. (There is an appendix at the end of the book which provides additional, more technical information about arguments.) The second chapter focuses on one of the central problems of meta-ethics: Does morality have an objective status, or does it somehow depend upon us? Various possibilities are explored—cultural relativism, personal relativism, moral subjectivism, and moral nihilism—and the conclusion is reached that there are indeed objective moral facts. The third chapter is devoted to normative ethics and focuses on the analysis of right action. It explains and critically evaluates egoism, altruism, utilitarianism, Kantian ethics, the divine command theory, the theory of moral rights, and virtue ethics. The remaining chapters cover sundry issues in applied ethics and political philosophy—abortion, euthanasia, meat eating, political authority, economic justice, crime and punishment, war and terrorism.

This book has several noteworthy features. One, of course, is the concentration on moral reasoning. Another is the inclusion of several topics from political philosophy. The chapter on political authority deals with the justification for governmental coercion. The chapter on wealth and poverty connects the problem of poverty with the institution of capitalist ownership, lays out both the utilitarian and the libertarian arguments for capitalism, examines the concept of property rights, and makes a case for democratic socialism. The chapter on punishment questions the right of governments to punish criminals and, after reviewing the traditional approaches to this problem, raises the possibility that governments cannot effectively deter crime without widespread rights violations. The chapter on war places the problem in its modern context: Can we consistently condemn terrorism and yet condone military action? There are also numerous references to historical and current events. There are discussions of honor killings in the West Bank, the "dump families" of Cambodia, the social organization of Kalahari Bushmen, the conditions of factory-farmed animals, slavery and indentured servitude in colonial America, brutal forms of execution, civilian casualties in the Iraq War—and much more. To help students build a philosophical vocabulary, there is a glossary at the end of the book.

Some of the material included in this book has appeared elsewhere. The first two chapters are based upon modules prepared for the Ethics Curriculum Project, a program of the Youth Ethics Initiative aimed at integrating ethics into the Miami-Dade County public school system. Sections of the sixth chapter are based on two previously published articles: "The Predation Argument," *Between the Species*, August 2005; and "Animals and the Ethics of Domination," *Between the Species*, August 2006. Some of the material in Chapter 9 appeared in "Buddhism, Punishment, and Reconciliation," *Journal of Buddhist Ethics*, May 2012.

This project evolved over a number of years, and I am grateful to my students for their feedback on the original version of this text. My debts to teachers, friends, family, and colleagues are numerous. In particular, I wish to thank Howard Pospesel—one of my teachers from the University of Miami—and Amy Lund and Mark Neunder—two of my friends and colleagues at Miami Dade College—for their comments and criticisms.

Charles K. Fink
Miami, Florida
June 2016

— arguments
— Moral syllogisms
— fallacies

1. Moral Reasons

The most fundamental critical-thinking skill is the ability to evaluate reasons for belief. Despite the skepticism people sometimes express about morality—a topic we will explore in the next chapter—people nonetheless have moral opinions and often try to support these opinions with reasons. How do we distinguish good moral reasons from bad ones? Is it possible to prove anything in ethics? In this chapter, we will discuss some of the concepts involved in evaluating moral arguments and lay the groundwork for the remainder of the book.

1.1. Arguments

Moral arguments often advance bold conclusions. In a famous article, Australian philosopher Peter Singer calls into question the morality of the consumer lifestyle with the following argument:

> [S]uffering and death from lack of food, shelter, and medical care are bad. . . . [I]f it is in our power to prevent something very bad from happening, without thereby sacrificing anything morally significant, we ought, morally, to do it. . . . When we buy new clothes not to keep ourselves warm but to look "well-dressed" we are not providing for an important need. We would not be sacrificing anything significant if we were to continue to wear our old clothes, and give the money to famine relief. By doing so, we would be preventing another person from starving. It follows . . . that we ought to give money away, rather than spend it on clothes which we do not need to keep us warm. (Singer 1972: 231, 233)

Singer claims that it is morally wrong to spend money on unnecessary things when this money could be used to help people suffering from extreme poverty (a category that includes, according to recent estimates, 1.2 billion people, or one-sixth of humanity). His argument for this claim can be reconstructed, step by step, as follows:

(1) Suffering and death from lack of food, shelter, and medical care are bad.

(2) If it is within our power to prevent something bad from happening without thereby sacrificing anything morally significant, we ought to do so.

(3) We would not be sacrificing anything morally significant if we did not spend our money on unnecessary things, such as unneeded clothes, but instead donated this money to effective humanitarian organizations. In this way, we could prevent suffering and death from lack of food, shelter, and medical care.

Therefore:

(4) Rather than spending our money on unnecessary things, we ought to donate this money to effective humanitarian organizations.

Should we accept this argument? Singer imagines a case in which a small child is drowning in a pond. You could easily save the child's life by stepping into the water and pulling the child to safety. You choose not to, however, because you don't want to ruin your new pair of suede shoes. You abandon the child, and the child drowns. Obviously, your behavior in this imaginary example is deplorable. If you are in a position to save a child's life without thereby sacrificing anything "morally significant" then you ought to do so. But consider this. Rather than spending money on a new pair of shoes, you could contribute this money to an effective humanitarian organization, such as UNICEF or Oxfam, which uses the funds it collects from donors to provide life-saving assistance to desperately poor people. (As many as 1.5 million children under the age of five die annually from diarrhea. A rehydration tablet, which can reverse the deadly effects of diarrhea, costs only pennies. Tuberculosis kills two million people every year, including 250,000 children. The disease can be cured in most cases for between $10 and $20 per patient.) Is there a morally significant difference between refusing to save a child's life because you don't want to ruin your new pair of shoes, and refusing to save a child's life because you would rather spend your money on a new pair of shoes? If not, then the spending habits of affluent consumers are morally indefensible. As Singer argues, rather than spending our money on unnecessary things, we ought to donate this money to charitable organizations.

An "argument," in the philosophical sense of the term, is something that embodies reasons for belief. When presenting an argument, what is argued for is called the "conclusion" of the argument, and the reasons given for believing the conclusion are called the "premises." In the above example, statement (4) is the conclusion of the argument, and statements (1), (2), and (3) are the premises. In some cases, the conclusion of an argument may only be implied, or a premise may be assumed without being explicitly stated. In such cases, it is necessary to fill in some of the steps in reasoning. Consider, for example, the following argument on the abortion issue, given by Baruch Brody:

> The most obvious reason for supposing that it is permissible to perform an abortion in order to save the life of the mother, even though the fetus is a human being, is that such an abortion would be a permissible act of defending oneself. After all, the fetus's continued existence poses a threat to the life of the mother which she can meet, if necessary, by the taking of the life of the fetus. (Brody 1973: 105)

Brody argues that it is permissible for a woman to have an abortion when pregnancy threatens her life. But what *exactly* is his argument? Fully spelled out, his reasoning runs as follows:

(1) It is permissible to kill in self-defense.
(2) When pregnancy threatens a woman's life, having an abortion (killing the fetus) is an act of self-defense.

Therefore:

(3) It is permissible for a woman to have an abortion when pregnancy threatens her life.

valid

Is Brody's argument a good argument? His argument satisfies one important condition: if the premises are true, then the conclusion has to be true. This is what is meant by describing an argument as "valid." It is less clear whether Brody's argument satisfies another important condition. Even if it is permissible for you to kill in self-defense, is this permissible when the attacker is an innocent person, or your own child, or both? Suppose someone has plotted to kill you by wiring a bomb to a light switch inside your house. When your daughter returns from school, she will instinctively flip the light switch, triggering the device, killing you. You are gagged and tied up in the living room, but you have been able to free one hand. You hear your daughter turning a key in the front door. You reach underneath the sofa, where you keep a gun stashed. Would it be permissible for you to kill your daughter to prevent her from flipping the light switch? Arguably not, which suggests that it is not *always* permissible to kill in self-defense. The problem with Brody's argument, then, is not whether the reasoning is valid, but whether all the premises are true. A good argument, or what is called a "sound" argument, satisfies two conditions: first, the reasoning is valid; and second, all the premises are true.

1.2. Validity

Since even false propositions have logical implications, the conclusion of an argument can validly follow from the premises even if the premises are false. Consider, for example, the following rather strange argument:

> All circus acrobats are alcoholics. Hillary Clinton is a circus acrobat.
> Therefore, Hillary Clinton is an alcoholic.

No one should be persuaded by this argument. But is it invalid? To describe an argument as valid means only this: that the conclusion is logically related to the premises in such a way that *if* the premises are true then (as a matter of logical necessity) the conclusion must be true. The above argument satisfies this definition: *if* all circus acrobats are alcoholics and Hillary Clinton is a circus acrobat, then Hillary Clinton must be an alcoholic. This argument is unsound, not because the reasoning is flawed, but because the premises are false. (To repeat: for an argument to be sound, the reasoning must be valid *and* all the premises must be true.)

Try to evaluate the following arguments as valid or invalid. (For additional exercises, see the Appendix: Argument Patterns.)

1. All Christians are monotheists. No monotheists are atheists. Therefore, no Christians are atheists.

2. All murderers are criminals. All criminals should be punished. Therefore, all murderers should be punished.

3. All Libras are psychics. All psychics read tarot cards. No Capricorns read tarot cards. So, no Capricorns are Libras.

4. All circus clowns are highly trained professionals. So Bobo must be a highly trained professional, since he is a circus clown.

5. If lying is against the will of God, then it is wrong. Lying is wrong. Therefore, it must be against the will of God.

6. Only people born in the United States can become president. Therefore, Donald Trump can become president, because he was born in the United States.

7. All Marxists are atheists, and all communists are atheists. So, all Marxists are communists.

8.   The moral standards that people should live by are the standards adopted by their culture. Therefore, there is no moral standard that all people should live by, because there is no moral standard that is adopted by every culture.

9.   You can't deny that aliens visited our planet thousands of years ago given that millions of people believe that this happened.

10. All Darwinians are evolutionists. No creationists are evolutionists. All fundamentalists are creationists. Therefore, no fundamentalists are Darwinians.

1.3. Moral Syllogisms

The following two arguments share something in common:

> It is wrong to kill an innocent human being. To commit euthanasia is to kill an innocent human being. Therefore, euthanasia is wrong.

> It is wrong to kill an innocent human being. To have an abortion is to kill an innocent human being. Therefore, abortion is wrong.

Though they reach different conclusions, both arguments rest on the same general principle: that it is wrong to kill an innocent human being. This is what is meant by a "moral syllogism." A moral syllogism is an argument in which we reach a moral conclusion on the basis of a general moral principle. This type of argument illustrates the role that rules play in moral reasoning. According to some ethicists, moral decision-making rests upon a handful of rules, or perhaps upon one basic principle. If this is true, then moral reasoning is fundamentally "syllogistic."

What questions should we ask when evaluating such an argument? A moral syllogism applies a moral rule to a particular situation or issue. So one question we should ask is whether there are relevant exceptions to the rule. (Is it *always* wrong to kill an innocent human being, as both of the above arguments assume? Or is it just ordinarily wrong?) Another question we should ask is whether the rule has been correctly applied. (Is it true that a human fetus is a human being, as the second argument assumes?) Let us see how these considerations come into play when evaluating the above two arguments.

There appear to be two reasons why it is ordinarily wrong to kill an innocent human being: one is that it violates the victim's right to life; the other is that it inflicts a tremendous loss upon the victim. Yet, neither one of these considerations would explain why voluntary euthanasia is wrong. First of all, rights can be waived, and when a patient requests death, that person waives his or her right to life. For this reason, voluntary euthanasia would not violate the patient's right to life. Second, it is not always the case that death is a loss. Death is a loss only when life is good, but the life of a terminally ill patient can be quite bad. Indeed, death can be good by comparison. (The word "euthanasia," from *eu-thanatos*, literally means "good death.") There are, in short, exceptions to the rule that it is wrong to kill an innocent human being, and voluntary euthanasia seems to fall into this category.

The problem with the second argument is not whether the rule against killing an innocent human being holds without exception, but whether it can be correctly applied to the abortion issue. Is a human fetus a human being? Or is it merely a potential human being? Many philosophers have challenged the claim that human life begins at conception. Henry Morgentaler presents one such challenge:

> At the moment of conception the sperm and the ovum unite, creating one cell. To proclaim that this one cell is already a full human being and should be treated as such is so patently absurd that it is almost difficult to refute. It is as if someone claimed that one brick is already a house and should be treated with the same respect a full house deserves. Even if you have a hundred bricks, or two hundred bricks, it is not yet a house. For it to be a house it needs walls, plumbing, electricity, and a functional organization. The same is true for a developing embryo. In order for it to be a human being it needs an internal organization, organs, and especially a human brain to be considered fully human. This entity is the result of sexual intercourse, where procreation is often not the goal, and whether it is called a zygote, blastocyst, embryo, or fetus, it does not have all the attributes of a human being and thus cannot properly be considered one. (Morgentaler 1996: 14)

For each of the following moral syllogisms, identify the general principle on which the argument is based. Are there relevant exceptions to the principle? Has the principle been correctly applied? Is the reasoning valid?

1. It is wrong to kill innocent people. Waging war inevitably involves killing innocent people. (On average, about 90 percent of the people killed in modern wars are innocent people.) Therefore, it is wrong to wage war.

2. It is wrong to cause unnecessary suffering. Using animals for food causes them to suffer unnecessarily. Therefore, it is wrong to use animals for food.

3. It is natural for people to eat meat. If something is natural then it cannot be morally wrong. Therefore, it cannot be morally wrong for people to eat meat.

4. It is permissible to use extreme forms of coercion to prevent people from committing serious crimes. (People are imprisoned to prevent them from committing serious crimes. Isn't this permissible?) Torture is an extreme form of coercion used to prevent people from committing serious crimes. (If a terrorist is tortured to extract information that is used to prevent a

planned attack, then the terrorist is prevented from committing the attack.) Therefore, it is permissible to use torture to prevent people from committing serious crimes.

5.   If torture is used as an interrogation technique, it is inevitable that innocent people—people falsely suspected of terrorism or other criminal activities—will be tortured. It is wrong to torture innocent people. Therefore, it is wrong to use torture as an interrogation technique.

1.4. Moral Analogies   *include under abortion*

A moral syllogism applies a general principle to a particular case. Another type of moral argument involves a comparison between cases and is "analogical" in character. Consider, for example, the following argument on the abortion issue, advanced by a contemporary American philosopher, Judith Jarvis Thomson:

> [Let] me ask you to imagine this. You wake up in the morning and find yourself back to back in bed with an unconscious violinist. A famous unconscious violinist. He has been found to have a fatal kidney ailment, and the Society of Music Lovers has canvassed all the available medical records and found that you alone have the right blood type to help. They have therefore kidnapped you, and last night the violinist's circulatory system was plugged into yours, so that your kidneys can be used to extract poisons from his blood as well as your own. The director of the hospital now tells you, "Look, we're sorry the Society of Music Lovers did this to you—we would never have permitted it if we had known. But still, they did it, and now the violinist is plugged into you. To unplug you would be to kill him. But never mind, it's only for nine months. By then he will have recovered from this ailment, and can safely be unplugged from you." Is it morally incumbent on you to accede to this situation? (Thomson 2007: 98)

Of course, Thomson believes that you would be justified in unplugging yourself from the violinist, even if this cost the man his life. If so, then wouldn't a woman be justified in "unplugging" herself from her fetus? Thomson implicitly reasons as follows:

(1)   In the case of the violinist, a woman would have the right to unplug herself from the violinist, even though this would be a death sentence for the man.

(2)   There is no relevant difference between this case and a case in which a woman is pregnant with an unwanted child and chooses to have an abortion.

Therefore:

(3)   A woman has the right to have an abortion when she is pregnant with an unwanted child.

This argument does not rest upon a moral rule—such as that a woman has the right to decide how her body is used—but upon a comparison between two cases. There may be important differences between them, but *if* the two cases are alike in all respects that matter, and *if* a woman in the situation imagined by Thomson would have the right to unplug herself from the violinist, then, by analogy, a woman has the right to have an abortion. This is what is meant by a "moral analogy." A moral analogy is an argument in which we reach a moral conclusion about one case by comparing it with another case that allegedly resembles it in all relevant respects. According to some ethicists, our moral intuitions about particular cases are fundamental to moral reasoning. Moral rules are simply generalizations that usually hold. If this is correct, then moral reasoning is not fundamentally syllogistic but analogical.

The basis for analogical reasoning in ethics is the principle of consistency. According to this, if we make a moral judgment about one case, then, to be consistent, we must make the same judgment about any other case exactly like it in all relevant respects. To see what this means, compare the following two cases (originally discussed by Judith Jarvis Thomson in "Killing, Letting Die, and the Trolley Problem"):

Trolley Case 1: A runaway trolley is about to strike five people tied to the track. You are standing beside the track, and you could easily divert the trolley down an alternate track by pulling a lever, but there is one person tied to the alternate track. If you pull the lever, this person will die. If you don't, five people will die. The choice is between one life and five lives. Should you pull the lever?

Trolley Case 2: A runaway trolley is about to strike five people tied to the track. You are standing on a bridge over the track, and you could prevent the accident by dropping a sufficiently large object in the trolley's path. Unfortunately, the only available object large enough to stop the trolley is an extremely large man who is standing next to you. (Imagine a Hulk-sized sumo wrestler.) If you nudge the man, who is standing on the edge of the bridge, he will topple onto the track preventing the accident, but he will be killed. In this case, only one person will die. If you don't push the large man onto the track, five people will die. The choice is between one life and five lives. Should you push the man onto the track?

Most people say that it would be right to pull the lever in the first case but wrong to push the large man onto the track in the second. This is true even though the outcome is the same in both cases. It is not obvious what the relevant differences are, if there are any, but we recognize that there *must* be such differences if we are right in judging the two cases differently. In other words, if the two cases are alike in all respects that matter, and if it is permissible to sacrifice one person to save five people in Trolley Case 1, then it must be permissible to do the same thing in Trolley Case 2. If the two cases are alike in all relevant respects, then consistency requires that we make the same judgment about them. (If you evaluate these cases differently, how do you account for this?)

Because of this consistency requirement, we can always reason analogically in ethics. When evaluating an analogical argument, the crucial question to ask is whether there are relevant differences between the cases being compared. If so, the argument is unsound. One objection to Thomson's "violinist" argument, for example, is that there is an important difference between the case imagined by Thomson and the typical abortion case. In Thomson's case, a violinist has been strapped to a woman's back without her knowledge or consent. In the typical abortion case, however, a woman has voluntarily engaged in intercourse, knowing what the consequences might be, and has become pregnant as a result. Thomson's case, therefore, is not strictly analogous to the typical abortion case. At most, Thomson's argument shows that abortion is permissible when a woman has been raped. (We will discuss Thomson's argument more fully in a later chapter.)

Try to evaluate the following moral analogies. Are the cases being compared alike in all relevant respects? If not, what are the important differences?

1. There is no moral difference between a lion eating a zebra and a human being eating meat. There is nothing wrong with a lion eating a zebra. Therefore, there is nothing wrong with a human being eating meat.

2. Cannibalism is morally revolting. But there is no difference between eating human flesh and eating animal flesh. In fact, human flesh *is* animal flesh. Therefore, it is morally revolting to eat animal flesh.

3. There are "transabled" people who strongly identify as disabled. They feel disassociated from their abled bodies, and some have gone so far as to inflict crippling injuries on themselves. Clearly, we should not condone someone's wish to become disabled, no matter how sincere or strongly felt this wish might be. But how do transabled people differ from transsexuals who also feel disassociated from their bodies? Just as we should not condone someone's wish to become disabled, neither should we condone someone's wish for sexual reassignment.

4. In America, we do not impose legal restrictions on procreation. No one—not even someone who is unemployed, or who has a criminal record—is legally barred from having children, and there are no legal restrictions on how many children a couple may have. But this is inconsistent with an immigration policy that permits only certain people to migrate to this country and restricts the number of such immigrants. Clearly, it doesn't matter *how* the population grows—internally, through increased birth rates, or externally, through immigration—or *how* the ethnic composition of the country changes. Therefore, to be consistent, America should not impose legal restrictions on immigration.

5.   Strangers may want to enter your home, but your home belongs to you, and
     so you have the right to bar them from entering. You don't even need to
     have a good reason. You may simply not want to associate with them. Can't
     we say the same thing about immigrants? There are many foreigners who
     would like to move to the United States. But whose country is this? Ameri-
     ca belongs to Americans. Just as homeowners have the right to bar strangers
     from entering their homes, Americans have the right to bar foreigners from
     entering their country.

6.   Adults do and should have the legal right to drink alcohol. But there is no
     difference between the use of alcohol and the use of narcotics. Therefore,
     adults should have the legal right to use narcotics.

7.   People should not have special privileges simply because of their race. It
     would be wrong, for example, to permit only white people to ride first-class
     on an airplane. But classism—treating wealthy people differently than poor
     or working class people—is morally indistinguishable from racism. There-
     fore, people should not have special privileges simply because they are
     wealthy.

1.5. Fallacies in Moral Reasoning

A "fallacy" is a logically defective argument. Logicians catalogue fallacies so
that we can avoid such mistakes in reasoning. The following are some common
fallacies associated with moral reasoning.

Appeal to Nature

This fallacy, as illustrated by the two examples below, occurs whenever it is
argued that something is moral because it is natural, or that something is immoral because it is unnatural.

> Human beings are by nature meat eaters. Therefore, there is nothing
> wrong with eating pork chops and hamburgers.

> Homosexuality is wrong because it is a perversion of nature.

These arguments are fallacious because there is no conceptual connection between what is natural and what is moral. (The first category has to do with how
things *are*, whereas the second has to do with how things *ought to be*.) For example, it is natural for women to experience pain and suffering during childbirth. Does this mean that such suffering is good, or that it is wrong for women
to have some form of pain-relief during childbirth? It is unnatural for human

beings to fly. Does this show that it is morally wrong for people to travel by airplane?

Appeal to the People

Does either one of the arguments below seem plausible to you?

> No one should criticize me for taking pencils, paper clips, or other office supplies. Who doesn't?

> Do women have the right to have abortions? Opinion polls show that they do. Overwhelmingly, American's support a woman's right to choose.

The moral principle underlying both arguments is that the right thing to do is to "follow the crowd." Clearly, this is a fallacy. In one form, this fallacy occurs whenever it is argued (as in the first example above) that something is right or permissible because many people do it. In another form, this fallacy occurs whenever it is reasoned (as in the second example above) that something is right simply because many people believe that it is right.

Appeal to Tradition

This fallacy occurs whenever it is reasoned that something is right or permissible because it has been practiced for a long time, or that something is wrong because it is contrary to an established tradition. The two arguments below illustrate this fallacy:

> Marriage has traditionally been an institution between a man and a woman. Therefore, same-sex marriages should not be condoned.

> America has traditionally been an English-speaking country. Therefore, English should remain the national language.

Both arguments are fallacious because the fact that people have engaged in some practice for a long time in no way justifies that practice. After all, people have practiced slavery, murder, religious persecution, robbery, and rape throughout human history.

Black-and-White Thinking

In an interview with *Playboy Magazine* (January 1981), we read the following brief exchange between David Sheff and John Lennon:

Sheff: "Why does anyone need $150,000,000? Couldn't you be perfect-
ly content with $100,000,000? Or $1,000,000?"

Lennon: "What would you suggest I do? Give everything away and
walk the streets?"

Here David Sheff implied, rather impolitely, that it was wrong for John Lennon
to horde his wealth. In response, Lennon argued that the alternative—giving
everything away and walking the streets—was ridiculous. The problem is that
Lennon imagined only two possibilities: hording his wealth or giving it all away.
Obviously, there were other options between these two extremes. This is what is
meant by the fallacy of black-and-white thinking (also called the fallacy of
"false dilemma"). In general, we commit this fallacy whenever we consider only
extreme alternatives, overlooking more plausible intermediate options. Another
example: "My father tells me that I'm neglecting my school work by playing
video games for eight hours every day. But it's ridiculous to think that I should
spend every waking moment studying!"

Argumentum ad Hominem

The following brief dialogue, or something like it, may sound familiar:

A: "I can't believe that you're late. Now we're going to miss the beginning of the movie."

B: "Don't criticize me for being late. The other night I waited in the res-
taurant for nearly an hour before you showed up."

The Latin *ad hominem* means "at the man." The *ad hominem* fallacy occurs
whenever an argument is directed at a person rather than at the person's views.
There are several forms of the fallacy. In one form (what is referred to as *tu
quoque*, meaning "you too"), this fallacy occurs, as in the above dialogue,
whenever someone attempts to deflect moral criticism by pointing out that the
person making the accusation is guilty of similar offenses. To give another example, suppose someone criticizes you for lying. You respond, "Who are *you* to
tell me not to lie? The other day you told your wife that you were working late
at the office when you were really out drinking beer with your buddies." Does it
follow from this that it is *not* wrong for you to lie? Of course not, but this is the
conclusion you are arguing for. (It may be hypocritical to criticize others for
their moral failures while making excuses for one's own, but even the hypocrite
can correctly point out other people's faults.)

Slippery Slope Fallacy

"This insane drive towards gay marriage isn't the last stop for the bus," writes talk-show host Michael Savage. He continues:

> It's about expanding marriage to include polygamy, polyamory, transsexual marriages, and open marriage. Perhaps bestiality will get a new image. Why not? There are also single people who want to marry themselves and, in turn, enjoy the benefits afforded married couples. (Savage 2003:161)

Sometimes, as in this example, it is argued that a practice should not be condoned because it will lead to other unacceptable practices. This is what is meant by a "slippery slope" argument. Such an argument is not always fallacious, but a mistake occurs whenever the potential for harm is exaggerated. Is it reasonable to believe that if same-sex marriages were legally permitted (as, in fact, they now are throughout the United States), this would lead to polygamy, polyamory, and bestiality?

Appeal to Religion

Consider the following two arguments:

Murderers should be put to death because the Bible says so.

There is nothing wrong with eating meat. In the Bible, it says that God gave us animals for food, and even Jesus ate fish.

People often appeal to religion to support their moral beliefs, but this is deeply problematic for a number of reasons. First, different religions accept different scriptures as authoritative: Jews accept the authority of the Old Testament; Christians, the whole Bible; Muslims, the Koran; Hindus, the Bhagavad-Gita; and there are many other possibilities. How can we know which of the world's religions is the *correct* religion? One problem with this kind of argument, then, is that it rests on an unproven and, perhaps, unprovable assumption: that the religion relied on is the correct religion. In fact, as T. Edward Damer argues, this assumption is probably false:

> Since each of the hundreds of conflicting theological or ecclesiastical positions is different *in some respect* from all the others, we know before we begin any examination of those positions that only one of them has the possibility of being true—and even that one may be seriously flawed. So it turns out that not only is it *possible* that your own religious position is false or indefensible, it is *probable* that it is. (Damer 2013: 10)

Second, even if we could know that the Bible (or the Koran, or some other religious text) was truly authoritative, people often disagree about how religious texts are to be interpreted. Peter Wenz explains the problem:

> Theocrats believe that society should follow God's commands, as theocrats understand them, to know with certainty the difference between right and wrong. I find this view untenable in part because religious people differ among themselves about God's will and the conduct He requires. . . . Consider first the influence of disparate group traditions on interpretations of the Bible, the Old and New Testaments. In Deuteronomy 12:23, God tells people when they eat meat they should not eat blood; "for the blood is the life; and you shall not eat the life with the flesh." Traditional Jews interpret the verse to require that meat be cooked well done. But the traditional interpretation among Jehovah's Witnesses holds that the verse forbids life-saving transfusions of whole blood. Jehovah's Witnesses often refuse blood transfusions because they think violating God's command jeopardizes their immortal souls. The tradition among most Christians, by contrast, is to ignore this passage. (Wenz 2007: 41)

Finally, if we argue that an action is right (or wrong) simply because it says so in the Bible, to be consistent we must accept *all* of the moral pronouncements of the Bible. This is problematic, as illustrated by the following passages from the Old Testament:

> If two men are fighting and the wife of one of them comes to rescue her husband from his assailant, and she reaches out and seizes him by his private parts, you shall cut off her hand. Show her no pity. (Deuteronomy 25:11-12)

> If anyone curses his father or mother, he must be put to death. (Leviticus 20:9)

> If a man commits adultery with another man's wife—with the wife of his neighbor—both the adulterer and the adulteress must be put to death. (Leviticus 20:10)

> If a man lies with a man as one lies with a woman, both of them have done what is detestable. They must be put to death; their blood will be on their own heads. (Leviticus 20:13)

> If a man has sexual relations with an animal, he must be put to death, and you must kill the animal. (Leviticus 20:15)

> A man or woman who is a medium or spiritist among you must be put to death. You are to stone them; their blood will be on their own heads. (Leviticus 20:27)

> Do not allow a sorceress to live. (Exodus 22:18)

The argument that murderers should be put to death because the Bible says so is logically indistinguishable from the argument that adulterers (or homosexuals or mediums or disrespectful children) should be put to death because the Bible says so. If you accept the first argument (or *any* argument like it), then you cannot consistently reject the second.

Students sometimes protest that such passages, taken from the Old Testament, do not reflect the teachings of Christianity. Should we, then, simply ignore the Old Testament? Isn't the Bible *as a whole* revered by Christians as the revealed word of God? If it is, then it must be conceded that God at one time demanded that people be put to death for homosexuality and witchcraft. Was this ever right? If it is argued that Old Testament commandments are not binding upon Christians, then what are we to make of the following passage in which Jesus himself proclaims that such commandments should never be relaxed?

> Do not think that I have come to abolish the Law or the Prophets; I have not come to abolish them but to fulfill them. I tell you the truth, until heaven and earth disappear, not the smallest letter, not the least stroke of a pen, will by any means disappear from the Law until everything is accomplished. Anyone who breaks one of the least of these commandments and teaches others to do the same will be called least in the kingdom of heaven, but whoever practices and teaches these commands will be called great in the kingdom of heaven. For I tell you that unless your righteousness surpasses that of the Pharisees and the teachers of the law, you will certainly not enter the kingdom of heaven. (Matthew 5:17-19)

Test your understanding of these ideas by trying to identify the following fallacies.

1. It is natural for a woman to put the needs of her children ahead of her own. Therefore, it is wrong for a woman to care more about her career than about her family.

2. Abortion is wrong because the Bible clearly states: "Thou shalt not kill."

3. Public opinion polls show that the majority of Americans support capital punishment. Therefore, it would be wrong to abolish the death penalty in favor of life imprisonment.

4. You tell me I should wear a seatbelt when I drive. But I never saw you wear one. So why should I?

5. There is nothing wrong with cheating on your income taxes. Who doesn't?

6. It is human nature to be selfish. So there is nothing wrong with always putting yourself first.

7. People have been using narcotics for thousands of years. How could there be anything wrong with it?

8. You say that I spend too much money on clothes. Do you think I should walk the streets naked?

9. You're telling me that I shouldn't eat meat. But look at you! You're wearing leather shoes and a leather belt! How can I take you seriously?

10. Liberals think that assault rifles should be banned. But they're wrong. If assault rifles are banned, then handguns will be banned. Before you know it, we will lose all of our Constitutional rights!

11. Many people are opposed to the death penalty. But it's ridiculous to think that murderers should not be punished!

12. You tell me that I should exercise regularly. But when's the last time you got off the couch?

1.6. Reconstructing Arguments

When evaluating an argument, it is often necessary to reconstruct the reasoning. Sometimes this involves supplying a missing premise. For example, consider the argument: "The bug that bit me wasn't a spider because it didn't have eight legs." The missing premise is obvious: "All spiders have eight legs." Sometimes an argument is fallacious because of a false but unstated premise. For example, the appeal to tradition is a fallacy because it assumes that if something has been practiced for a long time, then it must be the right thing to do. This, of course, is a mistake. Consider the following arguments and try to identify the missing premises.

1. Malcolm is an American. Therefore, he is not a Canadian.
2. All Christians go to Church. Therefore, Franz is not a Christian.
3. It won't rain today because it's Tuesday.
4. Achmed is from Pakistan. Therefore, he must be Muslim.
5. There are no mountain goats in Miami because all mountain goats live in mountains.
6. God exists because the Bible says so.
7. Sally drives a Lexus, so she can't be a college professor.
8. It is natural for adults to be protective of infants. Thus, infanticide is wrong because it is unnatural.
9. It's wrong to be dishonest. Therefore, it's wrong to cheat on a test.
10. Molly wears leather shoes, so she can't be a vegan.
11. It is wrong to intentionally make people suffer. Therefore, torture is wrong.
12. All marathon runners are athletes, and all musicians are stoners. So no marathon runners are musicians.

13. No philosophers are Nobel Prize winners, and Sam is an ethicist. Therefore, Sam is not a Nobel Prize winner.
14. Most young people have sex before they're married. Therefore, there's nothing wrong with premarital sex.
15. People have been hunting throughout human history. Therefore, there is nothing wrong with the sport.

For each of the following arguments, identify the premises and the conclusion and attempt to decide whether the argument is sound. Do the premises provide good reasons for believing the conclusion? If not, why not? (In some cases, it may be necessary to supply missing steps in reasoning.)

1. "It is widely assumed that parents do have the right to inflict violence on their children, for a variety of reasons. . . . I myself would say that all such acts of violence are to be condemned. . . . Since these are not cases of self-defense of the parent against the child, or even acts of revenge for the child's earlier violence, they are really no different, morally, from hitting another adult because he disobeys you or does something you think is wrong. Only violence can justify violence, and in the vast majority of cases parental violence against children has no such justification. Naughtiness and disobedience are simply not forms of violence." (McGinn 1992: 50-51)

2. "It is unclear . . . that we would always be justified in treating wrongdoers as they have treated others, since this would mean torturing those who have tortured others and raping those who are guilty of rape." (Lyons 1995: 318)

3. "Although the advantages of allowing a current market in human kidneys are obvious, it is equally obvious why the proposal has been viciously condemned as unethical: the people who would sell their kidneys are likely to be poor, while the people who would buy them are likely to be rich. Moreover, as the sale of a kidney is a drastic measure, the people who would sell their kidneys in such a market would not only be poor but *desperately* poor. Since this is so, the opponents of such markets allege, the only people who would sell in a market for human kidneys would be those coerced into doing so by their poverty. The buyers of the kidneys would thus be exploiting the poverty of the vendors to secure organs for the buyers' own use." (Taylor 2005)

4. "Miscarriages of justice are rare, but do occur. Over a long enough time they lead to the execution of some innocents. Does this make irrevocable punishments morally wrong? Hardly. Our government employs trucks. They run over innocent bystanders more frequently than courts sentence innocents to death. We do not give up trucks because the benefits they produce outweigh the harm, including the death of innocents." (van den Haag 2002: 286)

5. "[An] argument, based on purely economic issues, is the 'I don't want to pay for their oatmeal' position towards those on death row. There is no evidence to back up this argument. . . . A 'New Jersey Policy Perspectives' report, commissioned by New Jerseyans for Alternatives to the Death Penalty, found that convicting a killer and putting him or her to death costs about four times more than imprisoning him for life without parole. . . . Of course there's an argument that those sentenced to death should only get one appeal, but this perspective overlooks the 172 exonerations of innocent people—including 14 people who were at one time sentenced to death—that the Innocence Project has won." (Monkerud 2006)

6. "A school program to fight childhood obesity that includes yoga is drawing complaints from some Christian parents in the Quesnel area in B.C.'s Cariboo region. They say yoga is a religion, and shouldn't be taught in public schools. Chelsea Brears, who has two children in the school system, said her son was asked to do different poses and 'to put his hands together.' Brears, a Christian, said she doesn't want her children exposed to another religion during class time. 'It's not fair to take prayer out, and yet they're allowing yoga, which is religion, in our schools.'" (*CBS News*, January 9, 2007)

7. "But can't torture at least be used on someone who might know of an imminent terrorist act? Not without opening the door to pervasive torture. The problem with this 'ticking bomb' senerio is that it is infintely elastic. Why stop with the terrorist suspect himself? Why not torture his neighbor or friend who might know something about an attack? And why stop with an imminent attack? Aren't the potential victims of possible future attacks just as worthy of protection by torture? The slope is very slippery." (Ross 2004)

2. Moral Skepticism

One of the required lessons taught in American public schools concerns the distinction between "facts" and "opinions."[1] To illustrate the distinction, one worksheet provided to students lists the following as statements of fact:

> Abraham Lincoln was a United States president.
> Fire needs oxygen to burn.
> All people must breathe to live.

These are contrasted with the statements below, which are classified as mere opinions:

> Blue is the best color.
> Pizza tastes great.
> I don't like broccoli.

In the resource materials, value judgments are grouped together with statements of personal taste or preference and are invariably classified as mere opinions. It is perhaps not surprising, then, that moral judgments are put in the same category. According to the resource materials, for example, all of the following are mere opinions:

> Copying homework assignments is wrong.
> All men are created equal.
> It is worth sacrificing some personal liberties to protect our country from terrorism.
> Drug dealers belong in prison.

People do have these opinions, of course, but people also have the opinion that Abraham Lincoln was a United States president and that fire needs oxygen to burn. These are not *mere* opinions, however, because they are supported by objective facts. We are led to think, then, that moral opinions differ from these other opinions in that moral opinions lack such support. Is this true? Does morality have *no* basis in objective fact?

Many people think so, including, it seems, American educators. We will refer to the view that morality is just a matter of opinion—that there are no objective moral facts—as "moral skepticism." This is the view expressed by people when they say "What's right in one culture is not necessarily right in another" or "What's right for me may not be right for you" or "Who's to say what's right?" For the moral skeptic, either moral statements are not true or their truth is somehow relative or subjective. In this chapter, we will try to understand what this means and see whether moral skepticism, in one form or another, is philosophically defensible.

2.1. Cultural Relativism

Different cultures adopt different standards of etiquette and there are no independent, objective standards by which we might judge the behavior of all people. In America, people eat with forks and knives, whereas in India they commonly eat with their bare fingers. In China, people use chopsticks. There are no "correct" customs concerning how people should eat, just different customs. Might the same be said about morality? In America, people eat beef, whereas in India this practice is abhorred. In parts of Asia, people commonly eat dogs and cats, but in America and India this is considered wrong. According to the cultural relativist, there are no "correct" moral standards concerning what people should eat, just different standards. Because beef eating is an accepted practice in America, it is acceptable for someone who is culturally American to eat beef. But Indian culture is different. Because beef eating violates an Indian cultural norm, it is wrong for someone who is culturally Indian to eat beef. Similarly, it is permissible for someone who is culturally Chinese, Korean, or Vietnamese to eat dogs and cats, but not for someone who is culturally American, Indian, or French. Different cultures can and often do adopt different moral standards. For the cultural relativist, the standards that people should live by, and by which their behavior should be judged, are the standards adopted by their respective cultures.

It may be that morality is partly or even largely conventional. Consider how people dress, for example. Public nudity is considered wrong in modern societies, but it is customary in some aboriginal cultures. In Muslim societies, it is considered wrong for a woman to appear in public unless she is veiled, but in Western societies it is customary for women to dress much more revealingly. Should we think that some cultures are right and others are wrong concerning how people should dress? Or is this entirely conventional? We might raise simi-

lar questions about other cultural norms. Should marriage be an institution between a man and a woman? Or is heterosexual marriage just a social custom,
and so subject to change? Do people have a genuine right to the things that they
acquire under the property arrangements of their society? Or are these arrangements as conventional as the rules of a card game? (Consider one implication of
this concerning the problem of poverty. If property arrangements are entirely
conventional, then there is no basis in objective fact for the property claims of
affluent people. It would not be "wrong," at least not in an absolute sense, to
confiscate their wealth and redistribute it among the poor.) For the cultural relativist, however, it is not that morality is partly or even largely conventional, but
that it is *entirely* conventional.

Fully defined, cultural relativism involves, not one, but a number of related
claims: (1) There are no moral standards independent of what different cultures
believe is right or wrong. Because different cultures have different moral beliefs,
what is right in one culture is not necessarily right in another. (2) The right thing
for someone to do is to act according to the moral standards (moral beliefs) of
that person's culture. What *makes* an action right, in other words, is its cultural
acceptance. (3) In passing judgment on someone's behavior, we should apply
the moral standards of that person's culture, not our own. (4) There are no universal moral standards. That is, there are no moral standards that apply to all
people regardless of their cultural affiliations. (5) All cultures are equal. No culture is morally superior or inferior to another, because there are no culturally
independent standards by which such judgments can be made. To pass judgment
on another culture, to regard another culture as "primitive" or "backward," is
ethnocentric.

Of these claims, the first is central. Why accept it? The usual argument for
this rests on the premise that people in different cultures have different moral
beliefs:

(1) Different cultures have different moral beliefs.
(2) If different cultures have different moral beliefs, then what is right
     in one culture is not necessarily right in another.

Therefore:

(3) What is right in one culture is not necessarily right in another.

It is not difficult to find support for the first premise. For example, child marriage is culturally condoned in many countries, including Bangladesh, Ethiopia,
Chad, Niger, India, and Nepal. In Bangladesh, over 60 percent of girls are married by the age of eighteen and nearly 30 percent by the age of fifteen. A small
percentage are married by the age of eleven, in some cases to middle-aged men.[2]
This is sanctioned by Islam. It is said that the Prophet Muhammad married his
third wife, Aisha, when she was six years old and consummated the marriage
when she was nine.[3] At the time, Muhammed was in his fifties. In most coun-

tries, people believe that child marriage, especially when it involves young girls and middle-aged men, is seriously wrong. Examples like this—and there are many others—show that people's moral beliefs are, at least to some extent, culturally variable.

But why should we accept the second premise of the above argument? That is, why should we think that what is right or wrong critically depends upon people's beliefs? During the Middle-Ages, it was commonly believed that the sun (and all other heavenly bodies) revolved around the earth. Today we know that the earth orbits the sun. Yet from this we would not conclude that people in the Middle-Ages lived in a different universe than we do today. The nature of the universe does not depend upon people's beliefs. Why, then, should we think that the nature of morality depends upon people's beliefs? People in the Middle-Ages may have *believed* that it was right to burn heretics at the stake, but this does not show that it actually *was* right.

In critically evaluating cultural relativism, we must try to see whether it accurately represents our understanding of what moral standards are like. We know that social customs are conventional and that there are no correct standards concerning what eating utensils people should use, or what clothes they should wear in pubic, or what forms of greeting—bowing to one another or shaking hands, for example—are appropriate. Do we think that moral standards are like this? Do we think, for example, that whether a middle-aged man should be allowed to marry a young girl is simply a matter of social custom, like whether people should eat with forks and knifes? Or do these seem like very different issues?

To turn to a different example, consider the custom of honor-killings. In Muslim culture, if a woman brings shame to her family—by committing adultery, by becoming pregnant outside of marriage, or even by being raped—restoring the family's honor can require that she be put to death. Honor-killings are reported in many Middle Eastern countries. Here's one story from the West Bank:

> Rofayda Qaoud, raped by her brothers and impregnated, refused to commit suicide, her mother recalls, even after she bought the unwed teenager a razor with which to slit her wrists. So Amira Abu Hanhan Qaoud says she did what she believes any good Palestinian parent would: restored her family's "honor" through murder.
>
> Armed with a plastic bag, a razor and a stick, Qaoud entered her sleeping daughter's room . . . . "Tonight you die, Rofayda," she told the girl before wrapping the bag tightly around her head. Next, Qaoud sliced Rofayda's wrists, ignoring her muffled pleas of "No, mother, no!" After her daughter went limp, Qaoud struck her in the head with the stick. (Nelson 2003)

Or consider the custom of "female circumcision," practiced by both Muslims and Christians in parts of Africa and the Middle East. The procedure, almost always performed on a young girl, involves removing all or part of the external female genitalia. In most cases, it is performed by a female elder using a knife, a razor blade, or even a piece of glass. An estimated 125 million girls and women alive today been "cut" in this way and more than three million girls are currently at risk. Critics argue that the custom, which renders women incapable of experiencing sexual pleasure, is designed to ensure a girl's premarital virginity and post-marital fidelity, which explains why "uncut" women are seen as promiscuous. But this is not how the custom is understood within those cultures that practice it. Here it is seen as a rite of passage, marking a girl's transition into womanhood.[4]

Again, the question we are considering is whether moral standards are no different than social customs. You might believe that a Muslim woman, in accordance with the customs of her religion, should wear a headscarf (*hijab*) in public. But do you believe that she should be put to death if she brings shame to her family by being raped? Do you believe that an Ethiopian woman should have her daughter circumcised because this is mandated by her culture? The strongest condemnation that the cultural relativist can make of honor killings and female circumcision is that these practices are wrong, but only *relative* to the moral standards of America and other Western societies. If you believe that these practices are wrong *without qualification*, then you cannot consistently be a cultural relativist.

Against this you might protest: "Yes, *I* believe that these practices are wrong. But this is just what I believe. People from different cultures see things differently. Who's to say what's right?" But the objection raised here is not about the morality of certain practices but about the nature of moral standards. Do moral standards allow for the *possibility* that people can do something wrong even though their behavior is accepted by their culture? That's the question. If so, then cultural relativism is false; for it cannot be that what *makes* an action right is its cultural acceptance.

The objection raised here can be summarized as follows:

(1) If cultural relativism is true then the members of a given culture cannot do something wrong unless their behavior conflicts with the moral beliefs of their culture.
(2) The members of a given culture can do something wrong even if their behavior does not conflict with the moral beliefs of their culture.

Therefore:

(3) Cultural relativism is false.

We saw earlier that there may be some truth to cultural relativism. If morality is partly based on social conventions, then some actions are right or wrong only in a relative sense. Nonetheless, if it is possible for people to do something wrong even though their behavior does not conflict with the norms of their culture—and we have seen plausible examples of this—then cultural relativism is false.

2.2. Personal Relativism and Moral Subjectivism

People sometimes say "What is right for me may not be right for you." What is meant by this? One possibility is personal relativism. According to this view, there are no moral standards independent of what different individuals believe is right or wrong. In fact, what *makes* it right for someone to do something is simply that that person *believes* that it is right. If you believe that it is right to donate money to charity, then it is right *for you* to do this. But other people may not agree with this, and so it may not be right *for them*. If you believe that abortion is wrong, then it would be wrong *for you* to have an abortion. But some people believe that abortion is permissible, and so it would not wrong *for them*. In general, since different people have different moral beliefs, what is right or wrong varies from one person to another. (It will be noticed that the essential difference between personal relativism and cultural relativism is that for the cultural relativist the right thing for a person to do is whatever that person's *culture* believes is right, whereas for the personal relativist the right thing for a person to do is whatever that *person* believes is right.)

A related view ties morality to people's feelings or emotions rather than to their beliefs. According to moral subjectivism, moral statements describe people's attitudes of approval or disapproval—attitudes that vary from one individual to another. This is another way of understanding what people mean by "What is right for me may not be right for you." When *I* say that something is right, this means that *I* approve of it. When *you* say that something is right, this means that *you* approve of it. Because I might approve of something that you disapprove of, what is right for me may not be right for you. On this view, saying "Abortion is wrong" is like saying "Blue is the best color" or "Pizza tastes great." These statements may be true, but their truth is not grounded in objective fact. The statement "Pizza tastes great" can be translated as "I like the taste of pizza." This is true if, as a matter of fact, I like the taste of pizza. Similarly, "Abortion is wrong" can be translated as "I disapprove of abortion." This is true too if, as a matter of fact, I disapprove of abortion. These statements can be understood as "mere opinions" because the facts that make them true are not objective facts but facts about our subjective states.

The argument for personal relativism parallels the argument given earlier for cultural relativism:

(1) Different people have different moral beliefs.
(2) If different people have different moral beliefs, then what is right for one person is not necessarily right for another.

Therefore:

(3) What is right for one person is not necessarily right for another.

For example, I might believe that it is right to be a vegetarian, whereas you see nothing wrong with eating meat. So for me it is right to be a vegetarian, but not for you.

The first premise of the above argument is true—people do have different moral beliefs—but what about the second? The problem is obvious: that people have different beliefs about something does not mean that there are no objective facts about it. For example, I might believe that God exists, whereas you are an atheist. In some sense, "for me" God exists, whereas "for you" God does not. But this does not mean that there is no objective fact concerning the existence of God. Either God exists or God does not. One of us is right and the other is wrong. In the same way, I might believe that it is right to be a vegetarian, whereas you see things differently. "For me" it is right to be a vegetarian, whereas "for you" it is not. But from this it does not follow that there is no objective fact concerning the morality of meat eating. It is still possible that one of us is right and the other is wrong. The above argument, then, does not prove personal relativism.

Moral subjectivism and personal relativism are related views but also importantly different. Subjectivism, like relativism, connects morality to people's subjective states. But whereas relativism is a theory about the nature of moral standards, subjectivism is a theory about the meaning of moral language. The subjectivist, unlike the relativist, does not tell us what is right or wrong but rather what it *means to say* that something is right or wrong. Indeed, if the subjectivist is right, we could dispense with moral language altogether and instead talk explicitly about our feelings. For example, rather than saying that meat eating is "wrong" I might as well say that I disapprove of meat eating or that I have a negative attitude toward it.

In critically evaluating these views, let us consider the following two questions. First, is it possible for you to make moral mistakes? That is, can you to do something wrong even though you believe that what you are doing is right? Second, can you know whether to judge an action as right or wrong simply by examining your feelings? Or should your moral judgments be based upon objective facts?

Consider the first question. According to the personal relativist, the right thing for you to do is whatever you believe is right. It follows that you can't believe that an action is right and yet be mistaken in this belief. The fact that you *believe* that it is right *makes* it right. Yet obviously this is false. It is surely possible for you to do something wrong even though you believe that it is right. But if this is so, there must be *independent* moral standards—that is, standards independent of your personal moral beliefs—by which your actions can be judged wrong.

For a vivid illustration of this point, consider the following transcription of a tape-recorded statement made by serial killer Ted Bundy to one of his victims (recorded by Bundy himself):

> Why is it more wrong to kill a human animal than any other animal, a pig or a
> sheep or a steer? Is your life more to you than a hog's life to a hog? Why
> should I be willing to sacrifice my pleasure more for the one than for the other?
> . . . In any case, let me assure you, my dear young lady, that there is absolutely
> no comparison between the pleasure I might take in eating ham and the pleas-
> ure I anticipate in raping and murdering you. (Pojman 2000: 165)

Ted Bundy apparently saw nothing wrong with raping and murdering young
women for pleasure. If he did not, and if personal relativism is true, it follows
that he did nothing wrong in committing these violent crimes. On the other
hand, if he did do something wrong, then there must be independent moral
standards by which his behavior can be judged wrong, in which case personal
relativism is false.

The argument against personal relativism parallels the argument given earlier against cultural relativism:

(1) If personal relativism is true then people cannot do something wrong
    unless their behavior conflicts with their personal moral beliefs.
(2) People can do something wrong even if their behavior does not conflict
    with their personal moral beliefs.

Therefore:

(3) Personal relativism is false.

As with cultural relativism, there may be some truth to personal relativism.
What else can we do but what we believe is right? But this does not mean that
believing that something is right *makes* it right. If you can do something wrong
even though you believe that you are doing the right thing, then personal relativism is false.

Now consider the second question. Can you know whether to evaluate an
action as right or wrong simply by examining your feelings? Suppose you learn
that I took my neighbor's ladder from her backyard. Can you know, just by in-
specting your feelings, what to say about this incident? Or do you need to have
additional information? Suppose you learn that I snuck into my neighbor's yard
late one night and took her ladder because I needed it to paint my ceiling. Then
you would probably say that what I did was wrong. But suppose my house was
on fire and I needed the ladder to rescue my child from a second-story balcony.
Then you would probably say that it was right for me to take the ladder (or at
least permissible). For the subjectivist, however, such considerations are essentially irrelevant; the facts relevant to making moral judgments are facts about
our feelings, not about the objective world. If you approve of an action, then you
can truthfully say that the action is right—right regardless of your reasons. If
you disapprove of an action, then you can truthfully say that it is wrong—again,
regardless of your reasons. (Remember: For the subjectivist, all that it *means* for

you to say that an action is "right" or "wrong" is that you approve or disapprove of it.)

We can summarize this objection to subjectivism as follows:

(1) If subjectivism is true, then people can know whether an action is right or wrong simply by examining their feelings.
(2) People cannot know whether an action is right or wrong in this way.

Therefore:

(3) Subjectivism is false.

There may be some truth to saying "What is right for me may not be right for you." What I believe is right may not be what you believe is right. What I approve of may not be what you approve of. But these are not deep truths, because they reveal nothing about the nature of morality. That you and I have different beliefs or attitudes is perfectly compatible with the view that there are objective moral facts.

2.3. Moral Nihilism

The moral skeptic is someone who maintains that there are no objective moral facts. This can be understood in two ways. It can mean that there are moral facts, but these facts are not objective in nature. Or it can mean that there are no moral facts, period. So far, we have explored different ways of defending the first understanding. According to the cultural relativist, there are moral facts but these facts are determined by the norms of different cultures. For the personal relativist, there are moral facts but these facts are determined by the moral beliefs of different individuals. According to the moral subjectivist, there are moral facts but these are facts about people's feelings. Other skeptics take a different route, arguing that morality has no factual basis at all. This is what is meant by "moral nihilism."

One way of defending moral nihilism is to draw a sharp line between facts and values. For the nihilist, morality is concerned with values, not with facts. When we judge that something is good or bad, right or wrong, we are not *describing* a fact about it; rather, we are *ascribing* a negative or a positive value to it. People project values onto things, but things in themselves, independently of human judgment, are neutral. For example, it is a fact that hurricanes destroy property and cause floods, injuries, and deaths. But, according to the nihilist, it is not a fact that hurricanes are bad; rather, people *judge* hurricanes to be bad. The value resides in our judgment, not in the world. The world in itself is value-free.

One argument for moral nihilism focuses on the problem of establishing truth and falsity in ethics and resolving moral disagreements. Suppose you and I disagree about some matter of fact, such as whose face appears on a thousand dollar bill. There is a way to determine whether one of us is right about this and resolve the disagreement. (The answer, incidentally, is Grover Cleveland.) But suppose you and I disagree about some moral issue, such as whether war is ever justified. If there are moral facts, then it should be possible to establish what these facts are and resolve moral disagreements like this one. But, according to the nihilist, it is impossible to prove anything in ethics. This is supposed to show that there are no moral facts.

Succinctly stated, the argument runs as follows:

(1) If there are moral facts, then it should be possible to prove things in ethics.
(2) It is not possible to prove things in ethics. (As people sometimes rhetorically ask: "Who's to say what's right?")

Therefore:

(3) There are no moral facts.

The reasoning is clearly valid, but both premises can be challenged. Is it the case that all facts can be proven? Is it true that moral opinions cannot be rationally as well supported as other opinions?

Let us concentrate on the second question. To prove something (whether inside or outside the domain of ethics) is to provide good reasons for believing it. Whether it is possible to prove things in ethics thus depends on whether it is possible to provide good reasons for at least some of the moral judgments that we make. Is this possible? If we consider only complex moral problems, such as the problem of abortion, then it is tempting to accept the premise that it is impossible to prove anything in ethics. But most of the moral judgments that people make are not about such complex issues but about comparatively simple things. For example, suppose I borrowed a book from you and promised to return it the following day. Is this something I ought to do? Assuming that there are no other relevant facts to consider, don't you have good reasons to believe that I ought to return it? If I announced the next day that I loaned the book to someone else or that I sold it to a used bookstore, wouldn't you think I did something wrong, and wouldn't you have good reasons for thinking this? Most of the moral judgments we make are about uncomplicated issues such as this one. If we have good reasons for making such judgments, then it is possible to prove things in ethics.

Consider some additional examples. Might there be good reasons for believing that the following moral claims are true? What might these reasons be?

Your car has a dead battery, and you need a jump. Your neighbor should help you start your car.

You found someone's wallet lying on a sidewalk. You should return it.

While you were shopping in a supermarket, someone backed into your car, damaging the rear bumper. This person should accept responsibility for the accident.

Someone at work is spreading unfounded and malicious gossip about you, and this should stop.

You suspect that your husband is having an affair. He should be honest with you.

Consider the first claim. Suppose you have been a helpful neighbor. Just last week, when your neighbor's car wouldn't start, you drove her to work. Her car is now in good working condition, and she has a pair of jumper cables. Assuming that there are no other relevant facts to consider, don't you have good reasons for saying that your neighbor ought to help you start your car?

2.4. Moral Realism

Our discussion of moral skepticism seems to show that there is no important sense in which morality is just a matter of opinion. People can and often do have good reasons for the moral judgments that they make, and this is all that is involved in proving that such judgments are true. If people can prove that some of their moral beliefs are true, then people don't just have moral opinions, they have moral knowledge.

The alternative to moral skepticism is the view that there is objective truth in ethics. This is known as "moral realism." (The opposite view, moral skepticism, is often called "moral anti-realism.") For the moral realist, moral knowledge might be compared to mathematical knowledge. Mathematical knowledge is purely conceptual; it is based on our understanding of mathematical concepts—our concepts of numbers, addition, subtraction, and so on. Because we can understand such concepts, we can know things about mathematics. We can know, for example, that the square root of 625 is 25. Human beings may be unique in their ability to grasp mathematical concepts, but the facts of mathematics do not depend upon us. Even if we lacked the conceptual resources to understand it, it would still be true that the square root of 625 is 25. Similarly, the moral realist can argue, our knowledge of morality is based upon our understanding of moral concepts. Because we can understand such concepts, we can know things about morality. We can know, for example, that it is wrong to torture someone for amusement. Human beings may be unique in their ability to grasp moral concepts, but the facts of morality do not depend upon us. Morality, like mathematics, is not something that people invent. Even if people lacked the conceptual resources to comprehend it, it would still be true that torturing for amusement is wrong.

In this chapter, we have built a strong case against moral skepticism. Have we not, along the way, developed a positive argument for moral realism? The following observations have emerged from our discussion:

(1) It is possible for you to be mistaken about some of your moral beliefs. You might believe that something is right and yet be mistaken about this.

(2) Some moral judgments are true and others are false. Moreover, it is often possible to prove that a moral judgment is true by providing good reasons for accepting it.

(3) Whether an action is right or wrong is a fact about the action, not about our feelings or other subjective states.

(4) Doing the right thing sometimes requires acting contrary to culturally established conventions. For example, it would not be right to own slaves or to support the practice of slavery even if one lived in a slaveholding culture.

It does not necessarily follow from any one of these statements that moral realism is true, but it does follow from all of these statements taken together. From (1) and (2), it follows that there are moral facts. You cannot be mistaken about something in morality, for example, unless there are facts to be mistaken about. From (3) and (4) it follows that the facts of morality do not in any way depend upon us—upon what we believe, or what we feel, or the conventions that we establish. If there are, in this sense, "objective" moral facts, then moral realism is true.

Notes

1. See "K-5: Fact Versus Opinion," <http://teaching.monster.com/training/articles/2589-k-5-fact-versus-opinion>.
2. See the Human Rights Watch report: "Bangladesh: Girls Damaged by Child Marriage," <www.hrw.org/news/2015/06/09/bangladesh-girls-damaged-child-marriage>.
3. *Ṣaḥīḥ al-Bukhārī*, Volume 7, Book 62, Number 64. For an English translation, see <www.usc.edu/org/cmje/religious-texts/hadith/bukhari/062-sbt.php>.
4. See the report issued by the World Health Organization: "Female Genital Mutilation," <www.who.int/mediacentre/factsheets/fs241/en/>.

3. Normative Ethics

For the most part, the moral facts are clear. There are complex cases, such as abortion and capital punishment, but such cases are exceptional. Most of the moral judgments we make are about uncomplicated matters, such as whether to keep a promise or to help out a neighbor. Still it is difficult to avoid thinking about complex issues, and it is entirely possible that we hold muddled or inconsistent moral beliefs even about simple things. If we are to resolve complex moral problems and achieve clarity and consistency in our moral thinking, we must reflect upon the basic principles of morality. What is it ultimately that makes an action right or wrong?

3.1. Some Problem Cases

In thinking about this, it is helpful to consider cases that test our moral intuitions. The problem cases below are organized around the questions addressed in this chapter.

Does the rightness or wrongness of an action depend upon its consequences? Or do other considerations matter?

1. You have inherited millions of dollars from a somewhat eccentric uncle. Although this was not stipulated in any legal document, your uncle's last request was that you donate his entire fortune to the American Spiritualist Society. On his deathbed, you promised to honor his request. If you keep your promise, your uncle's fortune will be used to finance research on haunted houses, astral projection, and extrasensory perception. You would like to donate the money to UNICEF, which would use the funds to combat

malaria and tuberculosis in the Third World (which annually claim the lives of millions of poor people). What would be the right thing to do?

2. Your mother needs expensive medications for a heart condition but she has no insurance to cover the costs. You work for a large corporation with billions of dollars in assets. You know of a way to transfer money from the corporate account into your personal checking account. No one would know about the transfers, and the corporation and its investors would be unaffected. If this were the only way you could help your mother, would it be wrong for you to take the money?

3. There are plants growing in your backyard from which a cancer-curing drug can be extracted. The plants grow only on your property, and the drug cannot be produced from any other source. You refuse to allow drug companies or anyone else access to your plants. Would it be wrong for someone to steal your plants—or for the government to confiscate them—in order to extract the cancer-curing drug?

4. You have been married for over ten years and have a good relationship with your husband. Early in your marriage you had a brief affair. Your husband never knew about it, and you have always regretted your behavior. Although he has no grounds for suspicion, one day he asks you whether you have ever been unfaithful. You know that he has a right to the truth. But you also know that if you are honest with him, it will ruin your marriage. What should you do?

5. You are a minimum-wage maintenance worker in a luxury condominium complex. One of the residents has dropped an envelope containing a thousand dollars. The resident is an extremely wealthy woman, and the loss of a thousand dollars would make little or no difference in her life. However, an extra thousand dollars would make a big difference in your life. Would it be wrong for you to keep the money?

Even if the morality of an action does not depend solely upon its consequences, are some actions inherently right or wrong—that is, right or wrong regardless of their consequences?

6. You are offered a deal by a sadistic killer. The killer's victim is strapped to an electric chair. You are told that *you* could pull the switch—and assuming that you did so quickly, the victim would die quickly—or that the sadistic killer will pull the switch—who, you are assured, will pull the switch quite slowly, torturing his victim to death. What are you to do?

7. There is a young boy drowning in a pond and you are the only person in a position to help. As it turns out, if you save the child, he will grow up to be a

mass murderer. Whether or not you can know this, should you rescue the boy? Should you base your decision on whether rescuing the child will have the best consequences?

Does morality sometimes require that you sacrifice yourself for others? How should you weigh your own interests against those of others? Do your own interests count for more?

8. Your husband has developed a serious medical problem and needs constant care. You might stay at home with him and give him the care that he needs, but you are very reluctant to sacrifice several years of your life to be your husband's nurse. Would it be wrong for you to abandon your husband so that you could have a more fulfilling life?

9. You were a passenger on a cruise ship which has sunk to the bottom of the sea. You are not a strong swimmer and you are desperately treading water. One of the other passengers is clinging to the only life preserver. You are exhausted, and you know that unless you seize the life preserver from the passenger—a little old lady, whom you can easily overpower—you will drown. Of course, by doing this, she will drown. Would it be wrong for you to save yourself by taking the life preserver?

Is it ever right to do something simply because your religion requires it? Does morality somehow depend upon religion?

10. You have an extremely rare blood type. You receive a call from a hospital telling you that a patient with your blood type needs a transfusion. Unless you donate a pint of blood, the patient will die. You refuse, but only because you are a Jehovah's Witness and believe that God forbids blood transfusions. Given your religious beliefs, is it right for you to refuse?

11. In Western societies, people assume that freedom of religion is a basic human right. But in Muslim societies, apostasy (leaving the Muslim faith) is punishable by death. If, as Muslims believe, this is commanded by God, are they right to execute apostates?

We are obligated to behave in certain ways, but are we also obligated to think and feel in certain ways? Do our inner motives and intentions affect the moral character of our external behavior?

12. You are a consumer of pornography—hardcore, violent porn. Nightly you pore over your stash of porn and fantasize about raping and torturing women. You never act out your fantasies, though, and no one would even suspect that you are a sadist, at least in your imagination. If your behavior harms no one, are you doing something wrong?

13. You are a sniper. From your tenth-story window you take aim at a pedestrian strolling down a sidewalk. You pull the trigger with the intention of killing him, but your gun jams. The pedestrian turns a corner and disappears never realizing that he was nearly killed. No one was actually hurt. Did you do something wrong?

3.2. Consequentialism

In the first problem case above, you might believe that the right thing to do is to donate your uncle's fortune to UNICEF. Why? Maybe because you believe that this will have better consequences than will donating the money to the American Spiritualist Society. If you believe that this is what makes an action right—that it has better consequences than does any alternative action—then you are what is known as a "consequentialist." A consequentialist believes that whether an action is right or wrong is determined *solely* by its consequences—by its effects, outcomes, or results—and that the right thing to do is whatever has the best consequences.

You might not agree with this, however. In the case we're imagining, you might believe that the right thing to do is to donate your uncle's fortune to the American Spiritualist Society rather than to UNICEF. Why? Maybe because you believe that it is important to keep a promise—so important that it outweighs the good that you might do by donating the money to UNICEF. If so, then you are a "deontologist." A deontologist believes that whether an action is right or wrong is *not* solely determined by its consequences but that other considerations—such as keeping promises, or telling the truth, or respecting people's rights—are morally important too. For some deontologists, we should take into account the consequences of our actions when making moral choices. The consequences *do* matter, but so do other considerations. Other deontologists are more extreme and believe that consequentialist considerations should never enter our thinking when making moral decisions.

The basic idea of consequentialism—that what makes an action right or wrong are its consequences—can be developed in different ways. In what follows, we will take a critical look at three consequentialist theories: egoism; altruism; and utilitarianism.

Egoism

According to egoism, the right thing for a person to do is whatever has the best consequences *for that person*. The ancient Greeks, as we will see in a later section, seem to have held such a view inasmuch as their moral thinking centered on the question of how an individual can best achieve his or her own good. This view has been defended by various thinkers over the ages. In the twentieth century, perhaps the most popular advocate of egoism was novelist and essayist Ayn Rand.

To avoid confusion, bear in mind that the egoist is not claiming that you should never do good for others. You should do good for others *if* doing so directly or indirectly promotes your own good. If, for instance, it is in your own best interest to have lasting friendships, and if treating your friends well is a necessary means to this end, then you ought to treat your friends well. What the egoist does deny, however, is that it would ever be right for you to sacrifice your own interests for the good of others. You must always put yourself first. Suppose, for example, that your elderly grandmother is no longer able to care for herself. You might personally assume the responsibility of caring for her, or you might place her in a nursing home. Suppose it would be in your grandmother's best interest if you cared for her yourself, but it would be in your own best interest if you placed her in a nursing home. According to the egoist, what should you do? Assuming that there are no other alternatives to consider, the right thing for you to do is to place your grandmother in a nursing home.

This example does not reflect well on egoism. It *may* be that the right thing to do is to place your grandmother in a nursing home, but clearly it is not right to do this simply because it is in *your* best interests. Your grandmother's interests count for something too. If you completely disregard her interests, then, in reaching a moral decision, you are not considering all the morally important facts. To take a more extreme example (mentioned in the first chapter), suppose you discover a small child thrashing about in a pond, drowning. You can easily save the child, but you are wearing a new pair of suede shoes. If you dive into the pond, you will ruin your shoes. What should you do? Suppose you are indifferent to the child but you cherish your shoes. If you consider only your own interests, the conclusion you will reach is that you should not save the child. True, the child will drown, but according to the egoist, it is wrong for you to sacrifice your own interests—even your own trivial interests—for the good of others.

A theory of moral conduct attempts to systematize moral reasoning by supplying general standards on the basis of which we can reach moral conclusions about particular cases. Egoism offers one such standard: the right thing for a person to do is whatever has the best consequences for that person. If this standard is correct, it can be applied in any situation, real or imagined, to reach a moral conclusion about what is right or wrong in that situation. How can we tell whether egoism—or any moral theory for that matter—is correct? The most important consideration (but not the only one) is this: how well does the theory fit our core moral beliefs? The criterion is simple: the better the fit, the better the theory. Our core moral beliefs are the raw data that a moral theory attempts to explain and systematize.

Obviously, egoism does not fare well by this criterion, and it is not difficult to multiply counterexamples to the theory. If you could best promote your own interests by lying, cheating, and stealing, then according to the egoist, you should lie, cheat, and steal. How can the egoist escape this charge? Suppose you stand to inherent a vast fortune from your elderly uncle and you have devised a foolproof plan to murder him. The egoist seems to be committed to saying, not just that it would be morally *permissible* for you to murder your uncle, which is bad enough, but that it would be your moral *obligation*. To permit the old man to live when you could benefit greatly from his prompt demise would be immoral. The right thing for you to do, after all, is whatever best serves *your* interests, no one else's.

In defense of egoism, it is sometimes argued that it is in everyone's self-interest to live in a society in which people keep their promises, refrain from lying and violence, occasionally assist one another, and otherwise conform to the rules of common morality. If this is true, then egoism, fully worked out, may not be so counterintuitive after all. But consider an African tribe known as the Ik, first studied by anthropologist Colin Turnbull in the 1960s. According to one account:

> The Ik acknowledge no moral or social obligation to anyone or anything. Their standard of value is the self; their rule of life, to do whatever they wish. At age 3, children are put out of their parents' huts and thereafter sleep in the open, rain or shine. . . . A neighbor's suffering evokes not pity or kindness but malicious glee. On one occasion observed by Turnbull, when an emaciated little girl lay dying of hunger, her playmates put a bit of food in her hand and then, as she raised it to her mouth, beat her savagely. Similarly, mothers laugh when their infants fall and hurt themselves; if a leopard carries off a child, the parents' reaction is delight. (Ruggiero 2001: 47-48)

If the egoist is right, there is no moral basis for criticizing the Ik. Indeed, since "their standard of value is the self," the Ik would seem to exemplify what, for the egoist, is a morally ideal society.

Before going on, let us summarize the objections that have been raised against egoism. One objection concerns the sacrifices that we should sometimes make for others:

(1) If egoism is true, then morality never requires that we make personal sacrifices for the good of others.
(2) Morality does sometimes require that we make personal sacrifices for the good of others.

Therefore:

(3) Egoism is false.

Imagine this. You are sitting in your car at a stoplight, when you see a truck (whose brakes have failed) heading toward you. You have just enough time to pull out of the way, but there is a child playing on the sidewalk beside your car. If you pull out of the way, the child will be crushed. If you don't, your car will be demolished, but both you and the child will be unharmed. Should you sacrifice your car to save the child's life? For the egoist, the answer would seem to be "no."

Another objection to egoism concerns when it is permissible to harm others:

(1) If egoism is true, then it is right for us to harm others simply because it benefits us.

(2) It is never right for us to harm others simply because it benefits us.

Therefore:

(3) Egoism is false.

The following true story provides an illustration:

> A case occurred a few years ago in San Antonio in which an entire family tormented a small child. One of many "games" they played, "The Color Purple Game," consisted of taping the child's nose and mouth shut, watching the child struggle until it turned purple, and then removing the tape. (Luper and Brown 1999: 5)

If the egoist is right, then the family mentioned in this story did something wrong, but not because of how they treated the child. They did something wrong because they were eventually caught!

Altruism

Egoism is located at one extreme of the consequentialist spectrum. At the opposite extreme is altruism. For the altruist, the right thing for a person to do is whatever has the best consequences *for others*. Christian ethics, as reflected in the life and teachings of Jesus, is a form of altruism. "If you want to be perfect," Jesus once told a rich young man, "go, sell your possessions and give to the poor" (St. Matthew: 19:21). For Jesus, our benevolence should extend, not just to the poor, but to *all* others, even to our enemies. "Love your enemies," says Jesus, "bless them that curse you, do good to them that hate you, and pray for them which despitefully use you, and persecute you" (St. Matthew: 5:44). Buddhist ethics provides another example. In the Mahayana tradition of Buddhism, the meaning or purpose of life is not to attain salvation for oneself, but to become a savior for others. Fundamental to this tradition is the notion of a Bodhisattva—a being who, having renounced his or her personal salvation, strives to attain Buddhahood for the sake of others. Those who have fully realized this goal are no longer bound to *samsara*—a Sanskrit term referring to the cycle of birth, death, and rebirth. They choose, however, to remain within *samsara* and to manifest themselves in countless ways for the benefit of others. This ideal is eloquently expressed by the ancient Buddhist sage and poet Shantideva:

> May I be a guard for those who are protectorless,
> A guide for those who journey on the road.

For those who wish to go across the water,
May I be a boat, a raft, a bridge.

May I be an isle for those who yearn for landfall,
And a lamp for those who long for light;
For those who need a resting place, a bed;
For all who need a servant, may I be their slave. (Shantideva 1997: 51)

The following legendary story dramatically illustrates the bodhisattva ideal:

Dola Jigme Kalsang was a Tibetan sage of the nineteenth century. One day
while on pilgrimage to China, he came to the central square of a small town
where a crowd had gathered. As he approached, he found that a thief was about
to be put to death in a particularly cruel fashion: he was to be made to straddle
an iron horse that had been heated to red-hot. Dola Jigme pushed his way
through the crowd and proclaimed, "I am the thief!" A great silence fell; the
presiding mandarin turned impassively to the newcomer and asked, "Are you
ready to assume the consequences of what you have just told us?" Dola Jigme
nodded. He died on the horse and the thief was spared. (Ricard 2006: 207)

We may doubt whether anyone alive today even approximates the bodhisattva ideal, but one candidate is Zell Kravinsky. After amassing a $45 million
fortune in the 1990s, Kravinsky gave nearly all of it away to various charities,
keeping just enough to meet his family's living expenses. Together with his wife
and four children, he lived in a modest home and drove an old car. But this is
not all. After he learned that African Americans suffering from kidney disease
often have difficulty obtaining transplant organs from family members, he found
a hospital that allowed him to donate one of his own kidneys to a lower-income,
black recipient. (For more on Kranvinsky's life, see Singer's "What Should a
Billionaire Give—and What Should You?") Most people would say that Kravinsky's philanthropy went well beyond what morality requires. But according to
the altruist, Kravinsky simply fulfilled his basic obligation to do good for others.

Does altruism demand too much from people? Many people think so. One
way to formulate this objection is as follows:

(1) Just as it is wrong for you to regard someone else's happiness as
    unimportant, it is wrong for you to regard your own happiness as
    unimportant.
(2) Altruism requires that you focus exclusively on the happiness of
    others and so regard your own happiness as unimportant.

Therefore:

(3) What altruism requires is wrong.

Your neighbor might appreciate it if you spent your weekends cleaning her home, polishing her car, and washing her laundry, rather than relaxing after a long workweek. She might also appreciate it if you bought her groceries and paid her electric bill, even if this meant that you were hungry and could not afford electricity for yourself. If the altruist is right, shouldn't you be willing to make these sacrifices?

Utilitarianism

Our discussion of egoism and altruism establishes the following important point: that in making moral decisions, we must consider the interests of *all* those affected by our actions. This includes *both* oneself and others. If to this we add that the same interests must be counted equally, the moral conclusion we reach is this: that the right thing to do is whatever has the best consequences, *everyone considered and considered equally.* This is known as "utilitarianism." Unlike egoism or altruism, utilitarianism is both *universal* and *egalitarian* in its moral outlook. The utilitarian maxim is: "Each is to count for one, and none for more than one."

To illustrate the theory, consider one of our original problem cases. Given the choice between (1) keeping your promise to your uncle and donating his entire fortune to the American Spiritualist Society and (2) breaking your promise and donating the money to UNICEF, the utilitarian is committed to saying that you should choose the second option. This is not to say that promises don't matter. We should keep our promises *when* this has the best consequences. But, for the utilitarian, we have lost sight of what morality is all about if we think that we should keep a promise even when this prevents us from saving people's lives or otherwise doing the most good for the most people.

According to what is sometimes called "classical" utilitarianism—the utilitarianism of the two British founders of this school of thought, Jeremy Bentham and John Stuart Mill—our actions should aim at the greatest amount of happiness for the greatest number of people, where by "happiness" is meant pleasure and freedom from pain. This account of happiness is known as "hedonism." Thus, classical utilitarianism is sometimes called "hedonistic" utilitarianism. John Stuart Mill writes:

> The creed which accepts as the foundation of morals "utility" or the "greatest happiness principle" holds that actions are right in proportion as they tend to promote happiness, wrong as they tend to produce the reverse of happiness. By happiness is intended pleasure, and the absence of pain; by unhappiness, pain and the privation of pleasure. (Mill 1974: 297)

An important corollary of this principle is that other animals count as "persons" in a morally important sense. For if our actions must aim at maximizing pleasure and minimizing pain, *everyone* considered, then since other animals are capable of experiencing pleasure and pain, it follows that their interests must be taken into account as well. In fact, for the classical utilitarian, the suffering of a human being has no greater moral significance than the suffering of any other animal. If it is wrong to inflict pain upon someone because the experience of pain is bad, then it doesn't matter *whose* pain it is; the experience of pain is bad regardless of *who* experiences it, human or nonhuman.

If the utilitarian is right about this, it certainly has important implications concerning our treatment of nonhuman animals. As Jeremy Bentham once remarked:

> The day *may* come when the rest of the animal creation may acquire those rights which never could have been withholden from them but by the hand of tyranny. The French have already discovered that the blackness of the skin is no reason why a human being should be abandoned without redress to the caprice of a tormentor. It may one day come to be recognized that the number of legs, the villosity of the skin, or the termination of the *os sacrum*, are reasons equally insufficient for abandoning a sensitive being to the same fate. What else is it that should trace the insuperable line? Is it the faculty of reason, or perhaps the faculty of discourse? But a full grown horse or dog is beyond comparison a more rational, as well as a more conversable animal, than an infant of a day or a week, or even a month, old. But suppose they were otherwise, what would it avail? The question is not, Can they reason? nor Can they *talk*? but, *Can they suffer*? (Bentham 1948: 311n)

The idea that utilitarianism builds on is that the whole point of morality is to bring about the best possible state of affairs, everyone considered and considered equally. This is an attractive idea. If we have done the right thing, shouldn't we have improved the world somehow? Shouldn't there be less suffering or more happiness than there otherwise would have been? Still, many philosophers believe that this idea is seriously problematic, and the critical literature on utilitarianism is vast. Let us take a look at three objections to the theory: the ends-means objection; the incompleteness objection; and the problem of unforeseeable consequences.

Generally stated, the ends-means objection amounts to this: for the utilitarian, no action is inherently wrong; anything is permissible, depending upon its outcomes. Suppose, for example, that we could discover a cure for cancer and save millions of lives, but this required forced, invasive experiments on human beings—kidnapping hundreds of people, infecting them with cancer, confining them in cages, killing them, dissecting their remains. Most people would say that it would be seriously wrong to conduct such experiments. But for the utilitarian, the end justifies the means. Any action is acceptable, depending upon its consequences. If we could prevent a great evil, but only by committing a smaller evil (perhaps only a slightly smaller evil), we would be morally justified in doing so, according to the utilitarian.

Or consider the following infamous case (first discussed by Judith Jarvis Thomson in "Killing, Letting Die, and the Trolley Problem"). You are a surgeon with six patients. One patient simply needs to have her tonsils removed, while the remaining five need organ transplants: one needs a liver, another a heart, another a lung, and two others need kidneys. In fact, if these five patients do not receive organ transplants within the next hour, they will die. It turns out that the one patient (suffering only from bad tonsils) is a matching donor. Her organs could be used to save the five other patients, but only at the cost of her own life. You are in a position to kill this patient and use her organs in transplant procedures to save the five other patients. What should you do? Clearly, you can do the most good for the most people by saving the five patients, even though this entails directly killing one patient. So for the utilitarian, this would be the right thing to do. Most people, however, believe that this would be seriously wrong.

Utilitarians believe that we should be concerned only with the outcomes of our actions. But isn't there more to morality than this? According to the second objection to utilitarianism, while maximizing utility—maximizing happiness and minimizing unhappiness—may be the goal of morality, it also matters how we achieve this goal. For this reason, utilitarianism gives us an "incomplete" picture of the moral facts. For example, suppose you have promised to pay someone $500 to paint your house. Once the job is done, however, you determine that you could do more good for more people by donating the money to a local homeless shelter. Should the painter accept your utilitarian justification for breaking your promise?

The third objection to utilitarianism rests upon the following fact: that we are largely in the dark concerning the future consequences of our actions. Because of this, we can never reach a rational, well-founded conclusion about what to do on the basis of utilitarian considerations alone. Consider again the case of the drowning child. Can I know, or even reasonably believe, that rescuing the child will have the best consequences in the long run? Do I know—to consider just one among any number of possible outcomes—that the child will not grow up to be a mass murderer? Perhaps saving the child will have the best consequences, but perhaps it will not. But because I have no rational basis for believing that saving the child *will* have the best consequences, I have no utilitarian reason for saving the child.

To take a notorious example of utilitarian moral reasoning, consider President Harry Truman's decision to drop atomic bombs on two Japanese cities, Hiroshima and Nagasaki, at the end of the Second World War. According to his memoirs, Truman weighed the alternatives: either 500,000 Americans would be killed in ground combat against the Japanese, or a significant but smaller number of Japanese would be killed in the nuclear conflagration. In fact, about 120,000 people were killed in Hiroshima and Nagasaki and another 130,000 injured. Tens of thousands of others died slowly from radiation exposure and its effects.

One glaring problem with utilitarian moral reasoning, as this example illustrates, is that the calculations upon which such reasoning depends are largely conjectural. There was no official basis for Truman's claim that 500,000 Americans would be killed in ground combat against the Japanese, and it may well have been an unrealistic estimate. In Hiroshima alone, about 220,000 people eventually died because of the atomic blast and its effects. Were more innocent lives saved than lost because of Truman's decision? We will never know. The effects of our actions ripple throughout the future and influence events in ways we cannot possibly predict. Because of choices we make now, what will the world be like ten years, a hundred years, a thousand years in the future? There is simply no way of knowing, or even guessing. Yet, from a utilitarian perspective, unpredictable consequences are morally as important as predictable ones, and actions that have good predictable consequences might well have disastrous unpredictable ones.

3.3. Deontologism

Our discussion of utilitarianism suggests that whether an action is right or wrong is not determined exclusively by its consequences. This does not necessarily mean that the consequences are irrelevant, although "extreme" deontologists take this position. It may only mean that there are additional considerations—what these might be is an open question—that are relevant in distinguishing between right and wrong. This is the position of the "moderate" deontologist. In this section, we will examine three theories in the deontological tradition: Kantian ethics; the divine command theory; and the theory of rights.

Kantian Ethics

Kantian ethics—the ethics of the eighteenth-century German philosopher Immanuel Kant—is considered by many to be the main alternative to utilitarianism. While the utilitarian maintains that the sole aim of morality is to maximize happiness and minimize unhappiness, Kant believed that what morality requires is strict obedience to moral rules. For Kant, it is always wrong to lie, or to break a promise, or to kill an innocent person, or to violate any other rule of morality.

In Kantian ethics, the basis for all moral rules is a principle known as the "categorical imperative." Kant gave different but equivalent formulations of the principle. In one formulation, the categorical imperative says:

> Act only according to that maxim by which you can at the same time will that it should become a universal law. (Kant 2007: 83)

According to this, if you cannot consistently will that your "maxim" (or rule of conduct) become a universal law, then you are doing something wrong. You must choose to act in such a way that your conduct can serve as an example for all people to follow. For example, suppose you are contemplating whether to tell a lie, or to break a promise, or to steal something. Can you consistently will that everyone follow your example? Kant believed that you could not and, therefore, that such things are always wrong. Suppose, for example, that you hope to gain something by telling a lie. Can you consistently will that your maxim become a universal law—that *all* people lie whenever it is to their advantage? Notice that nothing can be gained by telling a lie unless people can be trusted. (Lies accomplish nothing unless people believe them.) So the maxim you are acting on, if you choose to lie, presupposes that people can be trusted, and yet if all people lied whenever it was to their advantage, no one could be trusted. Therefore, you cannot *consistently* will that your maxim should become a universal law; to will this would be to will both that people be trusted and that people *not* be trusted, which is contradictory.

Kant maintained, not only that we should refrain from treating people in certain ways, but that on occasion we should come to their assistance. He gives the following example to illustrate this implication of the categorical imperative:

[A man], who is in prosperity, while he sees that others have to contend with great wretchedness and that he could help them, thinks: What concern is it of mine? Let every one be as happy as heaven pleases or as he can make himself; I will take nothing from him nor even envy him, only I do not wish to contribute anything either to his welfare or to his assistance in distress! . . . But although it is possible that a universal law of nature might exist in accordance with that maxim, it is impossible to *will* that such a principle should have the universal validity of a law of nature. For a will which resolved this would contradict itself, inasmuch as many cases might occur in which one would have need of the love and sympathy of others, and in which by such a law of nature, sprung from his own will, he would deprive himself of all hope of the aid he desires. (Kant 2007: 84-85)

The second formulation of the categorical imperative says:

Act so that you treat humanity, whether in your own person or in that of another, always as an end and never as a means only. (Kant 2007: 86)

As Kant saw it, all human beings are equal in inherent worth. Some ways of treating people acknowledge this fact, while other ways of treating people deny their personhood and reduce them to the status of things. According to the second formulation of the categorical imperative, our fundamental moral obligation is to treat every person as someone of inherent worth and never as a mere thing.

This is an appealing idea, but what is it that sets human beings apart from mere things—a category which, for Kant, included not only inanimate objects but all other animals? For Kant, the inherent worth of human beings resides in the following fact: that unlike mere things, human beings are rational, autonomous beings, capable of governing their own lives and making rational choices. To treat someone "as an end" is to treat that person as a rational, autonomous being; to treat someone "as a means only" is to treat that person as a mere thing.

Consider what this means in the case of telling a lie. If I am to rationally govern my own life, I must have reliable information. If you lie to me, you undermine my ability to make rational choices. For example, suppose you are a dishonest salesperson, and you lie to me so that I will buy some product—say, a new television—that I would otherwise not purchase. In doing this, you are treating me "as a means only." You are not treating me "as an end," as a rational, autonomous being, because you are not providing me with the information that I need in order to make a rational, well-informed choice. Rather, your intention is to undermine my autonomy so that I will make a choice that serves *your* interests.

Another clear illustration of treating someone "as a means only" is provided by an earlier example. We saw that, for the utilitarian, we would be justified in killing one patient and using her organs in transplant procedures if in this way we could save the lives of several other patients. Would this be permissible for Kant? Obviously not, because to do this would be to treat the "donor" as a mere thing, as a medical resource, rather than as a person. And this is true no matter how many lives are saved. Even if we could save the lives of millions of people by killing just one, for Kant this would still be wrong. (Although Kant took the position that it is always wrong to kill an *innocent* person, interestingly, Kant believed that it is morally obligatory to execute murderers. We will discuss this implication of the categorical imperative in a later chapter.)

Enlarging upon Kant's analysis, one contemporary philosopher, Martha Nussbaum (1995: 257), has identified seven different ways of treating someone (or something) as a mere thing:

1.   *Instrumentality*: The objectifier treats the object as a tool of his or her purposes.
2.   *Denial of autonomy*: The objectifier treats the object as lacking in autonomy and self-determination.
3.   *Inertness*: The objectifier treats the object as lacking in agency, and perhaps also in activity.
4.   *Fungibility*: The objectifier treats the object as interchangeable (a) with other objects of the same type, and/or (b) with objects of other types.
5.   *Violability*: The objectifier treats the object as something lacking in boundary-integrity, as something that it is permissible to break up, smash, break into.
6.   *Ownership*: The objectifier treats the object as something that is owned by another, can be bought or sold, etc.
7.   *Denial of subjectivity*: The objectifier treats the object as something whose experience and feelings (if any) need not be taken into account.

Take an ordinary pencil, for example. I relate to a pencil as a useful tool. As such, it is subject to my will. It does not act upon me; I act upon it. It is passive, inert. It is also replaceable. There is nothing special or unique about it. It is a piece of property and I have the right to treat it however I want—to use it, abuse it, even destroy it. It has no boundary-integrity that I must respect. It has no experiences or feelings that I must take into account. It is *just* a thing. Of course, there is nothing wrong with objectifying a pencil, because a pencil *is* an object.

But to treat a person in this way is dehumanizing and, according to Kant, inherently wrong. Rape, for example, illustrates how an objectifier treats a person as a tool or instrument of his own sexual gratification, and in so doing reduces his victim to a sexual object. Slavery illustrates how objectifiers treat people as if they can be owned, bought, and sold, thereby reducing them to property.

To sum up: According to Kant, some actions are inherently right or wrong. In particular, morality requires that we treat human beings—understood as rational, autonomous beings—in ways that manifest respect for their dignity and inherent worth. This requires that we treat every human being as and end and never merely as a means. Doing this requires that we strictly adhere to certain rules of conduct. It requires, for example, that we never lie, that we always keep our promises, that we refrain from killing innocent people, and that we assist the needy. Such actions are right *regardless* of their consequences.

However, lingering in this summation of Kantian ethics are two rather obvious problems. First, Kant's position concerning the inviolability of moral rules seems implausible. Is it, for example, *always* wrong to lie? Consider the following example. Suppose you work as a janitor in a high-rise apartment building. One day, while you are rearranging boxes in the basement, you accidentally knock over a tank of deadly poison. The tank ruptures and begins to leak poison gas into the ventilation system. Within a few minutes the gas will engulf the entire building, killing everyone inside. Obviously, you must act quickly and warn others. The problem is that you don't speak English. In fact, the only English word you know is "fire." In desperation, you run through the hallways yelling "Fire!" hoping that people will believe, mistakenly, that the building is on fire and evacuate. Are you doing the right thing? How bizarre it would be to claim that even if everyone in the building must perish, it is it is nonetheless wrong to tell a lie.

A second problem with Kantian ethics concerns the possibility of moral conflict. Suppose I cannot keep one rule without breaking another. What then? If doing the right thing requires strict adherence to moral rules, and if it is impossible to *always* adhere to the rules of morality, then it is not always possible to do the right thing. For example, suppose I have promised to pick you up at a certain time and drive you somewhere, but along the way I see a family in a broken-down car—parents with small children, stranded in a dangerous part of town. I could stop and help, but if I did, I would be late and break my promise. On the one hand, I ought to keep my promise; but on the other, I ought to help the family. The problem, of course, is that I cannot do both. Either I keep my promise, in which case I fail to help the family; or I help the family, in which case I fail to keep my promise. No matter what I do, I am doing something wrong.

A situation like this—a situation of moral conflict—is known as a "moral dilemma." For those, such as Kant, who maintain that morality is based upon absolute moral rules, moral dilemmas are especially problematic. If there are *no* exceptions to the rules of morality—if we must *never* break a promise, if we must *always* help those in need, and so on—then in situations of moral conflict we cannot possibly avoid doing something wrong.

Kant's approach to the problem turns on the distinction between "perfect" and "imperfect" obligations. Roughly, a perfect obligation is one that requires something specific for its fulfillment, whereas an imperfect obligation is one that does not. The obligation not to break a promise, for example, is a perfect obligation (and so are other negative obligations, such as the obligation not to lie, not to steal, and so on). If I have promised to pick you up at a certain time, this is a perfect obligation which makes a specific demand on me. On the other hand, the obligation to help those in need is an imperfect obligation (and so are other positive obligations). As Kant interprets it, I am obligated to do "enough" for others, but it is up to me to decide when and how I do this. I might make regular donations to charity, for example, or volunteer at a homeless shelter, among other possibilities. But, because this is an imperfect obligation, it is not the case that I am obligated to assist someone simply because that person needs someone's assistance and I am in a position to help. In the situation we have imagined, for example, I am not obligated to help the family stranded on the side of the road. This does not mean that there are exceptions to imperfect obligations. If I have lived a completely miserly life, contributing little or nothing to the welfare of others, then I have neglected my obligation to assist the needy. But I have not neglected this obligation simply because I have not, in a specific situation, failed to help someone in need. Therefore, the situation we have imagined is not, from a Kantian perspective, a morally impossible one. If I keep my promise to you and in other ways fulfill my obligation to help those in need, then I have done nothing wrong. For Kant, then, the solution to moral dilemmas is this: when perfect duties seem to clash with imperfect ones—when, for example, I cannot help someone in need without breaking a promise— perfect duties prevail.

Does this solve the problem? Consider the following case. Suppose I have promised to meet you somewhere at exactly 12:00 noon, but along the way I hear the cries of a child who has fallen into a deep well. I could, with some effort, rescue the child, but if I did, I would be late for my appointment. Would it be right for me to abandon the child so that I would not break my promise? The problem, obviously, is that keeping a promise does not always take precedence over helping others. Sometimes it does, but sometimes it doesn't. Generally speaking, if I could save someone's life, or prevent some other great evil, by breaking a trivial promise, then it would be permissible for me to break the promise. According to Kant, however, we are never justified in breaking a promise no matter what the consequences. In light of this example (and other easily imaginable examples) Kant's "solution" to the problem of moral dilemmas is not really a solution.

The Divine Command Theory

Is there an important connection between morality and religion? Many people think so. In fact, a not uncommon view is that the essence of morality is "right-eousness," understood as obedience to God, and that the essence of immorality is "sin," understood as defiance of God. Among philosophers, this is known as the "divine command theory" of morality. On this view, whether an action is right or wrong is determined ultimately by God's will: what makes an action right is that God commands it, and what makes an action wrong is that God for-bids it.

A rather striking illustration of the divine command theory is provided by Chapter 22 of Genesis, where Abraham is tested by God. Abraham is instructed: "Take your son, your only son, Isaac, whom you love, and go to the region of Moriah. Sacrifice him there as a burnt offering on one of the mountains I will tell you about" (22:2). Abraham does not challenge the Lord. After reaching the designated location, Abraham "built an altar there and arranged the wood on it. He bound his son Isaac and laid him on the altar, on top of the wood. Then he reached out his hand and took the knife to slay his son" (22:9-11). An angel in-tervened. "Do not do anything to him," Abraham is told. "Now I know that you fear God, because you have not withheld from me your son, your only son." If there is a moral lesson in this story, what is it? Certainly, we are supposed to think that Abraham did the right thing, at least in the eyes of God. Yet, how can it be right for Abraham to sacrifice his son (or, at least, how can it be right for him to be willing to sacrifice his son) simply because God has commanded it? The divine command theory has an answer: the essence of morality is obedience to God. "Because you have done this," the angel tells Abraham, "and have not withheld your son, your only son, I will surely bless you and make your de-scendants as numerous as the stars in the sky and as the sand on the seashore" (22:16-17).

The divine command theory is one way to understand the relationship be-tween morality and religion, but it is not the only way, and it may not be the best way. In critically evaluating this theory, consider the following three questions. First, do we have good reasons for believing that God exists? If not, then the theory has no rational foundation. Second, even if we can know that God exists, what reliable source of information do we have concerning God's commands? Different religions accept different sources as authoritative—the Bible and the Koran are only two options—and possibly none of them is truly authoritative. If we don't know what God's commands are, then we can never apply the divine command theory to reach a moral decision. Third, even if we can know that God exists and that some religious source is reliable, is it the case that the standards of morality depend upon the will of God? Let us explore this last question more fully.

If the standards of morality depend upon God's will, then any arbitrary ac-tion would be right if God commanded it. To appreciate the problem, consider some of God's commandments from the Book of Deuteronomy in the Old Testament:

> A woman must not wear men's clothing, nor a man wear woman's clothing, for the Lord your God detests anyone who does this. (22:5)

> Do not plant two kinds of seed in your vineyard; if you do, not only the crops you plant but also the fruit of the vineyard will be defiled. (22:9)

> Do not wear clothes of wool and linen woven together. (22:11)

> Make tassels on the four corners of the cloak you wear. (22:12)

If what makes an action right is simply that God commands it, then these seemingly trivial commandments have the same moral force as the commandments against killing, lying, and stealing. In fact, if the divine command theory is correct, it is *just* as wrong to violate any of these minor commandments as it is to commit murder. Because there are no degrees of commanding, there are no degrees of right and wrong. All right actions are equally right, and all wrong actions are equally wrong.

This is bad enough, but there is another problem. If the *only* thing that makes an action right is that God commands it, then any deplorable action would be right if God commanded it. Consider another passage from the Book of Deuteronomy (21:18-21):

> If a man has a stubborn and rebellious son who does not obey his father and mother and will not listen to them when they discipline him, his father and mother shall take hold of him and bring him to the elders at the gate of his town. . . . Then all the men of his town shall stone him to death. You must purge the evil from among you. All Israel will hear of it and be afraid.

God is thought to be almighty. But could any being be powerful enough to make it right to stone children to death as punishment for disobedience? If some actions would be wrong even if God commanded them, then the divine command theory is false. The argument:

(1) If the divine command theory is true, then any action would be right if God commanded it.
(2) There are some actions (such as stoning children to death) that would be wrong even if God commanded them.

Therefore:

(3) The divine command theory is false.

It is pointless to argue that God would not command us to do something that was morally wrong. For (aside from scriptural evidence to the contrary) this assumes that there are standards of morality independent of God's will. Yet, if what makes an action right is that God commands it, then there are no moral boundaries to the commands that God might make.

Moral Rights

A theory of moral conduct attempts to identify some principle that is fundamental to moral decision-making. So far we have considered several such attempts. Whether or not a complete moral theory can be founded on the conception of rights—which seems doubtful—many philosophers believe that rights constitute an indispensable moral category. Many moral issues are framed in terms of rights: Does the fetus have a right to life? Do animals have rights? Do governments have a right to rule? Do all citizens have a right to employment, housing, medical care, and other social benefits? Such issues are framed in terms of rights because they involve relationships between powerful individuals or institutions—adults, human beings, governments—and those over whom power is exercised—fetuses, animals, citizens. Rights determine whether and how such power may be used.

From this it should be clear that "moral" rights do not necessarily coincide with "legal" rights. The citizens of Pakistan may have a moral right to practice any religion they choose, but they do not have the legal right to convert from Islam to another faith. (The punishment for apostasy is death.) A woman living in El Salvador may have a moral right to have an abortion, but she has no such legal right (not even if the procedure is necessary to save her life). Legal rights vary from one country to another and are entirely conventional. Moral rights are universal and have the same objective and independent status that all moral principles have.

Sometimes the expression "human rights" is used interchangeably with what is meant here by "moral rights," but this is problematic for at least two reasons. First, the expression suggests that consciousness, the desire to live, the ability to experience pain, and other psychological capacities are irrelevant to whether a being has rights; all that matters is whether that being is biologically human. If this is true, then even someone in a persistent vegetative state—who has permanently lost the capacity for conscious experience—has the same rights as anyone else. Second, if moral rights are human rights, then nonhuman animals have no rights at all, regardless of their mental capacities. Certainly, we cannot take this for granted. Exactly what beings are rights-holders, or "persons" in the morally important sense, is a complex and largely unresolved philosophical issue, but it is safe to assume that this category excludes some human beings—maybe human fetuses, and almost certainly anyone in a persistent vegetative state—and includes many nonhuman animals.

Every right involves a "claim" against others that they behave or refrain from behaving in certain ways. Because you have a right to life, for example, you have a claim against others that they refrain from causing your death. But what is distinctive about rights as a moral category is that rights regulate the legitimate use of force or power. This has a dual meaning. First, rights impose moral limits on the use of power. This is why the language of rights is often used when discussing the moral status of vulnerable individuals or groups. Second, rights license the use of force. If someone tries to kill you—threatening your right to life—you may use force, even lethal force, against the attacker, if necessary. If someone tries to steal one of your possessions—threatening your property right—you may use force against the thief. In general, if you have a right to something, then it is permissible for you (or the government, or someone acting on your behalf) to use force in defense of that right. A right can therefore be defined as an *enforceable* claim against others that they behave or refrain from behaving in certain ways.

Reflected in this definition is the distinction between "negative" and "positive" rights. Corresponding to every negative right is a negative obligation (or an obligation of forbearance). The right to life, for example, is a negative right. Respecting your right to life does not require that I keep you alive or do anything else for you, but only that I refrain from causing your death. Property rights are negative too. Respecting your property rights does not require that I give you anything, but merely that I leave your things alone. Corresponding to every positive right, on the other hand, is a positive obligation (or an obligation of beneficence). Respecting people's positive rights requires, not simply that they not be interfered with, but that they be provided with certain benefits. If parents have an enforceable obligation to provide their children with food, housing, medical care, education, and other benefits, then children have a positive right to parental care. Socialists sometimes claim that all citizens have positive rights to such benefits, but this claim is disputed. Indeed, some philosophers—in particular, libertarians—deny that there are *any* positive rights. (We will return to this issue in Chapter 8.)

All rights have three characteristic features. First, rights can be *transferred*. If you buy a book from me for $10.00, then strictly speaking we do not exchange property but property rights. In the exchange, I transfer my property right to the book and it becomes your rightful property; you transfer your property right to the money and it becomes my rightful property. Another important example concerns the institution of government. A "government" is often defined as an institution that has a monopoly on the legitimate use of force with a geographical area. How does a government come to have such a monopoly? We have seen that all rights are by nature enforceable. When people combine together to form a state, the explanation goes, they transfer their right of enforcement to the government. The government acts on behalf of its citizens in enforcing their rights. In this way, the government acquires a monopoly on the legitimate use of force within its territorial boundaries. (It will be noticed, though, that if this explanation is correct, the only legitimate power that a government has is to enforce people's rights.)

A second characteristic feature of rights is that rights can be *waived*. If something is your sole property, then you alone have the right to make use of it. If I take your car for a spin, then I violate your property right unless you grant me permission. By granting me permission, you waive your right to the exclusive use of the car. A more interesting example concerns the morality of euthanasia. It is sometimes argued that euthanasia is wrong because it is always wrong to kill an innocent person. However, if what makes it wrong to kill an innocent person is that it violates that person's right to life, then voluntary euthanasia would not be wrong. By consenting to euthanasia, a person would waive his or her right to life, in which case euthanasia would not violate that person's right.

The third characteristic feature of rights is that rights can be *forfeited*. This is an especially important consideration in connection with the ethics of punishment. If theft, kidnapping, and murder are wrong, then how can it be permissible to fine, imprison, or execute criminals? The usual answer is that, by committing crimes, criminals forfeit certain rights they would otherwise have. Which rights? The very rights that they violate by their criminal actions. If this is true, then the death penalty does not violate the right to life of murderers, since murderers forfeit their right to life by violating the right to life of their victims. There may be other objections to capital punishment, but it cannot be said that capital punishment is "murder" in same sense in which intentionally killing an innocent, unwilling person is murder. (We will return to the issue of rights forfeiture in Chapter 9.)

An important and unresolved issue in ethics concerns how to weigh rights against other moral considerations. One moderate deontological view combines utilitarianism with rights theory. According to this view, we should strive to maximize happiness and minimize unhappiness, but at the same time we must respect the rights of all those affected by our actions. People's rights impose deontological restrictions on how we can go about achieving morally worthwhile goals. But how stringent are these restrictions? Do utilitarian considerations sometimes outweigh people's rights? Or do rights represent absolute moral boundaries?

To say that rights are "absolute" means that it is *always* wrong to violate people's rights, no matter what is at stake. We have seen that rights restrict the use of power. Because power is so often abused, it is tempting to think that such restrictions are absolute. There are examples that support this conception of rights, such as the following:

The Journalist Case: A terrorist group threatens to detonate a bomb, killing dozens of people, unless the authorities meet their demand. Their demand is that a journalist, who has written articles ridiculing the Prophet, be publicly executed. If the authorities execute the journalist, one innocent person will die; but if they don't, dozens of innocent people will die. Should the authorities meet this demand?

Many people believe that it would be wrong to execute the journalist (even if the terrorists have acquired a nuclear bomb and threaten the lives of many thousands of people). This example suggests that it is wrong to violate people's rights no matter what the cost.

But other examples suggest that rights are sometimes outweighed by utility. Here's one:

> The Hijack Case: An airplane has been hijacked by a terrorist group. Their intention is to fly the airplane into a large office building. If they are successful, not only will everyone on the airplane be killed, but so will everyone in the office building. The authorities can prevent the terrorist attack, but only by blowing up the airplane, in which case *they* (not the terrorists) will murder the passengers. What should be done?

Many people think that it would be permissible for the authorities to blow up the airplane, even though they would be violating the passengers' rights. This seems plausible.

It is unclear, then, how to weigh rights, even the right to life, against consequentialist considerations. Why would it be permissible to violate people's rights—in fact, to commit mass murder—in the Hijack Case but not in the Journalist Case? The fact that the passengers will die soon anyway does not cancel out their rights. (Terminally ill patients do not lose their rights simply because they do not have long to live.) But if this is not the relevant difference between the two cases, what is? (For a possible solution to this puzzle, see Chapter 10.)

3.4. Virtue Ethics

For Plato, the study of ethics was essentially the study of character. It was concerned, in Plato's words, not "with the outward man, but with the inner, which is the true self and concernment of man" (Plato 1991: IV 444d). Aristotle adopted a similar view. For Aristotle, the ultimate goal in life is "happiness," "well-being," or "flourishing" (from the Greek *eudaimonia*). The virtues are character traits that promote human flourishing. "The good of Man," wrote Aristotle, "is an activity of the soul in accordance with virtue" (Aristotle 1973: 1098a 17-19). What distinguishes the ethics of Plato and Aristotle from the other theories discussed in this chapter is that, for Plato and Aristotle, the central question of ethics is not "What is right thing to do?" but rather "What sort of person should I be?"

Virtue ethics, as this is now known, is not just the study of virtue, but an attempt to explain moral conduct in terms of virtuous character. The basic idea is this: the right thing to do is what the good person does. As it stands, this criterion cannot be classified as consequentialist or deontological because it says nothing about what *makes* an action right or wrong. (We don't want to say that what makes an action right is simply that it is done by a virtuous person, because virtuous people, like the rest of us, do many things that have no moral significance. Is it morally obligatory to grow a beard because virtuous people sometimes have beards?) In what follows, I will outline two ways in which the ethics of virtue might be applied to the theory of moral conduct.

One way is suggested by the following observation. Not only do we use the language of the virtues and the vices to talk about *people*, we use the same language to talk about people's *actions*. There are kind people, and there are acts of kindness. There are cruel people, and there are acts of cruelty. There are honest people, and there are acts of honesty, and so on. This suggests the following deontological moral theory: that what makes an action right is that it is a virtuous act, and what makes an action wrong is that it is a vicious act. If this is correct, then to decide whether an action is right or wrong, we must determine whether it is an act of kindness or cruelty, honesty or dishonesty, greed or generosity, compassion or callousness, courage or cowardice, patience or impatience, or whether it exhibits some other virtue or vice.

To appreciate this account, consider the following three problem cases:

The Street Vendor Case: You're buying a magazine from a street vendor. You hand him what you think is a $5.00 bill, but it is really a $20.00 bill. When he hands you back more than $15.00 in change, you mistakenly believe that he has made a costly mistake, but you pocket the money anyway. Have you done something wrong?

The Dare Case: You're driving home late one night with a friend. As you approach an intersection, he dares you to close your eyes and drive through a red light. Foolishly, you accept the dare, close your eyes, and plunge through the intersection. Luckily, the street is empty and no one is hurt. Did you do something wrong?

The Assault Case: One night, you're awakened by cries for help. "I've been stabbed! Someone help me! Please help me!" The cries are coming from your neighbor's apartment. You consider calling the police, but why should you get involved? You decide to ignore the situation, cover your ears, and go back to sleep. The next day you're surprised to learn that no one was assaulted. What you heard was your neighbor's television. Did you do something wrong?

In each of these cases, it seems correct to say that you did something wrong, but it is difficult to explain why. Is there a utilitarian explanation? No, because no one was hurt by your actions. In the Dare Case, someone *might* have been injured or killed when you ran the red light, but luckily no one was. Is there an explanation in terms of people's rights? No, because no one's rights were violated either. In the Dare Case, no one's rights were even threatened, since the roads were deserted. In the Street Vendor Case, you did not violate the vendor's property rights, since you pocketed the correct change. Is there an explanation in terms of moral rules? If so, then what moral precept is violated in the Assault Case? Since no one was actually assaulted, you did not fail to help someone in need. How is it, then, that you did something wrong?

The virtue ethicist has a reply. In each of these cases, your behavior reflects badly upon your character. In the Vendor Case, you took advantage of someone else's mistake, or so you thought. An honest person would have discussed the discrepancy with the vendor. In the Dare Case, your behavior was reckless and irresponsible. A conscientious driver would not have accepted the dare. In the Assault Case, you behaved callously. A concerned neighbor would have investigated the disturbance or contacted the police. In each of these cases, a good person would have acted differently.

To see why this account should be classified as deontological, consider the following two cases:

The Heart Attack Case: You are walking along a sidewalk when a stranger collapses on the pavement at your feet, gasping for his pills. Fumbling through his coat pocket, you find a container that reads: "Heart Medication: Take one tablet in the event of a cardiac emergency." Believing that the man is having a heart attack, you force one of the pills into his mouth. Unfortunately, the container was mislabeled and you unintentionally give the man a deadly poison. If you had done nothing, he would have lived. Now he is dead, and you killed him. Did you do the right thing?

The Placebo Case: You stand to inherit a vast estate from your wealthy uncle. He is an elderly man, but in good health, except for a heart condition. You are impatient and unscrupulous, so you devise a plan to dispose of him. You locate his heart medication and replace each of the pills with a placebo—except for one, which, in your haste, you overlook. Sometime later, your uncle complains of chest pains and you solicitously give him the one pill you did not replace, believing it to be a useless sugar pill. To your great disappointment, you unintentionally save his life. Did you do the right thing?

These two cases are initially somewhat puzzling, but on reflection it seems correct to say that you did the right thing in the Heart Attack Case and the wrong thing in the Placebo Case. But how can this be, given that you killed the stranger but saved your uncle's life? One difference between the two cases concerns your motivations. In the Heart Attack Case, your motivation was caring or compassion. You acted from a basic desire to help someone in need. In the Placebo Case, however, your motivation was greed. You wanted to dispose of your uncle so that you could inherit his fortune. Another difference concerns your intentions. In the Heart Attack Case, your intention was to save the stranger's life, whereas in the Placebo Case, it was to hasten your uncle's death. In the Heart Attack case, even though what you did had bad consequences, you acted virtuously, because your motives and intentions were good. In the Placebo case, even though what you did had good consequences, you acted viciously, because your motives and intentions were bad. As these examples illustrate, whether an action is virtuous or vicious has to do with the internal states of the agent and not with the external consequences of the action.

Another way of applying virtue ethics to the analysis of moral action—which yields a consequentialist theory—is suggested by Plato's contention that the aim of living a moral life is to attain and maintain good character. As Plato wrote, speaking of the just or virtuous man:

> [H]e proceeds to act, if he has to act, . . . always thinking and calling that which preserves and cooperates with his harmonious condition [the condition of the just soul], just and good action, . . . and that which at any time impairs this condition, he will call unjust action. (Plato 1991: IV 443e)

For Plato, the rightness or wrongness of an action is to be explained in terms of its consequences—specifically, its effects upon the agent's character. As Plato saw it, we are not born virtuous; rather, we become virtuous by performing virtuous acts. Right conduct is conduct that promotes "the health and beauty and well-being of the soul," whereas wrong conduct is conduct that promotes "the disease and weakness and deformity" of the soul (Plato 1991: IV 444e).

To what extent do we mold our own character? In his autobiography, G. Gordon Liddy—former aid to Richard Nixon—tells the story of his "lifelong journey from physical and psychological weakness to strength" (Liddy 1996: 492). He relates the following story of how, as a young boy, he overcame his fear of thunderstorms:

> On a Saturday afternoon in September, the western sky blackened and the wind rose. Severe thunderstorms had been predicted over a wide front. . . . I left the house quietly by the back door and went around the back of the detached garage in the wooded area. . . . I brought with me a four-foot safety belt I'd fashioned by braiding a clothesline rope and fixing a D-ring on one end and a metal shape-link on the other. The tree I had chosen was a pin oak about seventy-five feet tall. . . . After ten minutes of climbing, I gained the highest point that would hold my weight—some sixty feet up—and I lashed myself to the trunk with the belt. . . . Open your eyes. *Open your eyes*, I commanded myself, OPEN YOUR EYES! I did. It was chaos. The earth danced as the tree trunk swayed and snapped back against the wind. Water streamed into my eyes and I had to fight to hold them open, not daring to let go of the tree long enough to wipe them. . . . With reckless abandon I released one hand and shook my fist at the wildly pitching sky. "Kill me!" I shouted, "Go ahead and try! I don't care! I don't care!" and I started to laugh uncontrollably as I rode the whirlwind. (Liddy 1996: 48-49)

Elsewhere Liddy explains how, as a child, he conquered his fear of rats. One day, after finding the carcass of a large, dead rat, he built a fire from broken twigs and branches. "For the next hour," he writes, "I roasted the dead rat. Then I removed the burned carcass with a stick and let it cool. With a scout knife I skinned, then cut

off and ate the roasted haunches of the rat. The meat was tasteless and stringy"
(Liddy 1996: 40).

Of course, courage is only one virtue, but Liddy's autobiography illustrates
Plato's contention concerning the development of virtuous character: that we
become virtuous people by performing virtuous acts—that we become courageous,
for example, by doing courageous deeds. If our highest good is, as Plato believed,
good character, then we can achieve our highest good only by behaving in virtuous
ways—not necessarily by lashing ourselves to trees during thunderstorms or eating
dead rats, but by acting courageously, honestly, generously, patiently, fairly, kindly,
and in other virtuous ways.

Plato's view seems reasonable. If it is good for you to develop your
mathematical, musical, artistic, or athletic abilities, why would it not be good for
you to develop your moral abilities? Did Gandhi waste his life on moral
development when he might have been a successful attorney? Did Mother
Teresa waste her time becoming a saint when she might have been a successful
artist, mathematician, or circus performer? True, Gandhi might have had a more
comfortable life if he had established a successful law practice. Mother Teresa
might have had a more exciting life if she had become a circus acrobat. But
would they have had better lives?

The view expressed here is essentially a form of egoism, though in an elevated
form. For the egoist, as we saw earlier, a person's sole fundamental moral
obligation is to promote her own good. According to Plato, a person's true good
resides in the moral goodness of her character—in what Plato referred to as the
"health and beauty and well-being of the soul." If, as the egoist maintains, a moral
life is a life well lived, and if the virtuous life is not just a good life, but the best
life that a person can have, then a person's supreme moral obligation is a live a
life devoted to moral development. This was apparently Plato's view.

Platonic ethics responds to the objections raised earlier in this chapter
against "crude" egoism. There may be many things to be gained by dishonesty,
by cruelty, by disloyalty, or by other immoral means, but moral goodness is not
among them. If Plato is right, it is in our own best interest to do the right thing,
because this is how we build good character. But this raises another objection.
According to Plato, what *makes* an action right or wrong has to do with how it
affects the agent's character. What makes it wrong for you to throw darts at a
cat, for instance, is that it is bad *for you* to be cruel. What makes it right for you
to give to the poor is that it is good *for you* to be generous and caring. But surely
there is more to it than this. It may be bad for you to throw darts at a cat, but it is
also bad for the cat. Isn't this part of the reason why it is wrong to throw darts at
a cat? It may be good for you to help the poor, but it is also good for the poor.
Isn't this part of the reason why it is right to help the poor? If part of the explanation of why some actions are right or wrong has to do with how these actions
affect others, then Platonic ethics is an oversimplification. There is more to morality than building good character. It also matters how others are affected by
our actions.

4. The Ethics of Abortion

In 2012, there were 699,202 abortions legally performed in the United States, according to the CDC. This is a large number, but it is considerably smaller than the previous year's total of 730,322 abortions. In fact, abortions have been on the decline every year since 1990, when the annual total was 1,429,247. Still, since 1970, nearly 52 million abortions have been legally performed in the United States. For some, this is legalized mass murder; for others, it is a woman's right.

Is abortion permissible? If so, when and for what reasons? Although people tend to classify themselves as "pro-life" (opponents of abortion) or as "pro-choice" (supporters of a woman's right to choose), this is not a very useful distinction. One philosopher, Michael Tooley (1973), makes the following, more nuanced, distinctions:

The "conservative" believes that abortion is permissible, if at all, only when pregnancy threatens the mother's life. The "extreme" conservative does not even allow for this exception but believes that abortion is *always* wrong.

The "moderate" believes that abortion is permissible, but only if a woman has a good reason, such as (1) when pregnancy is the result of rape or incest, (2) when the fetus has some abnormality, (3) when the mother is underage or is otherwise incapable—emotionally or financially—of assuming responsibility for a child, or (4) when having a child would have adverse life-long consequences for the mother.

The "liberal" believes that, at least prior to a certain stage in the development of the fetus, it is permissible for a woman to have an abortion for whatever personal reasons she might have. The "extreme" liberal goes further in maintaining that abortion is *always* permissible, even late in pregnancy.

According to Michael Tooley, what divides people on the abortion issue concerns the *reasons* that a pregnant woman might have for choosing an abortion. At one extreme, there are conservatives who say that abortion is wrong no matter what reasons a woman might have (although most conservatives allow for the one exception noted). At the opposite extreme, there are liberals who say that abortion is permissible for whatever reasons a woman might have, even trivial reasons. In the middle, there are moderates who say that abortion is permissible for some reasons but not for others. Some moderates come close to conservatives—maintaining that abortion is permissible, but only under the most extreme circumstances, such as when pregnancy results from rape—and others come close to liberals—maintaining that abortion is permissible under less than extreme circumstances, such as when having a child would impose economic hardships on the mother.

Unlike the conservative or the moderate, the liberal believes that, at least prior to a certain stage in the development of the fetus, it is permissible for a woman to have an abortion simply because she chooses not to be pregnant. There is, however, disagreement among liberals concerning what stage in the development of the fetus is crucial, and even whether it is possible to draw the line. The "classic" liberal believes that there is a definite cut-off point after which abortion is wrong, whereas the "non-classic" liberal denies this. Among the possible cut-off points proposed by classic liberals are (1) the acquisition of a human form, (2) cardiac activity (when the fetus has a heartbeat), (3) quickening or motility (when the fetus acquires the capacity for spontaneous movement), (4) viability (when the fetus can survive outside the mother's womb), and (5) birth. According to non-classic liberals, while an early abortion is permissible for any reason, there is a strong moral presumption against a late abortion. We cannot, however, draw a sharp line somewhere between these two extremes. Rather, as the fetus develops, the moral presumption against abortion gradually increases. As it increases, the range of circumstances under which abortion is permissible decreases, so much so that late in pregnancy abortion is justified only under the most extreme circumstances, if at all.

Pro-natalism vs. Anti-natalism

In what follows, we will take a critical look at these different positions on the abortion issue. But before doing this, we might want to consider whether there are general reasons why we should or should not choose to have children. It might be thought that this is a personal choice rather than a moral one, and parents rarely consider what this choice means for the children they create. But no one chooses to exist. This choice is made for us. And it may or may not be the right choice.

Many people are "pro-natalists." They believe that it is good to have children, at least when these children can be adequately cared for and can reasonably be expected to have happy lives. Swedish philosopher Torbjorn Tannsjo
defends a particularly strong version of this view:

> Most people live lives that are, on net, happy. For them to never exist, then,
> would be to deny them that happiness. And because I think we have a moral
> duty to maximize the amount of happiness in the world, that means that we all
> have an obligation to make the world as populated as can be. (Tannsjo 2015)

Tannsjo's reasoning appears to be this:

(1) We have a moral obligation to maximize happiness.
(2) To maximize happiness, we must create as many happy people as
    possible.

Therefore:

(3) We have a moral obligation to create as many happy people as
    possible.

This argument will resonate with classical utilitarians, who believe that our fundamental moral obligation is to maximize happiness and minimize suffering.
But even non-utilitarians can accept the first premise of the above argument.
The seriously questionable premise is the second. Is it true that to maximize the
amount of happiness in the world we must maximize the number of happy people?
    Imagine two situations: (1) a situation in which 35 billion people (five times
the current population) have minimally happy lives (that is, lives barely worth
living); and (2) a situation in which 700 million people (one-tenth the current
population) have radiantly happy lives. Which is a better situation? It seems
obvious that the second situation is a better situation—in fact a *much* better situation. Even though there are more happy people in the first situation than in the
second, there is actually more happiness in the second situation because the
people in that situation are happier. Against the pro-natalist, then, we can reasonably argue that we do not increase the amount of happiness in the world by
creating additional happy people; we do this by increasing the amount of happiness that people experience, or even by decreasing the world's population, if this
results in a higher quality of life for future generations.
    But suppose we could dramatically increase the world's population without
thereby decreasing people's quality of life. Suppose, for example, that we could
add ten billion people to the current population and maintain the same level of
happiness for everyone. Wouldn't this be a better state of affairs? Not necessarily. One thing to bear in mind is that even if we do increase the amount of happiness in the world by creating additional people, we also increase the amount of

suffering. In choosing whether or not to procreate, then, we must weigh the obligation to maximize happiness against the obligation to minimize suffering. And this might well lead to the conclusion that, all things considered, it is better not to have children.

This is the view of the "anti-natalist." In defense of this view, South African philosopher David Benatar brings our attention to certain grim facts about life:

> [W]hen we look closely we notice just how much suffering there is. Consider, for example, the millions living in poverty or subjected to violence or the threat thereof. Psychological distress and disturbance is widespread. Rates of depression are high. Everybody suffers frustrations and bereavements. Life is often punctuated by periods of ill-health. Some of these pass without enduring effects but others have long-term sequelae. In poorer parts of the world, infectious diseases account for most of the burden of disease. However, those in the developed world are not exempt from appalling diseases. They suffer from strokes, from various degenerative diseases and from cancer. (Benatar 2015: 3)

There is much that can be done to decrease the amount of suffering in the world: eradicating poverty, reducing crime, resolving social conflicts, improving healthcare, and so on. But, realistically speaking, the only way to eliminate suffering altogether is *not* to have children. As Benatar observes:

> It is curious that while good people go to great lengths to spare their children from suffering, few of them seem to notice that the one (and only) guaranteed way to prevent all the suffering of their children is not to bring those children into existence in the first place. (Benatar 2006: 6)

Most people are glad that they exist, and this counts in favor of the decision to procreate. But we cannot blithely assume that this by itself justifies the decision. If we choose to have children, we are morally responsible for all of the predictable consequences of that choice, and it is perfectly predictable that the people we bring into existence will suffer, both physically and emotionally. Not only this, it is also predictable that they will die. As Marilynn Robinson poetically notes: "By some bleak alchemy what had been mere unbeing becomes death when life is mingled with it" (Robinson 1980: 215). We do not inflict unbeing upon people by choosing not to have children, but we do impose a death sentence upon the people we bring into existence, because if they never lived, they would never die. By choosing to have children, then, we are morally responsible for two great harms that inevitably befall the people we create: suffering and death. This certainly counts against the decision to procreate.

4.1. The Conservative Position

In this section we will examine four arguments in support of the conservative position: the argument from religion; the argument from innocence; the argument from potentiality; and the argument from the wrongness of killing.

The Argument from Religion

Religion is one prominent source of opposition to abortion. It is often taken for granted by Christians that the Bible condemns abortion, and that for this reason abortion is wrong. It is true that the sixth of the Ten Commandments condemns killing. But does this prohibition apply to the fetus? And even if it does, can we uncritically accept the moral pronouncements of the Bible?

The Bible allows killing all forms of life, including human life, for many reasons. Nowhere does the Bible explicitly condone or condemn abortion. There is, however, the following telling passage in Exodus (21:22-23):

> If men struggle with each other and strike a woman with child so that she has a miscarriage, yet there is no further injury, he shall surely be fined as the woman's husband may demand of him, and he shall pay as the judges decide. But if there is any further injury, then you shall appoint as a penalty life for life, eye for eye, tooth for tooth, hand for hand, foot for foot, burn for burn, wound for wound, bruise for bruise.

This passage is relevant to the abortion issue because it directly addresses the issue of whether the fetus has a moral status comparable to that of an adult woman. If the fetus did, then the penalty for inflicting a miscarriage upon a woman would be "life for life," which it is not. The penalty is a fine. (A word of caution, though. Some scholars insist that the Hebrew word rendered here as "miscarriage" should be translated instead as "premature birth." If this is true, then the meaning of the passage is drastically altered. Perhaps all we can say is that the Bible provides no clear guidance on the abortion issue.)

Yet, even if the Bible did categorically condemn abortion, how would this support the conservative position? As follows:

(1) If the Bible condemns a certain practice, then that practice is wrong.
(2) The Bible condemns abortion.

Therefore:

(3) Abortion is wrong.

In the first chapter, we saw that a religious appeal like this is fallacious; we cannot adequately justify a moral belief simply by citing passages from the Bible (or some other religious text).

This is not, however, the only religious argument against the practice of abortion. It is sometimes argued that abortion is wrong because it is contrary to God's design for human sexuality. Fully spelled out, the argument runs as follows:

(1) God has designed sexuality for the purpose of procreation.

(2) Sexual activity that conforms to God's design—sex between a husband and a wife for the purpose of procreation—is good, whereas sexual activity that does not—such as homosexuality and premarital sex—is bad. Also, anything that interferes with God's design—such as contraception—is wrong.

(3) Abortion interferes with God's design for sexual activity.

Therefore:

(4) Abortion is wrong.

For many people, this argument may prove too much. If the argument shows that abortion is wrong, it also shows that *any* form of sexual behavior that does not have procreation as its intended outcome—including masturbation, homosexuality, and recreational sex—is wrong.

The Argument from Innocence

The argument from innocence, in one form or another, is the argument most commonly given by conservatives. The basic idea is that abortion is wrong because it is wrong to kill an innocent human being. Carefully laid out, the argument runs as follows:

(1) A human fetus is an innocent human being.
(2) Every innocent human being has a right to life.

Therefore:

(3) A human fetus has a right to life.

Therefore:

(4) Abortion—that is, intentionally causing the fetus's death—violates the fetus's right to life.
(5) This rights violation is not outweighed by other moral considerations. (In particular, it is not outweighed by the mother's right to decide how her body is used.)
(6) If nothing outweighs this rights violation, then abortion is wrong.

Therefore:

(7) Abortion is wrong.

As it stands, this is an argument for the extreme conservative position that abortion is *always* wrong. The conservative might qualify the fifth premise, however, so that the mother's right to life overrides the fetus's when pregnancy threatens the mother's life. (By further qualifying this premise, the argument might be transformed into a defense of the moderate position that abortion is permissible when pregnancy results from rape or incest, or when the fetus is defective.)

The reasoning in this argument is valid, but the premises are controversial. Of the unsupported premises, by far the most controversial is the first. Is it true that human life begins at conception? There are three standard defenses of this premise, which we will now explore.

The Genetic Defense

Why should we think that a single-cell zygote or an amorphous cluster of cells (which is what the human fetus is during the earliest stages of its development) is an *actual* human being rather than just a *potential* one? What is the important difference between a spermatozoon or an ovum (the two cells that join to form a zygote) and the zygote itself? Perhaps the answer is this: that unlike a spermatozoon or an ovum, a human zygote contains a full complement of human genes. As one philosopher, John T. Noonan, writes:

> The positive argument for conception as the decisive moment of humanization is that at conception the new being receives the genetic code. It is this genetic information which determines his characteristics, which is the biological carrier of the possibility of human wisdom, which makes him a self-evolving being. A being with a human genetic code is man. (Noonan 1973: 15)

The argument:

(1) Anything with a complete human genetic code is a human being.
(2) At conception, a human fetus has a complete human genetic code.

Therefore:

(3) At conception, a human fetus is a human being.

There is one rather glaring problem with this argument, however. Every cell of the human body contains within its nucleus a full complement of human genes. From the first premise, therefore, it follows that every cell of a person's body is a human being!

The Potentiality Defense

A human skin cell contains a complete human genetic code, and so does a human zygote. Why should we say that a zygote but not a skin cell is a human being? According to some conservatives, the answer is this: that the zygote, unlike the skin cell, has the potential to mature into an adult human being. (The conservative is not saying that the zygote has the potential to develop into a human being; for this would be to concede that human life does not begin at conception but sometime later. The zygote cannot be a potential human being and, at the same time, an actual human being. Rather, the contention is that the zygote is already a human being, and that the important difference between a skin cell and a zygote is that the zygote, unlike the skin cell, has the potential to develop into an *adult* human being. This is consistent with conservative's claim that the zygote is already human.) The argument:

(1) Anything that has the potential to mature into an adult human being is already a human being.
(2) At conception, a human fetus has this potential.

Therefore:

(3) At conception, a human fetus is a human being.

The second premise is uncontroversial, but why should we accept the first? A coconut has the potential to develop into an adult coconut tree. But this does not mean that the coconut is already a coconut tree. Why, then, should we think that a human zygote is a human being simply because it has the potential to develop into an adult human?

The Continuity Defense

The most subtle and perhaps most ingenious defense of the premise that human life begins at conception is the continuity defense. If, the conservative asks, human life does not begin at conception, when *exactly* does it begin? On the continuum from zygote to infant, when does the fetus become a human being? There does not appear to be a good answer to this question. Should we say that the crucial stage is when the fetus acquires a human form? When it has a heartbeat? When it can survive outside the mother's womb? The problem is that, no matter where we draw the line, such a small developmental difference cannot make such a huge difference in the status of the fetus. The only non-arbitrary answer to the question of when human life begins, according to the conservative, is that it begins at conception. The argument:

(1) If the fetus is not a human being at conception, then there must be some stage in its development when it becomes a human being.
(2) But there is no stage in its development when the fetus becomes a human being.

Therefore:

(3) The fetus is a human being at conception.

In analyzing this argument, consider the different cut-off points proposed by classic liberals on the abortion issue. Is it reasonable to say that human life begins (1) when the fetus acquires a recognizable human form, (2) when the fetus has a heartbeat, (3), when the fetus acquires the capacity for spontaneous movement, (4) when the fetus has the capacity to survive outside the mother's womb, or (5) at birth?

Let us examine, briefly, each of these five proposed cut-off points. First, is having a human form necessary for being human? Consider someone who, because of disease, injury, or a serious birth defect, has lost or never acquired a human form. (There are many legendary sideshow performers, such as the Caterpillar Man and the Elephant Man, who fall into this category.) Would someone, for this reason alone, fail to be human? Or imagine a strange type of algae that congeals in human-like clumps. Should these clumps of algae be considered human beings because of how they look? What about manikins? Are they human beings because of their human-like appearance? Second, a functioning heart is only one component of a living human being. Why should human life commence when the fetus has a heartbeat rather than when other organs (the brain, liver, kidneys, spleen) are formed and begin functioning? Third, the capacity for spontaneous movement has historically been linked with the acquisition of a soul. But why should we think that the soul exists? (What exactly is a soul?) And even if it does exist, why should we think that the capacity for spontaneous movement (motility or quickening, as it is sometimes called) marks the occasion when the fetus acquires a soul? And even if it does, why is this relevant to the abortion issue? Fourth, the capacity to survive outside of the mother's womb is where the United States Supreme Court drew the line in the famous (or infamous) Roe vs. Wade decision. But is it reasonable to say that a fetus becomes a human being when it acquires this capacity? Suppose you and I are on a camping trip and you fall and break your leg. We are miles away from the nearest town and you are completely dependent upon me for your survival. Would you cease to be fully human for this reason? Would I be justified in slitting your throat because you could not survive without me? Fifth and finally, why should birth mark the occasion when human life begins? Why should a change of *location* mark the difference between a nonhuman fetus and a human being? Why should a premature infant be a human being but not a more developed fetus? It is not at all obvious how the classic liberal might answer these questions, which supports the conservative's contention that the only defensible answer to the question "When does human life begin?" is that it begins at conception.

These considerations notwithstanding, the liberal has a simple response to the continuity defense. There is a difference between a single grain of sand and a heap of sand. But *exactly* how many grains must be added to a single grain to form a heap? There is a difference between a coconut and a coconut tree. But in the transition from one to the other, *exactly* when does a coconut tree come into being? These questions are unanswerable because they rest on false assumptions. The first question assumes that if there is a difference between a single grain of sand and a heap of sand, there must be some precise number of grains that form a heap. But this is not true. Similarly, the second question assumes that if there is a difference between a coconut and a coconut tree, there must be a sharp line that can be drawn separating the two. But, again, this is not true. Some concepts are "vague" concepts in the sense that they do not have precise boundaries. The concept of a heap is one example. There is a difference between a single grain of sand and a heap of sand, but there is no precise number of grains that constitute a heap. The concept of a tree is another example. There is a difference between a coconut and a coconut tree, but in the transition from one to the other, there is no precise point when a coconut tree comes into existence. Perhaps something similar can be said in the case of a human being. In other words, it may be that a single-cell zygote is not a human being but develops into one (just as a coconut develops into a coconut tree) even though there is no stage in this developmental process which can be identified as the precise moment when human life begins.

The first premise of the argument from innocence is that human life begins at conception. As we have seen, there are grave problems with the traditional arguments used to support this premise. But even if these problems can be solved, there is an ambiguity in the claim that human life begins at conception. What is your "life" in the sense that matters? Is it your *biological* life? Or is it your *conscious* life? To appreciate the difference, imagine that a killer has shot you in the head. The killer's intention was to kill you, but he wasn't quite successful. You are alive, but you have suffered such extensive brain damage that you will never regain consciousness. You are, and will remain for the rest of your life, in a persistent vegetative state. (The well-publicized case of Terri Shiavo illustrates what is meant by a "persistent vegetative state." Because of oxygen deprivation, Shiavo's cerebral cortex was utterly destroyed. Although she "lived" for many years in this condition, it was physically impossible for her to regain consciousness.) In this situation, you are "alive," but only in the biological sense. Your conscious life is over. This raises the question: By shooting you in the head, did the killer actually murder you? Did he violate your right to "life" in the sense that matters?

If so, this has important implications concerning whether and when the fetus has a right to life. If the right to life is not the right to a *biological* life but the right to a *conscious* life, then it makes little sense to ascribe a right to life to the fetus until its brain is sufficiently complex to sustain consciousness; until this time the fetus is not "alive" in the sense that truly matters. (It is unclear exactly when this happens, but the basis of the central nervous system is not formed until about twelve weeks after conception.) There are, then, grounds for challenging the second premise of the argument from innocence: that every innocent human being has a right to life.

We may conclude that it is not reasonable to accept the conservative position for the reasons given by this argument. The two main premises are open to serious challenges and it is not clear how they can be defended. Let us, then, turn our attention to different arguments.

The Argument from Potentiality

The argument from potentiality is based upon the assumption that even if the fetus is not, from conception, a human being, it is nonetheless a *potential* human being, and it is this potential that makes abortion wrong:

(1) Whether or not human life begins at conception, a human fetus is at least potentially a human being.
(2) It is wrong to destroy anything with this potential.

Therefore:

(3) Abortion is wrong.

The reasoning is valid, and the first premise is true, but there are two serious problems with the second premise. First, if abortion is wrong simply because it destroys something with the *potential* to become a human being, then why shouldn't ordinary contraception, which also prevents a human being from forming, be morally wrong? Aren't the potentials the same in both cases? If contraception is not wrong, then abortion cannot be wrong for the reasons stated in this argument. Second, while it is (usually) wrong to destroy an *actual* human being, why should it be wrong to destroy a *potential* one? If every human being has a moral status, then the fact that a human fetus is *potentially* a human being only suggests that the fetus *potentially* has a moral status, not that it has one already. Why, then, should it be wrong to destroy a human fetus? Would it be wrong to destroy one of the many thousands of frozen embryos currently stored in fertility clinics around the world? After all, every frozen embryo is at least potentially a human being. Or consider this. Suppose Dr. Frankenstein has stitched together a human being from various cadaver parts. All that he needs to do to bring his creation to life is to hoist it to the top of his castle tower during a lightening storm. But suppose he has second thoughts about his experiment and decides to destroy the creature before bringing it to life. The creature is undoubtedly a potential person, but would it be wrong for Dr. Frankenstein to destroy it?

The Argument from the Wrongness of Killing

Our final argument for the conservative position, unlike the previous two, is not based upon the moral status of the fetus but upon an analysis of killing. In "Why Abortion is Immoral," American philosopher Don Marquis argues against the morality of abortion on the basis of the following simple idea: that what explains why it is wrong to kill an adult human being also explains why abortion is wrong. Since the explanation is the same in both cases, and since it is (nearly always) wrong to kill an adult human being, it follows that it is (nearly always) wrong to kill a human fetus.

Marquis writes:

> What primarily makes killing wrong is neither its effect on the murderer nor its effect on the victim's friends and relatives, but its effect on the victim. The loss of one's life is one of the greatest losses one can suffer. The loss of one's life deprives one of all the experiences, activities, projects, and enjoyments that would otherwise have constituted one's future. Therefore, killing someone is wrong, primarily because the killing inflicts (one of) the greatest possible losses on the victim. (Marquis 2007: 92)

He ties this to the abortion issue as follows:

> The claim that the primary wrong-making feature of a killing is the loss to the victim of the value of its future has obvious consequences for the ethics of abortion. The future of a standard fetus includes a set of experiences, projects, activities, and such which are identical with the futures of adult human beings and are identical with the futures of young children. Since the reason that is sufficient to explain why it is wrong to kill human beings after the time of birth is a reason that also applies to fetuses, it follows that abortion is prima facie seriously wrong. (Marquis 2007: 95)

These considerations suggest the following argument in support of the conservative position:

(1) Killing is wrong, when it is, primarily because it inflicts one of the greatest possible losses upon the victim—the loss of her life.

(2) Abortion inflicts this loss upon the fetus. (If killing someone as a child or as an adult is wrong because it deprives the victim of the rest of her life, then killing someone as a fetus must also be wrong because it deprives the victim of her *entire* life.)

Therefore:

(3) Abortion is wrong. (In fact, if a complete life is worth more than any portion thereof, then abortion is *more* seriously wrong than murdering a child or an adult.)

Marquis gives a plausible explanation of why killing is wrong, but it does not account for certain moral beliefs. For instance, suppose someone's health has deteriorated, and her quality of life is quite low, and she is not expected to live for more than a few months. Then it would seem that on Marquis' account, it would not be seriously wrong to kill this person, even if she did not wish to die. It would not be seriously wrong because in this case the victim would not lose something of great value (by comparison with what a healthy human being would lose.) This does not seem right, however. Most people would say that killing someone under these circumstances would still be seriously wrong even if her life, objectively considered, did not have great value; it would be seriously wrong because her life was still valuable *to her*.

This suggests an explanation of why killing is wrong that is similar to Marquis' account, but importantly different. Perhaps killing is wrong, when it is, primarily because it deprives the victim of the rest of her life—something which *she* greatly values, whether or not the rest of her life has great value, objectively considered. The important difference between this account and Marquis' is that the fetus cannot plausibly be said to have values; if the fetus cannot have values, it cannot value the rest of its life; and if the fetus cannot value the rest of its life, an abortion would not deprive it of something that it values, in which case an abortion would not be wrong.

This is one problem with Marquis' argument. A second problem concerns Marquis' claim that the "future of a standard fetus includes a set of experiences, projects, activities, and such which are identical with the futures of adult human beings and are identical with the futures of young children." Marquis assumes that there is a single, continuous person who endures through the stages of fetus, child, and adult. But this is far from obvious. It may be that a "person" does not come into existence until late in pregnancy, or even after birth, as some liberals maintain. If the fetus is not a person, then it is not the case that abortion deprives "someone" of his or her future; the person whose future would be deprived does not yet exist. (There is a difference between depriving you of your future, and depriving someone who does not yet exist, but who might exist sometime in the future, of that person's future. For example, there is a difference between killing an adult human being and practicing contraception.)

A third problem with Marquis' argument is that it does not take into consideration the rights of the mother. The liberal can argue that even if Marquis' account is correct, it does not follow that it is wrong to kill in every case in which a great loss is inflicted upon the victim. (For instance, killing in self-defense is permissible, even if the attacker has many valuable years of life to look forward to.) It may be that the rights of the mother have greater moral weight than whatever considerations the conservative might raise, such as the loss inflicted upon the fetus. (Judith Jarvis Thomson's "violinist" argument, discussed below, is relevant in this connection.) If so, then even if abortion would deprive the fetus of something of great value, a woman may nonetheless have the right to have an abortion.

4.2. The Moderate Position

Let us now turn to the moderate position on the abortion issue. We have seen that what distinguishes the moderate from the conservative is that the moderate believes that abortion is permissible for reasons not limited to medical necessity. For the moderate, having an abortion is not like having a tattoo removed, for which a woman does not need a moral justification. Nor does having an abortion have the same moral gravity as killing an innocent person. It would be wrong for a woman to have an abortion for trivial reasons, but it would not be wrong if she had a good reason.

Jane English (though herself not a moderate but a liberal) argues along these lines in "Abortion and the Concept of a Person." She imagines a case in which a mad scientist has been able to hypnotize people and use them for his nefarious purposes:

> To consider a somewhat fanciful example, suppose you are a highly trained surgeon when you are kidnapped by [a] hypnotic attacker. He says he does not intend to harm you but to take you back to the mad scientist who, it turns out, plans to hypnotize you to have a permanent mental block against all your knowledge of medicine. This would automatically destroy your career which would in turn have a serious adverse impact on your family, your personal relationships and your happiness. It seems to me that if the only way you can avoid this outcome is to shoot the innocent attacker, you are justified in so doing. You are defending yourself from a drastic injury to your life prospects. I think it is no exaggeration to claim that unwanted pregnancies (most obviously among teenagers) often have such adverse life-long consequences as the surgeon's loss of livelihood. (English 2002: 109)

The moderate position seems reasonable, but questions arise concerning the moral status of the fetus. Either the fetus is a "person" in the morally important sense, or it is not. If it is, then having an abortion *does* have the same moral gravity as killing an innocent person. If it does not, then having an abortion *is* like having a tattoo removed. While you might be justified in killing an innocent person in the purely imaginary case discussed by Jane English, would you be justified in killing an innocent person—say, a three-year-old girl—because she was conceived through an act of rape or incest? Because she has Down syndrome or spina bifida? Because you were emotionally or financially incapable of assuming responsibility for her? These would not be good reasons to kill an innocent person; but if the fetus is not a person, then a woman does not need a good reason to have an abortion. For the moderate, we are not required to treat the fetus as a person, nor are we permitted to treat it as a mere thing. The moderate relegates the fetus to some limbo-world between the categories of "person" and "mere thing," but it is far from clear what this means. In the absence of a satisfactory explanation of the moral status of the fetus, the moderate position is untenable.

4.3. The Liberal Position

Let us consider, finally, the liberal position on the issue. According to the liberal, abortion is permissible (for whatever reasons a woman might have), at least prior to a certain stage in the development of the fetus. For the classic liberal, there is a definite cut-off point after which abortion is wrong. For the non-classic liberal, there is not. Rather, as the fetus develops, the moral presumption against abortion gradually increases. As it increases, increasingly stronger reasons are required to justify abortion.

The obvious problem for the classic liberal is that of identifying some stage in the development of the fetus when it becomes a person or acquires a full moral status—a problem we touched upon earlier in this chapter. It may not, however, be necessary or even possible to identify such a stage. If the concept of a person is vague, then there may be no definite answer to the question as to when (if ever) a fetus is a person. This, roughly, is the position of the non-classic liberal. Jane English, who defends this position, argues that even if the fetus is not a person, as it develops it comes to *resemble* a person, and as this resemblance increases so does the moral presumption against abortion. Thus, because a newly formed fetus is most unlike a person, an early abortion is morally acceptable. In the middle months of pregnancy, when the fetus has come to resemble a person, abortion is permissible only when continuing the pregnancy would cause harm to the mother. In the final months, when the fetus resembles a person to an even greater degree, abortion is permissible only to save the mother's life or to protect her from serious harm. English writes:

> Even if a fetus is not a person, abortion is not always permissible, because of the resemblance of a fetus to a person. I agree . . . that it would be wrong for a woman who is seven months pregnant to have an abortion just to avoid having to postpone a trip to Europe. In the early months of pregnancy when the fetus hardly resembles a baby at all, then, abortion is permissible whenever it is in the interests of the pregnant woman or her family. The reasons would only need to outweigh the pain and inconvenience of the abortion itself. In the middle months, when the fetus comes to resemble a person, abortion would be justifiable only when the continuation of the pregnancy or the birth of the child would cause harms— physical, psychological, economic or social—to the woman. In the late months of pregnancy, even on our current assumption that a fetus is not a person, abortion seems to be wrong except to save a woman from significant injury or death. (English 2002: 112)

The most important, and also the most controversial, claim that the liberal makes is that, at least up to a certain point, abortion is a morally neutral act or otherwise morally unobjectionable. For the extreme liberal, this is true throughout a woman's pregnancy. There are two arguments commonly used to support the liberal position. The first argues against the personhood of the fetus, and the second argues that even if the fetus is a person, its rights are outweighed by those of the mother.

The Argument from Personhood

According to this argument, having an abortion (at least up to a certain stage in the fetus's development) is a morally neutral act, like removing a tattoo, because the fetus does not count as a "person" in the morally important sense. There are several versions of this argument. The pattern of reasoning is roughly this:

(1) A being is a person only if it has certain characteristics or capacities. (Different versions of the argument identify different characteristics or capacities.)

(2) The fetus (at least prior to a certain stage in its development) lacks these features.

Therefore:

(3) The fetus (at least up to a certain point) is not a person.

(4) If the fetus is not a person, then having an abortion is a morally neutral act.

Therefore:

(5) Having an abortion (at least prior to a certain stage in the development of the fetus) is a morally neutral act.

What features must a being have in order to qualify as a person? The answer is far from clear. One philosopher, Mary Anne Warren, approaches the problem in this way:

> Imagine a space traveler who lands on an unknown planet and encounters a race of beings utterly unlike any he has ever seen or heard of. If he wants to be sure of behaving morally towards these beings, he has to somehow decide whether they are people, and hence have full moral rights, or whether they are the sort of thing which he need not feel guilty about treating as, for example, a source of food. (Warren 2000: 262)

What might the space traveler discover about these beings that would tell him whether they are persons or mere things? Warren (2000: 263) suggests the following criteria for personhood:

1. consciousness (of objects and events external and/or internal to the being), and in particular the capacity to feel pain;

2. reasoning (the *developed* capacity to solve new and relatively complex problems);

3. self-motivated activity (activity which is relatively independent of either genetic or direct external control);

4. the capacity to communicate, by whatever means, messages of an indefinite variety of types, that is, not just with an indefinite number of possible contents, but on indefinitely many possible topics;

5. the presence of self-concepts, and self-awareness, either individual or racial, or both.

Clearly, a human fetus fails to possess any of these characteristics (except for the first, once the central nervous system is formed and functioning), from which

Warren draws the conclusion that "a fetus is a human being which is not yet a person, and which therefore cannot coherently be said to have full moral rights" (Warren 2000: 264). If this is correct, then having an abortion, even a late-term abortion, is a morally neutral act.

Another liberal, Peter Singer, argues that

> we accord the life of a fetus no greater value than the life of a nonhuman animal at a similar level of rationality, self-consciousness, awareness, capacity to feel, etc. Since no fetus is a person, no fetus has the same claim to life as a person. Moreover it is very unlikely that the fetuses of less than 18 weeks are capable of feeling anything at all, since their nervous system appears to be insufficiently developed to function. If this is so, an abortion up to this point terminates an existence that is of no intrinsic value at all. In between 18 weeks and birth, when the fetus may be conscious, though not self-conscious, abortion does end a life of some intrinsic value, and so should not be taken lightly. But a woman's serious interests would normally override the rudimentary interests of the fetus. Indeed, even an abortion late in pregnancy for the most trivial reasons is hard to condemn in a society that slaughters far more developed forms of life for the taste of their flesh. (Singer 1979: 118)

Peter Singer's argument in this passage is analogical:

(1) There is no morally important difference between a human fetus and a nonhuman animal at a comparable level of mental development.
(2) The life of a nonhuman animal with no conscious experience at all (such as a clam or an oyster) has no intrinsic value.

Therefore:

(3) The life of a human fetus with no conscious experience (a human fetus less than 18 weeks old) has no intrinsic value.

Singer poses the following dilemma for meat-eating conservatives. If it is permissible to kill a nonhuman animal, such as a cow or a pig, who is mentally much more sophisticated than a fully developed human fetus, simply for the taste of its flesh, how can it be seriously wrong to have abortion, even a late-term abortion, for trivial reasons?

The Argument from a Woman's Rights

In the first chapter, we briefly discussed the most well-known version of this argument, given by Judith Jarvis Thomson in "A Defense of Abortion." Here you are asked to imagine that you wake up in the morning to find that an unconscious violinist has been strapped to your back. His circulatory system has been plugged into yours so that your kidneys can be used to extract poisons from his blood. To make matters worse, the violinist cannot be unplugged from you for the next nine months, or he will die. The question Thomson poses: Do you have to let your body be used as a dialysis machine? Does morality require it? Thomson believes that it would be permissible for you to unplug yourself from the violinist and that, by analogy, it would be permissible for a woman with an unwanted pregnancy to "unplug" herself from her fetus.

Critics have pointed out that Thomson's argument supports, at best, the moderate position that abortion is permissible when pregnancy results from rape. (In the example imagined by Thomson, the violinist is strapped to your back without your consent.) But suppose a woman voluntarily engages in sexual intercourse, knowing what the consequences might be, and becomes pregnant as a result. Under these circumstances, a woman would be responsible for the presence of the fetus developing inside her. Wouldn't this give the fetus a right to the use of the woman's body? Thomson anticipates this objection, and argues against it as follows:

> If the room is stuffy, and I therefore open a window to air it, and a burglar climbs in, it would be absurd to say, "Ah, now he can stay, she's given him a right to the use of her house—for she is partially responsible for his presence there, having voluntarily done what enabled him to get in, in full knowledge that there are such things a burglars, and that burglars burgle." It would be still more absurd to say this if I had had bars installed outside my windows, precisely to prevent burglars from getting in, and a burglar got in only because of a defect in the bars. It remains equally absurd if we imagine it is not a burglar who climbs in, but an innocent person who blunders or falls in. (Thomson 2007: 106)

Thomson's case for the liberal position rests upon an important feature of property rights: that people have an exclusive right to the use of their possessions. I can request to read one of your books, or to spend the night in your home, or to borrow your car, or to wear your sweater, but you have the right to refuse. Unless you freely grant me permission, I violate your property rights if I make use of your things. Doesn't a woman have the exclusive right to the use of her body? Even if the fetus is a person with a right to life, a woman has rights too, and it is at least unclear whether the fetus's rights outweigh those of its mother.

These considerations suggest a different formulation of the argument from a woman's rights (one that is syllogistic rather than analogical in character). Libertarian thinker Murray Rothbard formulates the argument as follows:

> The proper groundwork for an analysis of abortion is in every man's absolute right of self-ownership. This implies immediately that every woman has the absolute right to her own body, that she has absolute dominion over her body and everything within it. This includes the fetus. Most fetuses are in the mother's womb because the mother consents to the situation, but the fetus is there by the mother's freely granted consent. But should the mother decide that she does not *want* the fetus there any longer, then the fetus becomes a parasitic "invader" of her person, and the woman has the perfect right to expel this invader from her domain. Abortion should be looked upon, not as "murder" of a living person, but as the expulsion of an unwanted invader from the mother's body. Any laws

restricting or prohibiting abortion are therefore invasions of the rights of mothers. (Rothbard 1998: 98)

Rothbard's reasoning appears to be this:

(1) People have the right to prevent others from using their property.
(2) A woman's body is her property.

Therefore:

(3) A woman has the right to prevent others—in particular, her fetus—from using her body.
(4) The only way that a woman can prevent her fetus from using her body is by having an abortion.

Therefore:

(5) A woman has the right to have an abortion.

Suppose I am a guest in your home, but I have overstayed my welcome. Don't you have the right to expel me? If I refuse to leave, wouldn't this be a violation of your property rights? Similarly, doesn't a pregnant woman have the right to expel an unwanted fetus from her womb? If the government, by criminalizing abortion, forced a woman to remain pregnant, wouldn't this be a violation of her property rights (akin to forcing people to permit unwanted guests to stay in their homes)?

In assessing Rothbard's argument, consider the following two questions. First, are property rights absolute, as Rothbard assumes, or can they sometimes be overridden or nullified? Second, even if a woman does have the right to have an abortion, might it be wrong for her to exercise that right? Suppose, once again, that I am an unwelcome guest in your home. Other things being equal, you have the right to expel me. But suppose other things are not equal. Suppose there is a blizzard outside and I would freeze to death unless I stayed indoors. Do you have the right, under these circumstances, to force me out? If not, then people do not always have the right to prevent others from using their property, contrary to the first premise of Rothbard's argument. Suppose, however, that you do have the right to expel me from your home. Wouldn't it be wrong for you to exercise that right, knowing that I could not survive outdoors? If I am a passenger on your lifeboat, wouldn't it be wrong for you to throw me overboard simply because you wanted to have room to stretch your legs? Even if you have the right to do so—because the lifeboat is your property—wouldn't it be wrong for you to exercise that right? If so, then Rothbard's argument is irrelevant to the *moral* problem of abortion, for it does not show that it is morally permissible for a woman to have an abortion. At most, the argument shows that it would be wrong for the government to criminalize abortion insofar as this would violate a woman's property rights (which is, in fact, the conclusion that Rothbard argues for.)

Both Thomson and Rothbard assume that a woman's body is her property. But this is not as obvious as it might initially seem. To characterize a woman's body as her property is to say, in part, that she has the exclusive right to the use of it, which implies that no one else, including her fetus, may make use of it without her consent. This is the important point made by both Thomson and Rothbard. But the concept of property has other implications. Property is something that can be bought, sold, traded, auctioned, abandoned, given or thrown away, rented, loaned, leased, stolen, and vandalized, among other uses (or abuses). Whether a woman's body is her property is thus tied to a number of questions. Can a woman rightfully sell her body? Can she, for example, sell her body to a pimp in order to settle a debt? (If a woman's body is her property, what grounds are there for condemning this form of sexual slavery?) Should a woman have the legal right to use her body as collateral in taking out a loan, permitting a bank to seize possession of it if she defaults? Can a woman abandon her body or throw it away, permitting anyone to take possession of it? Can she loan her body to someone, or make a gift of it? If a woman has been beaten or raped, has her body has been "vandalized"? Does a prostitute or a surrogate mother "rent" or "lease" her body? If a woman has been abducted, has her body been "stolen"?

If the answer to many or all of these questions is "no," then a woman's body is not, strictly speaking, her "property." This does not mean that a woman's body does not "belong" to her, but a belonging is not necessarily property. (There is a sense in which a woman's fetus "belongs" to her, but it would be bizarre to suggest that she is entitled to treat it as property—for example, by selling it to the highest bidder.) If a woman's body is not her property, then one cannot reasonably argue in support of abortion on the basis of a woman's right of self-ownership.

5. The Ethics of Euthanasia

Ramon Sampedro, a ship mechanic from Galicia, Spain, was paralyzed from the neck down as the result of a swimming accident that occurred when he was 25. He described himself as "a head attached to a corpse." Unable to end his own life, he fought a legal battle in the Spanish courts for nearly 30 years for his right to die. It is estimated that every year approximately 130,000 people worldwide suffer traumatic spinal cord injury and live for 40 years or more bound to a wheelchair. Many quadriplegics are happy to be alive, but Sampedro was not. He spoke eloquently of his wish to die:

> Why die? Because every journey has its departure time and only the traveler has the privilege and the right to choose the last day to get out. Why die? Because at times the journey of no return is the best path that reason can show us out of love and respect for life, so that life may have a dignified death.

Eventually, Sampedro devised a way to commit suicide (from potassium cyanide poisoning). One of his close friends, Ramona Maneiro, was later arrested and charged with assisting him in his suicide. She was subsequently released, due to a lack of evidence, and no further charges were ever filed in connection with his death. Several years later, Maneiro admitted that she had provided Sampedro with the cyanide-laced drink and a straw. She said, "I did it for love."[1]

The word "euthanasia" literally means "good death" (from the Greek *euthanatos*), and refers to the act of killing a patient, or letting a patient die, when it is believed that the patient's life is not worth prolonging. The following two examples illustrate what is meant by the term:

> In 1992, a physician, Dr. Cox, openly defied the law and assented to a seventy-year-old patient's persistent request for active euthanasia. His patient, Mrs. Boyes, was so ill that she "howled like a dog" if anyone touched her. Conven-

tional medicine did not relieve her agony. Eventually, after repeated requests to die, Dr. Cox gave her an injection of potassium chloride. Dr. Cox received a suspended sentence for his actions.[2]

Terri Schiavo was 26 years old when she collapsed in 1990. While her potassium level was later found to be abnormally low, an autopsy drew no conclusion as to why she had lost consciousness. Whatever the cause, her brain was deprived of oxygen long enough to leave her in a "persistent vegetative state," a condition that is not to be confused with brain death. She could breathe without mechanical assistance. But doctors concluded that she was incapable of thought or emotion. Between her collapse and her eventual death, the nation bore witness to an increasingly acrimonious battle between her husband, Michael Schiavo, and her parents, Robert and Mary Schindler. Mr. Schiavo wanted to detach the feeding tube that gave her nourishment. Terri never would have wanted to be kept alive that way, he said. The Schindlers insisted that the tube be kept in place. That, they said, is what their daughter would have wanted. Florida courts consistently sided with the husband, and Terri's feeding tube was removed in 2005.[3]

There are different forms of euthanasia, some of which are more controversial than others. The two examples above illustrate the distinction between "active" and "passive" euthanasia. To commit active euthanasia (as in the first example) is to directly kill a patient. To commit passive euthanasia (as in the second example) is to let a patient die. A widely held view is that passive euthanasia is sometimes acceptable whereas active euthanasia is always wrong. This, in particular, is the position of the American Medical Association, which reads:

> The intentional termination of the life of one human being by another—mercy killing—is contrary to that for which the medical profession stands and is contrary to the policy of the American Medical Association.
> The cessation of the employment of extraordinary means to prolong the life of the body when there is irrefutable evidence that biological death is imminent is the decision of the patient and/or his immediate family. (Rachels 1980: 38)

What lies behind this position is the belief that (1) the distinction between killing someone and letting someone die is in itself a morally important distinction, and (2) even though the outcome is the same, it can be permissible to let someone die when it would be wrong to kill that person. Before going on, let us see what considerations support this belief and try to determine whether it is defensible.

5.1. Active and Passive Euthanasia

Consider the following imaginary example (discussed by Fischer and Ravizza in their introductory essay to *Ethics: Problems and Principles*):

The Drug Case: We have a limited quantity of a life-saving drug. To be treated effectively, one patient will require the entire quantity of the drug, whereas five other patients will each require only one-fifth of the entire quantity. Would it be right to let one patient die in order to save the lives of five others?

Intuitively, it would be right to give the drug to the five patients, even though this would indirectly involve letting one patient die. But compare this example to the following one (first discussed in the third chapter):

The Transplant Case: You are a surgeon with six patients. One patient simply needs to have her tonsils removed, while the remaining five need organ transplants: one needs a liver, another a heart, another a lung, and two others need kidneys. In fact, if these five patients do not receive organ transplants within the next hour, they will die. It turns out that the one patient with bad tonsils is a matching donor. Her organs could be used to save five lives, but only at the cost of her own. You are in a position to kill this patient and use her organs in transplant procedures to save the lives of the other five. Would it be right to kill this one patient in order to save the lives of five others?

Clearly, it would be wrong to kill one patient in order to save the lives of five others. Yet, given that the outcome is the same, why should it be right to save five lives at the cost of one in the first case but not in the second? What is the relevant difference? Arguably, the difference is that in the Transplant Case you would be directly killing a patient, whereas in the Drug Case you would merely be letting a patient die. Examples such as these support the position of the American Medical Association.

It is doubtful, however, whether the distinction between killing and letting die explains why we evaluate these two cases differently. For consider a modified version of the Transplant Case:

The Case of the Bleeding Accident Victim: Suppose six people are involved in a car accident. Five of them have sustained serious internal injuries. In fact, unless they receive organ transplants within the next hour, they will die. One accident victim needs a liver, another a heart, another a lung, and two others each need a kidney. Now, suppose the sixth victim is slowly bleeding to death but could easily be saved by applying a tourniquet. Otherwise she is fine and will easily recover from her injuries. You are a skilled surgeon and the only physician on the scene. You are in a position to let this one accident victim bleed to death and then harvest her organs for transplant. Unless you do this, the five remaining accident victims will die. Would it be permissible for you to let this one accident victim bleed to death so that her organs could be used to save the lives of five others?

In this modified example, unlike the original one, you would not be killing one person to save the lives of five other people; you would merely be letting one person die. Still, this omission (letting someone die) in the modified case seems just as wrong as the commission (directly killing someone) in the original case. This suggests that the distinction between killing and letting die is not *in itself* a morally important difference. (If this is not the relevant difference between the first two cases, what is?)

Some philosophers, such as James Rachels (1980), have argued that, other things being equal, killing someone is morally equivalent to letting someone die (as suggested by the comparison between the original and the modified transplant cases). If this is correct, then the medical establishment cannot reasonably condone passive euthanasia but condemn active euthanasia. If Rachels is right, active euthanasia is permissible in every situation in which passive euthanasia is permissible.

5.2. Arguments for Active Euthanasia

The heart of the euthanasia controversy concerns the morality of active euthanasia. When, if ever, is it permissible to intentionally kill a terminally ill patient? There are several common arguments in support of the practice. We will discuss three: the argument from passive euthanasia; the argument from autonomy; and the argument from mercy.

The Argument from Passive Euthanasia

As we just noted, James Rachels believes that killing someone is morally equivalent to letting someone die. This suggests an analogical argument in support of active euthanasia:

(1) Passive euthanasia is sometimes acceptable.
(2) Other things being equal, there is no morally important difference between active and passive euthanasia.

Therefore:

(3) Active euthanasia is sometimes acceptable.

This argument is strengthened by the fact that active euthanasia is sometimes more humane than passive euthanasia. How can it be right, Rachels asks, to allow a terminally ill patient to die a slow, agonizing death (which is sometimes what passive euthanasia entails) but wrong to end that patient's life quickly and painlessly? If passive euthanasia is an acceptable practice, and if active euthanasia is more humane than passive euthanasia, then surely active euthanasia is an acceptable practice.

The Argument from Autonomy

To be autonomous is literally to be "self-governed." People are autonomous beings in the sense that they have the ability to rationally govern their own lives. Respect for personal autonomy is one of the fundamental principles of common morality. (According to Immanuel Kant, respect for autonomy is the central concern of ethics, although, interestingly, Kant condemned suicide.) This principle does not require that we respect every decision that a person makes, because even rational people can sometimes make irrational or uninformed decisions. But suppose a patient makes a rational, well-informed decision to die and requests a lethal injection from a physician. Then, out of respect for the patient's autonomy, shouldn't the physician administer the drug? Isn't this at least permissible? The argument:

(1) If a patient makes a rational, well-informed decision to die and requests euthanasia, then it is permissible for a physician to honor that request.
(2) A patient can make a rational, well-informed decision to die and request euthanasia.

Therefore:

(3) It can be permissible for a physician to honor a patient's request to die.

This is a compelling argument, but someone might reasonably object that while it is important to respect a patient's autonomy, there are other, more weighty considerations that count against euthanasia. We will explore what these other considerations might be later in the chapter.

The Argument from Mercy

As James Rachels points out, "Terminal patients sometimes suffer pain so horrible that it is beyond the comprehension of those who have not actually experienced it." According to the argument from mercy, active euthanasia is sometimes justified because it puts an end to such suffering. The story of Jonathan Swift, as recounted by Rachels, provides an illustration:

> The great Irish satirist Jonathan Swift took eight years to die, while, in the words of Joseph Fletcher, "His mind crumbled to pieces." At times the pain in his blinded eyes was so intense he had to be restrained from tearing them out with his own hands. Knives and other potential instruments of suicide had to be kept from him. For the last three years of his life, he could do nothing but sit and drool; and when he finally died it was only after convulsions that lasted thirty-six hours. (Rachels 1980: 40)

Rachels (1980: 43) argues that no moral objection can reasonably be raised against performing euthanasia in cases such as this. Stated in general terms, the argument runs as follows:

(1)   If an action promotes the best interests of everyone concerned and violates no one's rights, then that action is morally acceptable.
(2)   In at least some cases, active euthanasia promotes the best interests of everyone concerned and violates no one's rights.

Therefore:

(3)   In at least some cases, active euthanasia is morally acceptable.

Euthanasia would have promoted the best interests of Jonathan Swift and, we may assume, anyone who cared about him. Moreover, if all those involved in the situation waived their rights and, in particular, if Jonathan Swift waived his right to life and wanted to die, then no one's rights would have been violated. In this case, what possible moral objection could there be to euthanasia? There are those who take the position that it is *always* wrong to kill an innocent person. Those who accept this rule would object to the first premise of the argument, but it is difficult to see why this rule applies in the case of Jonathan Swift and other cases like it.

5.3. Arguments against Active Euthanasia

There are several standard arguments against the practice of active euthanasia, which we now turn to: the argument from innocence; the argument from divine dominion; the argument from fallibility; and the slippery slope argument.

The Argument from Innocence

The argument from innocence rests upon the principle that it is always wrong to kill an innocent human being. "A patient is an innocent person," writes Joseph V. Sullivan, a Roman Catholic Priest.

> The fact that the patient is incurably ill, wills euthanasia, and is useless to the community, does not in any way change the fact of the person's innocence. For a man to take the life of an innocent person directly, even his own life, for any reason whatsoever, apart from a divine command, has always been against the conscience of the West. (Sullivan 1989: 203)

Sullivan's argument:

(1)   It is wrong to kill an innocent human being.
(2)   To commit active euthanasia is to kill an innocent human being.

Therefore:

(3) It is wrong to commit active euthanasia.

The reasoning is clearly valid, and the second premise is true. But what about the general moral principle on which the argument rests? As we noted in the first chapter, there appear to be two reasons why it is ordinarily wrong to kill an innocent person: one is that it violates the victim's right to life and the other is that it inflicts a tremendous loss upon the victim. If this account is correct, then while it might be ordinarily wrong to kill an innocent person, it is not always wrong. In particular, it is not wrong in a situation in which a patient consents to euthanasia—thereby waiving his or her right to life—and in which the patient would, in fact, be better off dead (as in the case of Jonathan Swift). There are, in short, exceptions to the rule against killing an innocent person. For this reason, the argument from innocence does not prove that active euthanasia is always wrong.

But what about a situation in which a patient is not suffering, or is incapable of consenting to euthanasia, or both? The case of Terri Schiavo, mentioned at the beginning of the chapter, provides an illustration. Schiavo's parents argued that their daughter was conscious and wanted to live, but as an autopsy later revealed her cerebral cortex—the area of the brain that supports consciousness—had been liquefied. Despite what her parents wanted to believe, Schiavo experienced nothing. If, as argued in the previous chapter, to be "alive" in the sense that matters is to have a conscious life, then Schiavo did not have a valuable life. Her life might have been valuable to her parents, but it was not valuable to her, and it was not valuable in itself. Moreover, if the right to life is the right to a conscious life rather than to a biological life, as also argued in the previous chapter, then Schiavo no longer had a right to life. For these reasons, the rule against killing an innocent person did not apply in the case of Terri Schiavo, and it would not apply in other cases like it. To end the life of a patient in a persistent vegetative state does not inflict a loss upon the patient, nor does it violate the patient's right to life.

The Argument from Divine Dominion

In his discussion of euthanasia, J. Gay-Williams suggests that "Man as trustee of his body acts against God, its rightful possessor, when he takes his own life" (Gay-Williams 1996: 232). Joseph V. Sullivan develops the point:

> Man has not full dominion over his life. He has only the use of it; and the natural law obliges man while using a thing that is under the dominion of another not to destroy it. The life of man is solely under the dominion of God. Wherefore, as man may not take his life, neither may another man take it . . . since another man would have even less dominion over it. (Sullivan 1989: 197)

According to these writers, active euthanasia is wrong because a patient's body does not belong to the patient but rather to God. The argument:

(1) A patient's body belongs to God.

Therefore:

(2) To commit active euthanasia is to destroy something that belongs to God.
(3) It is wrong to destroy something that belongs to someone else.

Therefore:

(4) It is wrong to commit active euthanasia.

The reasoning is valid, but the two unsupported premises can be challenged. Obviously, the argument will be unacceptable to the atheist, who denies the existence of God. But even if we grant God's existence, can one person's body belong to another person, as the first premise assumes? This is the assumption on which slavery is based—an odious assumption, if ever there was one. The third premise of the argument is simply false, for it is not always wrong to destroy someone else's property. If you were being tortured on a rack, it would not be wrong for you to destroy the contraption, even if this were someone else's property. (Aren't terminally ill patients sometimes put to torture by their own bodies?)

The Argument from Fallibility

"Contemporary medicine has high standards of excellence," writes J. Gay-Williams,

> and a proven record of accomplishment, but it does not possess perfect and complete knowledge. A mistaken diagnosis is possible, and so is a mistaken prognosis. . . . In such circumstances, if euthanasia were permitted, we would die needlessly. Death is final and the chance of error too great to approve the practice of euthanasia. (Gay-Williams 1996: 233)

Compactly stated, the reasoning appears to be:

(1) It is wrong to approve of any practice if some people will die needlessly as a result of that practice.
(2) If active euthanasia is approved, then (owing to the fallibility of medical science) some people will die needlessly as a result of that practice.

Therefore:

    (3) It is wrong to approve of active euthanasia.

The reasoning is valid, and the second premise is plausible. There are, however, grave problems with the first premise. Every year close to 5,000 American workers are killed on the job, or die as a result of work-related injuries, and more than 30,000 Americans are killed in automobile accidents. Is it the case that people should not be permitted to work or to drive because some people will die needlessly as a result? Consider also that patients sometimes die because of the mistakes that physicians make in performing routine tasks, such as prescribing medications. Is it the case that physicians should not be permitted to practice medicine at all because of the possibility that some of their patients will die needlessly?

The Slippery Slope Argument

Some writers have argued against active euthanasia on purely consequentialist grounds. J. Gay-Williams argues that the practice of euthanasia would likely have a corrupting effect on the medical profession:

> Doctors and nurses are, for the most part, totally committed to saving lives. . . . Euthanasia as a practice might well alter this. It could have a corrupting influence so that in any case that is severe doctors and nurses might not try hard enough to save the patient. . . . The result would be an overall decline in the quality of medical care. (Gay-Williams 1996: 233)

Joseph V. Sullivan suggests that the practice of euthanasia would have serious social consequences and lead to an overall decline in the respect for human life:

> Once the respect for human life is so low that an innocent person may be killed directly even at his own request, compulsory euthanasia will necessarily be very near. This could lead easily to killing all incurable charity patients, the aged who are a public care, wounded soldiers, captured enemy soldiers, all deformed children, the mentally afflicted, and so on. Before long the danger would be at the door of every citizen. (Sullivan 1989: 205)

The reasoning:

    (1) If active euthanasia were permitted, this would have disastrous social consequences or lead to morally unacceptable practices.

Therefore:

    (2) Active euthanasia should not be permitted.

Is it reasonable to accept the premise of this argument? This is an empirical question, and the burden of proof is upon Gay-Williams and Sullivan to support their contentions with empirical evidence. Active euthanasia has been tolerated in the Netherlands for decades and was officially legalized in 1997. Belgium legalized the practice in 2002. Has such legislation led to an overall decline in the quality of medical care or in the respect for human life? Although this issued has been studied, there is no evidence that the open practice of euthanasia has the consequences that Gay-Williams and Sullivan predict. Furthermore, even if Gay-Williams and Sullivan are right in thinking that legalizing euthanasia would have negative social consequences, certainly the refusal to practice euthanasia has negative consequences, since many patients suffer needlessly as a result. Which set of consequences is worse? Once again, the burden of proof is upon Gay-Williams and Sullivan to show that the practice of euthanasia would have worse consequences than the refusal to practice it.

Notes

1. EXIT, Voluntary Euthanasia Society of Scotland <www.euthanasia.cc/vess.html>, Rick Hansen Spinal Cord Injury Registry <www.rickhansenregistry.org/page192. html>. Ramon Sampedro's life is the subject of the Spanish film *The Sea Inside*.
2. EXIT, Voluntary Euthanasia Society of Scotland <www.euthanasia.cc/vess.html>. Quotation edited.
3. Clyde Haberman, "From Private Ordeal to National Fight: The Case of Terri Schiavo," *The New York Times*, April 20, 2014 <www.nytimes.com/2014/04/21/us/from-private-ordeal-to-national-fight-the-case-of-terri-schiavo.html?_r=1>. Quotation edited.

6. The Ethics of Meat Eating

In the United States alone, more than nine billion farm animals are slaughtered every year for food. In 2014, this figure included 30 million cattle, 106 million pigs, 236 million turkeys, and an astonishing 8,666 million chickens.[1] During their short lives, farm animals are often caged, branded, castrated, beaten, electrocuted, or treated in ways that, under other circumstances, would qualify as animal abuse. Although we don't ordinarily think of our food choices as moral choices, these facts suggest that meat production poses a serious moral problem. Are farm animals *just* food, no different than vegetables? Or do they belong in an altogether different category? Are they, in a morally important sense, "persons"? If so, what does this entail concerning our food choices? Are we morally obligated to become vegetarians?

6.1. Animals and Culture

How we think about these questions is greatly influenced by culture. The Judeo-Christian tradition teaches us that human beings are created in the image of God and are alone endowed with an immortal soul. Our privileged place in nature is assured by the book of Genesis, where we are told that human beings have been granted dominion over all the animals of the earth:

> Then God said, "Let us make man in our image, after our likeness; and let them have dominion over the fish of the sea, and over the birds of the air, and over the cattle, and over all the earth, and over every creeping thing that creeps upon the earth." (1:26)

> And God blessed Noah and his sons, and said to them, "Be fruitful and multiply, and fill the earth. The fear of you and the dread of you shall be upon every beast of the earth, and upon every bird of the air, upon everything that creeps on the

ground and all the fish of the sea; into your hand they are delivered. Every moving thing that lives shall be food for you; and as I gave you the green plants, I give you everything." (9:1-3)

Not only were animals delivered into our hands for food, but also for blood sacrifice. "For the life of the creature is in the blood," we read in Leviticus, "and I [the Lord] have given it to you to make atonement for yourselves on the altar" (17:10). For whatever reason, the Lord of the ancient Israelites demanded the spilling of blood as atonement for sin: "It is the blood that makes atonement for one's life" (Leviticus 17:10); "Without the shedding of blood there is no forgiveness" (Hebrews 9:22). Since there was much to be forgiven, a great deal of animal blood was shed. We can only imagine how many animals were butchered in these rituals. One indication is found in 1 Kings (8:63), where it is reported that Solomon once sacrificed 22,000 cattle and 120,000 sheep and goats over a period of fourteen days as a fellowship offering.

Christianity, though it rejected animal sacrifice, did little to elevate the status of animals. Even vegetarianism was denounced as a heresy. Constantine, the first Christian emperor of Rome, had little tolerance for this particular heresy and ordered that those convicted of the practice have molten led poured down their throats (Hill 1996: 34-35). Pope Pius IX prohibited the establishment of an animal welfare office in Rome, arguing that people have obligations to one another, but not to animals (Linzey 1995: 19). St. Thomas Aquinas, by far the most influential theologian in the history of the Catholic Church, summed up the Christian attitude toward animals in a few words: "[B]y divine providence [animals] are intended for man's use in the natural order. Hence it is not wrong for man to make use of them, either by killing them or in any other way whatever" (Aquinas 1989: 8)

Our attitudes towards animals are embodied in language. "Not only is our language male-centered," writes Carol J. Adams, "it is human-centered as well." She continues:

> Language distances us . . . from animals by naming them as objects, as "its.". . . [J]ust as the generic "he" erases female presence, the generic "it" erases the living, breathing nature of animals and reifies their object status. The absence of a non-sexist pronoun allows us to objectify the animal world by considering all animals as "its." (Adams 1994: 64)

Notice that it is appropriate to say, "A wolf is fiercely protective of *its* young," but not, "My neighbor is fiercely protective of *its* young." When children begin to conceptualize the world, they soon learn that while human beings belong in the personal category of "he" and "she," other animals are consigned to the impersonal category of "it"—the category of pencils, rocks, toys, machines and all other mere things.

While the generic "it" objectifies animals, other stereotypes—the cowardly chicken, the stubborn mule, the filthy pig—reinforce negative attitudes toward them, and so do such pejoratives as "bitch," "worm," "rat," and "weasel." When we describe hardened criminals as "animals," not only do we express contempt for them, we also imply that they are not deserving of respect or compassion. And even when we acknowledge the sobering truth that human beings are, after all, just animals—genetically almost indistinguishable from chimpanzees—our animal cousins are stigmatized as "lower" or "subhuman" animals. (For comparison, imagine the implications of describing other races as the "lower" races or describing women as "submen.")

Language is also used to camouflage the true nature of the human-animal relationship. Human beings enslave other animals, imprison them, mutilate them, kill them, dismember them, and eat them. But this is not how we commonly think about our relationship to animals. We speak of animal "domestication" rather than of animal enslavement. We describe hunting and fishing as forms of recreation, as "sports," rather than as animal abuse. We conceptualize animal muscle as "food"—as hamburger, steak, or beef (not cow muscle), as ham or pork (not pig muscle), as poultry (not chicken or turkey muscle), as mutton (not sheep muscle), as venison (not deer muscle), as chicken or fish (not *a* chicken or *a* fish).

Industries that exploit our animal "resources" also shape people's attitudes, sometimes in insidious ways. The National Cattlemen's Beef Association has created a website, "Cool 2B Real," to promote meat consumption among teenage girls. "The site," explains one article, "which looks like a cross between a Barbie fan page and a Taco Bell ad (beef-filled tacos and gigantic hamburgers dot the screen), extols teenage girls to 'Keep it Real'—'real' as in a person who eats beef, preferably three or four times a day" (Reaves 2003). An advertisement for Florida's Gatorland, typifies our consumer culture's perception of animals. Here an alligator is represented, not as a whole, living being, but as a collection of undetached consumer goods. Various parts of the animal are identified by arrows accompanied by such comments as "Small stuffed alligator heads sell for $14.98 at Gatorland," and "Teeth: Gatorland strings them into necklaces, $3.98 each," and "Toenails: Make dandy backscratchers, which Gatorland sells for $4.98 each." The owner of Gatorland is quoted as saying, "We try to sell everything except the grunt." And one could not ask for a clearer illustration of our consumer culture's commodification of animals than the "GloFish," a genetically engineered glow-in-the-dark aquarium fish. One advertisement reads: "GloFish are available in six stunning colors: Starfire Red, Electric Green, Sunburst Orange, Cosmic Blue, Galactic Purple, and Moonrise Pink."

If this is how animals are conceptualized in our culture, why should we have qualms about killing them for food? "The death of the other animals is an accepted part of life," writes Carol Adams,

> either envisioned as being granted in Genesis 1:26 by a human-oriented God who instructs us that we may dominate the animals or conceptualized as a right because of our superior rationality. For those who hold to this dominant viewpoint in our culture the surprise is not that animals are oppressed (though this is not the term

they would use to express human beings' relationship to the other animals), the
surprise is that anyone would object to this. (Adams 1994: 65)

Consider the following comparison.[2] For centuries, Africans were abducted from
their native lands and sold into slavery in the Americas and Europe. Certainly,
they were not viewed as persons in the full sense. Indeed, there were respected
European thinkers who refused to classify them as human beings! Just as Rene
Descartes claimed that animals were nothing more than unthinking, unfeeling
machines, Voltaire placed Africans midway between apes and human beings.
David Hume insisted that Africans only mimic human beings in the way in
which, for instance, parrots mimic human speech. With the boundary firmly
drawn between "us" and "them" and Africans relegated to a subhuman status,
the practice of slavery was easily condoned. Racism, which persists to this day,
is the legacy of our slaveholding past. Do people harbor a similar attitude toward
animals? Does "speciesism" serve the same social function that racism served—
to rationalize domination?

6.2. Speciesism

The racist is someone who believes that race-membership in itself is important
in deciding how individuals should be treated. Today, most people recognize
that this is a serious moral mistake. If two people are alike in all respects except
race-membership, morality requires that they be treated the same. For example,
it would be wrong for an employer to pay one employee more than another
simply because they belonged to different races. It would be wrong for a judge
to sentence one criminal to ten years in prison but to release another on parole
simply because the first criminal was black but the second white. The moral
principle that condemns such racist practices is the principle of equal treatment:
that different individuals should be treated the same unless there are differences
between them that justify treating them differently. Race-membership, most
people will agree, is not in itself a morally important difference between individuals. Hence, we are not justified in treating people differently simply because
of their racial differences.

What about species-membership? For example, can it be right to use chimpanzees in biomedical research—to cage them, infect them with diseases, run
invasive tests on them—but wrong to treat human beings in this way? Certainly,
there are important differences between humans and chimpanzees, considered as
groups, but there are also individual humans who are not importantly different
from chimpanzees. Could it be right to use chimpanzees in biomedical research
but not mentally disabled people at the same intellectual level? All that can be
said in defense of such differential treatment is that chimpanzees are just animals whereas mentally disabled people are still human beings. But how does
this differ from the racist's claim that blacks may be treated differently simply
because they are not white? Why should species-membership *in itself* matter but
not race-membership? (You might say that there is an important difference. A

human being, regardless of race, is still a human being but a chimpanzee is not. But the question is why we should think that species-membership, unlike race-membership, is morally important. Why not say that chimpanzees should be treated no differently than human beings because a primate, regardless of its species, is still a primate?) On the surface, speciesism is no more defensible than racism. Both involve the belief that, regardless of the similarities and differences between individuals, it is a being's *group-membership* that ultimately matters in deciding how that being should be treated.

Speciesism, like racism, violates the principle of equal treatment. If the members of two groups are not importantly different, it cannot be right to treat the members of one group in ways in which it would be wrong to treat the members of the other group. For example, if it is wrong to run invasive experiments on mentally disabled humans, then it is wrong to run such tests on chimpanzees. The mere fact that disabled humans belong to one group but chimpanzees to a different group is morally unimportant. If this is correct, then speciesism is no more defensible than racism (or any other form of prejudice based upon group-membership).

The analogical argument presented here can be summarized as follows:

(1) Speciesism is no more morally defensible than racism.
(2) Racism is morally indefensible.

Therefore:

(3) Speciesism is morally indefensible.

The crucial premise is the first. If species-membership, unlike race-membership, is morally important, why? If we discovered creatures on another planet who were indistinguishable from human beings except that they were not biologically human, should we treat them differently simply because of this biological difference? Or think of it in this way: If you demand that *you* be treated as an individual and not simply as a representative of your race (or religion, or gender, or ethnicity), then, to be consistent, you must extend the same consideration to others, even to other animals.

6.3. The Moral Case for Vegetarianism

For her book *Slaughterhouse*, Gail Eisnitz interviewed workers from meatpacking facilities around the country. This is some of what she was told:

> "A lot of times the sticker just can't do his job right," Walker said. "He doesn't get a good bleed." Still, within seconds of being stuck, the cows arrived at the two head-skinners, who stripped all the hide from the animals' heads.
> "A lot of times the skinner finds out an animal is still conscious when he slices the side of its head and it starts kicking wildly. If that happens, or if a cow is

already kicking when it arrives at their station, the skinners shove a knife into the back of its head to cut the spinal cord."

This practice paralyzes the cow from the neck down but doesn't deaden the pain of head skinning or render the animal unconscious; it simply allows workers to skin or dismember the animal without getting kicked.

• • •

"After they left me, the hogs would go up a hundred–foot ramp to a tank where they're dunked in 140 degree water [a standard procedure in pork processing]. That's to scald their hair off," he explained. "Water any hotter than that would take the meat right off the bones. You stick a live hog, it tightens up the muscles around that slit and holds the blood in. There's no way these animals can bleed out in the few minutes it takes to get up the ramp. By the time they hit the scalding tank, they're still fully conscious and squealing. Happens all the time." (Eisnitz 1997: 28-29, 71)

Eisnitz's book exposes some of the routine abuses that occur in commercial meat production. Her account may not be representative of how farm animals are generally treated, but no one who has explored the literature on this topic could possibly doubt that farm animals endure intense and prolonged suffering because of the methods employed by the meat industry in the process of raising, transporting, and slaughtering animals. And it is not just farmhands, truckers, and meatpackers who are responsible for such suffering. By purchasing meat products and financially supporting the meat industry, consumers are directly responsible as well. It has been estimated that the average American, over the course of a lifetime lasting 75 years, consumes the equivalent of eleven cows, 32 pigs and sheep, and 2,600 chickens, turkeys, and ducks.[3]

This suggests the following moral syllogism against meat eating:

(1) It is wrong to cause pain and suffering for trivial reasons.
(2) The practice of eating meat causes pain and suffering for trivial reasons.

Therefore:

(3) The practice of eating meat is wrong.

The reasoning is obviously valid. What about the premises? There may be some hesitation to apply the first premise to the suffering of farm animals. But what it feels like for a farm animal to be scalded or skinned alive is more or less what it feels like for a human being to be scalded or skinned alive. If you would not condone the infliction of such pain on human beings for trivial reasons, then—keeping in mind our discussion of speciesism—you cannot consistently condone the infliction of such pain on farm animals for trivial reasons. There may also be some hesitation to apply the second premise to all cases of meat consumption. After all, subsistence hunters do not cause animals to suffer for trivial reasons inasmuch as meat is necessary for their survival; and even outside of this context, some people may have important reasons for eating meat. Also, on small farms and in many rural areas around the world, animals are not subjected to the brutalities of the modern meat industry. Still the premise does apply in cases in which (1) people choose to eat meat simply because they enjoy the taste of meat, and (2) the meat that they consume has been produced by means of the intensive farming methods adopted in America and other industrialized countries. In all likelihood, therefore, the second premise applies in *your* case. If so, then you can validly draw the conclusion that it is wrong for *you* to eat meat.

Peter Singer, who has written more influentially on this topic than any other philosopher, explains the obligation to become a vegetarian in the following way:

> Becoming a vegetarian is not merely a symbolic gesture. Nor is it an attempt to isolate oneself from the ugly realities of the world, to keep oneself pure and so without responsibility for the cruelty and carnage all around. Becoming a vegetarian is a highly practical and effective step one can take toward ending both the killing of nonhuman animals and the infliction of suffering upon them. (Singer 1990: 162)

Vegetarianism, for Singer, is a form of boycott undertaken for the express purpose of ending the suffering of animals on factory farms. "Until we boycott meat," Singer writes, "and all other products of animal factories, we are, each one of us, contributing to the continued existence, prosperity, and growth of factory farming and all other cruel practices used in rearing animals for food" (Singer 1990: 162). By boycotting the products of animal factories, we undercut in one stroke the only reason why these practices exist: the consumer demand for meat.

6.4. The Moral Case against Vegetarianism

The most common objection to ethical vegetarianism—that is, vegetarianism for ethical reasons—concerns the morality of the predator-prey relationship. According to one version of the objection, ethical vegetarians fail to recognize that human beings are by nature predatory animals (while not carnivores, at least omnivores). If it is natural for human beings to eat meat, how could it be wrong? Related to this is the charge that ethical vegetarians are in the awkward position of condemning, not just human predation, but all forms of natural predation. If we should interfere in the operations of the meat industry or abolish recreational hunting because of the misery which these practices inflict upon animals, shouldn't we also interfere in the operations of nature and protect prey animals from wild predators? The objection raised here is sometimes called the "predation argument." In what follows, we will examine three versions of the argument.

The Predation Analogy

One version of the predation argument—the "predation analogy"—rests upon a comparison between human predation and predation in the wild. For many people, there is no significant difference between what human beings do in eating meat and what natural predators do in killing prey for food. Clearly, a wolf does nothing wrong in killing sheep for food, so why should it be wrong for human beings to eat meat? As Kent Baldner writes, "If killing for food is morally justifiable for natural predators, the same should be true for human predators, whether they are individual hunters or corporate factory farmers" (Baldner 1990: 2). Set forth as an analogical argument, we have:

(1) It is morally acceptable for wild animals to kill prey.
(2) There is no significant difference between human predation and predation in the wild.

Therefore:

(3) It is morally acceptable for human beings to kill animals for food.

Although this is a common defense of meat eating, it is not terribly difficult to refute. Is it plausible to maintain that whatever behavior is acceptable for wild animals is also acceptable for human beings? This seems doubtful. "It is odd," Peter Singer once remarked, "how humans, who normally consider themselves so far above other animals, will, if it seems to support their dietary preferences, use an argument that implies that we ought to look to other animals for moral inspiration and guidance" (Singer 1990: 224). The problem concerns the second premise. Is it true that human predation is not importantly different from predation in the wild? Against this it will be argued that human beings are moral agents—that is, beings capable of understanding moral principles and guiding their conduct accordingly— whereas other animals (presumably) are not. Animals lack the conceptual resources to form moral judgments about their behavior. For this reason, it may be permissible for wolves to kill sheep for food, but not for human being to do so. Because wolves are not moral agents, their behavior cannot be evaluated morally. But because human beings are moral agents, their actions are subject to moral judgment. Therefore, behavior that is morally neutral for wolves, such as killing sheep, may be morally wrong for human beings.

A different response to the predation argument is suggested by Stephen Sapontzis. Rather than arguing that there are important moral differences between humans and other animals, Sapontzis suggests that the predatory practices of wild animals might be judged morally wrong even if these animals are not moral agents. Consider the example of a small child—someone who is also not a moral agent— tormenting a cat. Sapontzis writes:

The child may be too young to recognize and respond to humane moral obligations. However, while this may influence our evaluation of his/her character and
responsibility for his/her actions, it does not lead us to conclude that there is nothing wrong with his/her tormenting the cat. To take another example, if we determine that someone is criminally insane, i.e., is incapable of distinguishing right
from wrong, this affects our evaluation of his/her responsibility for his/her actions
and whether he/she deserves punishment for them. However, it does not lead us to
conclude that there was nothing wrong with those actions. (Sapontzis 1984: 28)

Sapontzis's point is that whether or not someone is a moral agent is relevant to certain kinds of moral judgments, such as assignments of moral responsibility, but not
to the moral evaluation of that person's actions. If a young girl torments a cat, what
the child does is wrong whether or not she realizes it or should be held accountable
for her actions. And if a cat torments a bird, this is wrong too whether or not the cat
realizes it or should be held accountable for her actions. The child and the cat simply don't know any better, but this doesn't render their actions morally neutral. Similarly, a wolf who preys upon sheep may not know any better, but this doesn't make
the wolf's actions morally neutral. If Sapontzis is right, then, interestingly, it is not
the second premise of the above argument that is suspect, but rather the first.

The Predation Syllogism

Let us now turn to a different version of the argument. Sometimes the predation
argument is based upon the morality of living according to one's nature. If human
beings are by nature omnivores, how can it be wrong for them to eat meat? Fully
spelled out, we have the following syllogistic argument:

  (1) It is not wrong for natural predators to kill other animals for food.
  (2) Human beings are natural predators (that is, meat eaters by nature).

Therefore:

  (3) It is not wrong for human beings to kill other animals for food.

This version of the argument—the "predation syllogism"—does not rest upon a
comparison between human predation and predation in the wild. Rather, it rests
upon the general moral principle, expressed in the first premise, that if an animal is
by nature a meat eater—as, it is assumed, human beings are—then there is nothing
wrong with that animal killing other animals for food. This might be true even if
there are important moral differences between human behavior and animal behavior. So this version of the argument is not necessarily open to the same criticisms as
the first one.

    Still, there are at least three objections that can be raised against this argument.
First, as we saw in the opening chapter, there is no obvious conceptual connection
between what is natural and what is moral. To argue, as it is argued here, that it is

permissible to eat meat simply because it is natural is a logical fallacy. Second, although some biologists argue that human beings possess both herbivorous and carnivorous characteristics, there are many reasons, rooted in our physiology and evolutionary past, for believing that humans are not true omnivores. If we are not, then the second premise is false and the argument collapses. A third objection has to do, not with the argument itself, but with its application to meat eating in America and other industrialized nations. No one could reasonably claim that the factory-farming methods employed in these countries are in any sense "natural." Therefore, it may be permissible in principle for human beings to use animals for food, but in actual practice, because of the methods employed by the meat industry, it may still be wrong. The argument seems to provide at best a defense of the subsistence hunting practices of hunter-gatherers, not of factory farming.

The Predation *Reductio*

Yet another version of the predation argument—for us, the final version—is known as the "predation *reductio*." A *reductio* (more precisely, a *reductio ad absurdum*) is an argument which attempts to refute some position by "reducing it to absurdity"— that is, by deducing from it some absurd or ridiculous consequence. The predation *reductio* is an argument which attempts to refute ethical vegetarianism by deducing from it an absurd consequence involving the abolition of natural predation. "Among the most disturbing implications drawn from conventional indiscriminate animal liberation/rights theory," writes J. Baird Callicott, "is that, were it possible for us to do so, we ought to protect innocent vegetarian animals from their carnivorous predators" (Callicott 1992: 258). This charge, in one form or another, is often leveled against ethical vegetarianism. Fully developed, the predation *reductio* proceeds as follows:

(1) Let us assume, along with ethical vegetarians, that other animals are members of the moral community and, consequently, that there is a moral obligation to alleviate animal suffering and otherwise protect animals from harm.
(2) Wild predators harm prey animals.

Therefore:

(3) If ethical vegetarians are right, then there is a moral obligation to prevent predation in the wild.
(4) But it is absurd to suppose that there is such an obligation.

Therefore:

(5) Ethical vegetarians are wrong—that is, other animals are not members of the moral community.

The moral principle underlying this argument is uncontroversial: if others are in need of assistance, and we are in a position to help, then we should. By "others" in this context is meant other members of the moral community (or "persons" in the morally important sense of the term). According to ethical vegetarians, this category includes a large class of nonhuman animals. Hence, just as we should come to the assistance of another human being in need, we should come to the assistance of another animal equally in need. Consider, for instance, what our reaction would be if another human being were attacked by a wild animal. To stand by and do nothing would obviously be wrong. We have a moral obligation to protect people from harm, whether this results from crime, accidents, disease, natural disasters, or wild animals. Hence, we have an obligation to protect people from predators. The problem, for the ethical vegetarian, is that if other animals count as persons, by parallel steps in reasoning, we reach the conclusion that prey animals should be protected from natural predators. Yet, how could anyone reasonably maintain that there is an obligation to abolish natural predation? Since this conclusion is unacceptable or obviously false, the assumption on which it rests must be false. Animals, in other words, are not members of the morally community.

The predation *reductio* cannot be easily dismissed, as some philosophers have tried to do. "The short and simple answer," writes Peter Singer, after raising the question of prey protection, "is that once we give up our claim to 'dominion' over the other species we should stop interfering with them at all. We should leave them alone as much as we possibly can. Having given up the role of tyrant, we should not try to play God either" (Singer 1990: 226). Yet this quick response is hardly consistent with Singer's claim that animal suffering should be counted equally with human suffering. We are not "interfering" with prey animals by protecting them from predators; we are showing as much concern for their suffering as for the suffering of our fellow humans.

Singer admits that this short and simple answer is inadequate. It is conceivable, he concedes, "that human interference will improve the conditions of animals, and so be justifiable." But, he goes on:

> Judging by our past record, any attempt to change ecological systems on a large scale is going to do far more harm than good. For that reason, if for no other, it is true to say that, except in a few very limited cases, we cannot and should not try to police all of nature. We do enough if we eliminate our own unnecessary killing and cruelty toward other animals. (Singer 1990: 226)

Surely, Singer would not say that we "do enough" for other human beings if we eliminate our own unnecessary killing and cruelty toward them. So why is it that we do enough for other animals by refraining from such things? Why, in other words, should we intervene on behalf of other humans but simply leave other animals alone? It may be true that by intervening on a large scale in the operations of nature we would do more harm than good; but from this it does not follow that we should do nothing, or intervene in only a "few very limited cases." This is black-

and-white thinking. In any event, Singer's response misses the point. The important question is whether ethical vegetarianism entails a moral obligation to protect prey animals. Even if this obligation is overridden in most cases by other considerations, the point of the predation *reductio* is that it is absurd to suppose that there is any such obligation to begin with. If it is an implication of Singer's moral views that there *is* such an obligation, even one that is usually overridden, then he must somehow dispel the apparent absurdity of this.

Tom Regan approaches the problem in a different way, arguing that there is no obligation to prevent predation in the wild because wild predators are not moral agents and, therefore, cannot violate the rights of prey. He writes:

> *Only moral agents can have duties*, and this because only these individuals have the cognitive and other abilities necessary for being held morally accountable for what they do or fail to do. Wolves are not moral agents. . . . [They] cannot *themselves* meaningfully be said to have duties to anyone, nor, therefore, the particular duty to respect the rights possessed by other animals. In claiming that we have a prima facie duty to assist those animals *whose rights are violated*, therefore, we are not claiming that we have a duty to assist the sheep against the attack of the wolf, since the wolf neither can nor does violate anyone's rights. (Regan 1983: 285)

It may or may not be true that wolves violate the rights of sheep, but surely this is not of decisive importance. Again, consider what our reaction would be if a human being were attacked by a wild animal. Certainly, Regan would not argue that because a wild animal is not a moral agent and cannot, therefore, violate anyone's rights, this releases us from any obligation to come to that person's assistance. We have a moral obligation to protect *all* members of the moral community from harm, whether or not this harm comes from moral agents. If sheep are members of the moral community, it follows that we have a moral obligation to protect them from predatory wolves, whether or not wolves violate their rights.

Let us examine the charge that the obligation to prevent natural predation is morally absurd. What exactly does this mean? There seem to be two possibilities. First, it might mean that the obligation to protect prey animals from natural predators is inherently absurd, like the obligation to protect rocks from natural erosion or to protect water from evaporation. It simply makes no moral sense at all. Second, it might mean that such an obligation, while morally meaningful, is nonetheless incompatible with our deepest moral convictions. It should not surprise us that ethical holists, such as Kent Baldner and Baird Callicott, whose moral outlook is shaped by the land ethic of Aldo Leopold, would insist that the obligation to protect prey animals from natural predators is morally absurd. According to Leopold, "A thing is right when it tends to preserve the integrity, stability, and beauty of the biotic community. It is wrong when it tends otherwise" (Leopold 1987: 224-25). For Leopold, the suffering endured by prey animals is not in itself a moral reason for interfering in the operations of nature. It is the good of the whole community of life that has moral importance, not the good of any individual living being. If the predator-prey relationship, in all its multifarious forms, contributes to the "integrity, stability, and beauty" of nature, as arguably it does, then, for Leopold, it should be preserved.

Is the obligation to protect prey animals morally absurd in either one of these senses? There are examples which suggest otherwise. Consider an insect, known as *cephenomyia trompe*, whose larvae feed and grow in the nostrils of reindeer, slowing suffocating the animals to death.[4] If such parasitism could be eliminated, without significant cost to ourselves, and without disturbing the balance of nature, should we do so? While we might hesitate to interfere in the lifecycle of *cephenomyia trompe*, how can we not have compassion for an animal dying slowly from suffocation? Would it be inherently absurd, or incompatible with our deepest moral convictions, to suggest that reindeer should be spared this ordeal? If animal suffering counts for something in the moral balance, then the fact that animals suffer from predation constitutes a good moral reason for preventing it, and one that we should act on, unless other considerations weigh against it. As Singer notes, there are reasons for thinking that any attempt to alter ecological systems on a large scale would do more harm than good.[5] Still it is not *inherently* absurd to suppose that there is an obligation to protect animals from natural predators, even if this obligation has limited practical application. Nor (except, perhaps, in the case of ethical holists) does it conflict with our deepest moral convictions. If one of these convictions is that we should strive to reduce the amount of suffering in the world, then assisting prey animals, in some cases at least, is one way in which this can be accomplished.

Notes

1. According to the Humane Society of the United States, <http://www.humanesociety. org/news/resources/research/stats_slaughter_totals.html>.
2. Many writers, going back to Henry Salt and Jeremy Bentham, have made this comparison. For a book-length discussion of the many parallels between human slavery and animal exploitation, see Marjorie Spiegel, *The Dreaded Comparison: Human and Animal Slavery*.
3. www.wfad.org/mediacenter/NRVictims6.pdf.
4. This example is discussed by Arne Naess in "Should We Try To Relieve Clear Cases of Extreme Suffering in Nature?"
5. Although Singer is not specific about these reasons, two are rather obvious. First, as already noted, extending protection to prey animals would in all likelihood involve condemning an indefinite number of predators to death by starvation. Second, successfully segregating predators from prey would require greatly restricting the freedom of these animals, and so diminish the quality of their lives. An additional consideration is that the energy and resources invested in any large-scale effort to protect prey animals would almost certainly be better utilized in the preservation and restoration of wildlife habitats. As a general policy, we do more good for animals by protecting them from human encroachment than by protecting them from natural predators.

7. The Ethics of Political Authority

For better or for worse, virtually all people live under some form of government. Some governments are more intrusive than others, but all governments restrict people's freedoms. In the United States, freedom of religion is recognized as a basic right, but in Pakistan apostates can be put to death. In Amsterdam, the use of marijuana, hashish, and psilocybin mushrooms is legally tolerated, but not in the United States and in most other countries. The Supreme Court recently ruled in favor of same-sex marriage, but in Iran homosexuals are hanged. All governments fund their operations by levying taxes on their citizens and many require some form of direct participation, such as military service or jury duty. Because government is ubiquitous, people tend to take the institution for granted and not ponder the alternatives. Yet, even if government is inevitable or inescapable, is it morally defensible?

The question raised here concerns the "legitimacy" of government. To say that a government is legitimate, or that it has legitimate power or authority over its citizens, means that (1) citizens have an obligation to *obey* the government—that is, to do what they are told, to follow the law, simply because this is what the government commands—and (2) the government has the right to *force* people to submit to its rule by punishing disobedience. People ordinarily have a right to live their lives as they choose, so governmental coercion requires a justification. Does any government have legitimate authority over its citizens? If so, how?

7.1. Plato's Defense of Political Authority

Plato was one of the first philosophers to critically examine the notion of political authority. His position, as formulated in one of his early philosophical dialogues, the *Crito*, is that political authority is both unconditional and unrestricted: *all* governments have the right to rule, and citizens are obligated to do *whatever* their government commands. Concerning the duties of citizens, Plato writes:

> [I]f you cannot persuade your country you must do what it orders, and patiently submit to any punishment that it imposes, whether it be flogging or imprisonment. . . . And if it leads you out to war, to be wounded or killed, you must comply, and it is right that you should do so. You must not give way or retreat or abandon your position. Both in war and in the law courts and everywhere else you must do whatever your city and your country command. (Plato 1985: 50c)

Plato argues for this position through the dialogue's main character, Socrates, who has been condemned to death by an Athenian tribunal. In the *Crito*, we find Socrates in prison, awaiting execution. One of his devoted students has bribed a prison guard, paving the way for Socrates to escape and flee Athens. But Socrates refuses. In an earlier dialogue (the *Apology*) Socrates refuted the charges brought against him. It is understood, then, that Socrates has been unjustly sentenced to death, and yet Socrates argues that he is morally obligated to accept the verdict.

The Argument from Parental Authority

Socrates imagines the laws of Athens speaking to him:

> [S]ince you have been born and brought up and educated; can you deny . . . that you were our child and servant, both you and your ancestors? . . . [W]e maintain that anyone who disobeys is guilty of doing wrong . . . because we are his parents. (Plato 1985: 50e)

Plato's reasoning appears to be:

(1) Children have an obligation to obey their parents.
(2) The government plays the role of a parent in relation to its citizens.

Therefore:

(3) Citizens have an obligation to obey their government.

There are three rather obvious objections to Plato's argument. First, while good parents might have a claim to the obedience of their children, bad parents do not. Therefore, the strongest conclusion that Plato is entitled to is that citizens ought to obey *some* governments—that is, *good* governments. Second, parental authority has its limits. Children are not obligated to do something dangerous, criminal, or foolish simply because their parents command it. Plato's argument, therefore, does not show that citizens have an obligation to do *whatever* their government commands. Finally, there is an important difference between the institution of government and the institution of parenthood. The responsibility of a parent is to care for those who are too young to care for themselves. Once children reach adulthood and are capable of making responsible decisions for themselves, parents have no rightful authority over them. Why, then, should a government have rightful authority over its adult citizens?

The Argument from Gratitude

Plato's second argument draws upon the sense of gratitude that people often feel toward their country. Socrates again imagines the laws speaking to him:

> Are you not grateful to those of us laws which were instituted for this end, for requiring your father to give you a cultural and physical education? . . . [W]e have brought you into the world and reared you and educated you, and given you and all your fellow citizens a share in all the good things at our disposal. . . [W]e maintain that anyone who disobeys is guilty of doing wrong . . . because we are his guardians. (Plato 1985: 50e, 51d-50e)

Plato's argument can be reconstructed as follows:

(1) Citizens owe it to their government to be obedient.
(2) Debts ought to be repaid.

Therefore:

(3) Citizens ought to obey their government.

This argument is also deficient. Good governments provide important services for people, but so do many institutions and business enterprises, such as hospitals and electric companies. Should you be grateful to your electric company for providing you with electricity? This is an important service, but you also pay for it, and having paid for it, you owe nothing. Why should citizens feel grateful to a government for services that are funded by their tax dollars? Why, after having paid for such services, do citizens still owe something to their government? And why, of all possible forms of payment, do citizens owe it to their government to be obedient? There appear to be no good answers to these questions.

The Argument from Tacit Agreement

In the *Crito*, Plato advances three arguments in support of governmental authority. So far, we have examined two. Of the three, by far the most compelling is the argument from tacit agreement. Centuries later, John Locke and other social contract theorists would give essentially the same argument in support of the legitimacy of government. According to these theorists, government is established by means of a social contract, and the legitimacy of this institution derives from the obligation that people have to keep their agreements. Plato is not a social contract theorist, but he does argue that by remaining within a country, when they are free to leave, citizens make a tacit promise to obey their government.

The laws of Athens address Socrates:

> [A]ny Athenian, on attaining to manhood and seeing for himself the political organization of the state and us its laws, is permitted, if he is not satisfied with us, to take his property and go away wherever he likes. If any of you chooses to go to one of our colonies, supposing that he should not be satisfied with us and the state, or to emigrate to any other country, not one of us laws hinders or prevents him from going away wherever he likes, without any loss of property. On the other hand, if any one of you stands his ground when he can see how we administer justice and the rest of our public organization, we hold that by so doing he has in fact undertaken to do anything that we tell him. (Plato 1985: 51d-51e)

Socrates has "undertaken, in deed if not in word, to live [his] life as a citizen in obedience to" the Athenian government. The laws tell him that by failing to obey, Socrates would be "guilty of doing wrong . . . because after promising obedience, he is neither obeying us nor persuading us to change our decision" (Plato 1985: 51e)

Plato's argument:

(1) Citizens make a tacit agreement to obey their government.
(2) Agreements ought to be kept.

Therefore:

(3) Citizens ought to obey their government.

To get a feel for Plato's reasoning, suppose you're playing chess with a friend. Although your friend may not have explicitly agreed to abide by the rules of the game, you would certainly think that she did something wrong if she cheated. By choosing to play the game, your friend has made a *tacit* agreement—an agreement "in deed if not in word"—to play by the rules. According to Plato, by choosing to be a citizen of a country, a person makes a tacit agreement to abide by the laws of that country. Just as it is wrong to cheat at chess, it is wrong to break the law.

There are many personal relationships—marriage, friendship, parenthood—that entail certain responsibilities. By voluntarily entering into these relationships, people undertake an obligation to fulfill these responsibilities, whether or not they explicitly agree to it. Plato is suggesting that by remaining a citizen of a country, when one is free to leave, one undertakes an obligation to fulfill the responsibilities of citizenship, and chief among these responsibilities is the civic duty to obey the laws of that country. This line of reasoning makes sense if a country has a legitimate government. The problem, though, is that Plato's argument is supposed to *explain* the legitimacy of government, not presuppose it. To see the problem, suppose you live in a city controlled by gangs. Each gang claims some neighborhood as its own "turf" and defends it against rival gangs. Your neighborhood is claimed by the Jets. You have lived on Jet turf your whole life, and you own a small grocery store in the neighborhood. Like other business owners, you reluctantly pay a monthly fee to the Jets for "protection" against rival gangs. You reluctantly accept the situation, because every neighborhood in the city is controlled by a gang. If the Jets were ousted, some other gang would move in and take over. Of course, the Jets have no legitimate claim to their position of power. But suppose one of the gang members has been studying Plato. He tells you that since you have freely chosen to remain in the neighborhood when you might have fled long ago, you have given your tacit consent to Jet government. You are told:

> Anyone on attaining to manhood and seeing for himself how the Jets run the neighborhood, is permitted, if he is not satisfied with us, to take his property and go away wherever he likes. On the other hand, if any one of you stands his ground when he can see how we administer justice and the rest of our public organization, we hold that by so doing he has in fact undertaken to do anything that we tell him.

How would you respond? Probably, you would point out that the neighborhood does not belong to the Jets. It belongs to the people who live and work there. And you have the right to live in your own neighborhood without being bullied by the Jets. Couldn't you respond to Plato's argument in the same way? Doesn't a country rightfully belong to its people rather than to its government? If so, then don't people have a right to live in their own country without being bullied by the government?

The Argument from Inequality

In the *Crito*, Plato argues that *every* government has legitimate authority over its citizens. We have seen that his arguments for this are less than convincing. In a separate dialogue, the *Republic*, Plato argues for a narrower conclusion: that people ought to obey wise rulers. His argument can be set forth as follows:

(1) Citizens ought to promote the good of society.
(2) Citizens promote the good of society by obeying wise rulers.

Therefore:

(3) Citizens ought to obey wise rulers.

Unlike the arguments considered previously, this is not an argument for the legitimacy of all forms of government, certainly not democratic government. It is an argument for the legitimacy of *elitist* government or "meritocracy"—that is, a form of government in which only the most qualified individuals, the wise, have political power.

Social organization is highly complex, and there are different roles that people play within society, each requiring its own set of skills. Plato, in his classic tripartite analysis of the state, identified three basic roles or social classes: that of the ruler, whose function is to govern society; that of the soldier, whose function is to enforce the decisions of the ruler; and that of the common worker or producer, whose function is to provide for the material needs of society. According to Plato, every individual by nature, and largely by heredity, belongs to one of these three social classes. Justice, on his analysis, is the health of society, and this resides in the harmonious balance of the three social classes each performing its characteristic function well. If citizens are obligated to promote the good of society—that is, its health or well-being—and if this is best served by elitist government, then citizens are obligated to submit to the rule of the most qualified leaders.

Plato's distrust of democracy is understandable. If you were seriously ill, would you want it decided democratically whether you needed an operation? Or would you want a qualified physician to make this decision? If you were having a house built, would you want it decided democratically what materials to use or how to install the plumbing? Or would you want qualified builders to make such decisions? If the democratic process cannot be trusted in such cases, why should it be trusted when making important and complex decisions about economics, or foreign policy, or crime prevention, or nuclear deterrence? As Carl Cohen writes:

> Consistent democratic theory . . . will ascribe the right to vote to *all* humans, without regard for age or mental health. . . . If they specify any set of humans who are not entitled to vote—idiots, felons, the insane, infants—they must explain how democratic theory can justify that deprivation. There are very good reasons to discriminate in the distribution of political power, but the consistent democrat must be systematically blind to them. (Cohen 1982: 49)

Any responsible democrat must exclude at least *some* people from the democratic process—idiots, the insane, children. But why? Isn't it because such individuals are not qualified to make important political decisions? Yet, if idiots, the insane, and children should be excluded from the democratic process because of their lack of qualifications, then shouldn't *anyone* who lacks the necessary qualifications be excluded? In other words, isn't it the case that only the most qualified people should govern society?

True, it would make little sense for people to entrust their healthcare to the democratic process. But do physicians have the authority to make decisions for their patients and have these decisions enforced? Perhaps in the case of idiots, the insane, or children, but not in the case of ordinary adults. Ordinary adults have the right to manage their own affairs, including their own healthcare, even if they sometimes make bad decisions or fail to follow the advice of experts. Don't ordinary adults also have the right to manage their political affairs? Idiots, the insane, and children should be excluded from the democratic process, not because they lack the necessary qualifications to make important political decisions, but because they are incapable of making responsible decisions to begin with. The same cannot be said about ordinary adults. Therefore, it is not unreasonable or arbitrary to exclude the first group but not the second from the democratic process.

The objection raised here concerns the final step in the argument from inequality. Governments are *coercive* institutions, not advisory boards, and the problem of political authority concerns the legitimate use of coercion. To say that a government has the right to rule means, not only that its citizens ought to accept its decisions, but that it has a right to enforce these decisions. Plato's argument may show that people have an obligation to accept the counsel of the wise. But from this it doesn't follow that the wise have the right to enforce their decisions, because not all obligations are enforceable. For this reason, the argument from inequality, as it stands, does not establish the legitimacy of elitist government.

7.2. Hobbes's Defense of Political Authority

Imagine a world without police, court systems, armies, or other mechanisms of social control. Such a world is what social contract theorists refer to as "the state of nature." What would it be like? According to one social contract theorist, the seventeenth-century British philosopher Thomas Hobbes, "without a common power to keep them all in awe," people would be at war, "and such a war, as is of every man, against every man" (Hobbes 1958: 106). In a famous passage of his *Leviathan*, Hobbes writes:

> In such condition, there is no place for industry; because the fruit thereof is uncertain; and consequently no culture of the earth; no navigation, nor use of the commodities that may be instruments of moving, and removing such things as require much force; no knowledge of the face of the earth; no account of time; no arts; no letters; no society; and which is worst of all, continual fear, and danger of violent death; and the life of man, solitary, poor, nasty, brutish, and short. (Hobbes 1958: 107)

There are social goods—Hobbes mentions industry, navigation, science, arts, letters, and security—that require the institution of government. If people are better off with government than they would be without it, then the institution of government is justified because of its social utility. This is the heart of Hobbes's defense of political authority.

Since the appearance of Hobbes's *Leviathan*, the argument from social utility has become a stock argument in support of government. The thinking, briefly, is that it is the function of government to maintain social order and otherwise promote public welfare, and any government that narrowly fulfills this function has a legitimate claim to the allegiance of its citizens. As Stephen Nathanson writes:

> Government is desirable because it enforces the limitations on people's freedom that create security for all. Government is legitimate because it is something people would consent to if they think through the implications of living without government in the state of nature. Since people would consent to a government if they were offered a choice, then the government's claim to its powers is neither arbitrary nor contrary to people's wishes. (Nathanson 2000: 71)

Louis P. Pojman argues along similar lines:

> [I]nsofar as the state promotes justice and the public good, it merits our commitment. Since morality involves promoting the human good, including justice, and the state is instituted to help us carry out those tasks, we have a general obligation to cooperate with its edicts. . . . We have a general obligation to obey the laws of our land because it is vital to our protection and the overall public good, including the efficient carrying out of justice. (Pojman 2002: 41)

In what follows, I will outline Hobbes's classic statement of the argument from social utility and then consider reasons why anarchists question both the necessity and the desirability of government.

The Argument from Social Utility

An essential step in Hobbes's overall argument is establishing that the state of nature would be "anarchy" in the worst sense of the term. Many people would accept this claim without argument, but Hobbes does not take it for granted. His argument rests upon four premises:

(1) Human beings are rational egoists.

Of all "the voluntary acts of every man," Hobbes insists, "the object is some *good to himself*" (Hobbes 1958: 112). According to Hobbes, people are rational egoists, not only in the weak sense that people are capable of weighing the reasons for alternative actions and choosing those actions that best serve their own interests, but in the strong sense that people are motivated *entirely* by self-interest. (We shall return to this important claim later in the chapter.)

(2) All people have the same basic needs.

Hobbes mentions not only physical needs, such as for food, water, and shelter, but also emotional needs, such as for safety and glory. (Hobbes might have mentioned needs that promote social harmony and cohesion, such as the need for companionship. Instead, he emphasizes those needs that create competition and conflict. To achieve complete safety, for example, a person must crush all potential enemies, and to achieve glory, a person must demonstrate his superiority to others.) Hobbes also maintained that, without the threat of punishment, "our natural passions . . . carry us to partiality, pride, revenge, and the like" (Hobbes 1958: 139). For Hobbes, people are selfish and vicious by nature and will act morally only when it is to their own advantage to do so, which requires the credible threat of punishment.

(3) Resources are scarce.

Because people are egocentric, they concentrate narrowly on their own individual needs, yet the resources available to satisfy these needs are less than plentiful. Therefore, people must compete with one another to satisfy their needs.

(4) People are more or less equal in their ability to satisfy their needs.

In the competitive struggle, no one person has a decisive advantage over all the others. There are no winners or losers.

On the basis of these four premises, Hobbes concludes that life in the state of nature would be a perpetual war, "and such a war, as is of every man, against every man." To the skeptic, Hobbes points out that this conclusion is further supported by experience. First, Hobbes notes that even people who live with all the protections provided by government nonetheless arm themselves, bolt their doors, and keep their possessions under lock and key. This strongly suggests that people cannot be trusted. Second, Hobbes points out that nations in the international community exist without a sovereign power to keep them in awe, and the result is that "kings, and persons of sovereign authority, because of their independency, are in continual jealousies, and in the state and posture of gladiators" (Hobbes 1958: 108).

Of course, it would be to each person's advantage to forgo the advantages of "force and fraud" if others could be could be trusted to do the same—an essential step in creating a civil society. But given the bleak picture that Hobbes paints of human nature, when would it be reasonable for people to trust one another? For Hobbes, there is but one possible answer: "[T]here must be some coercive power, to compel men equally to the performance of their covenants, by the terror of some punishment, greater than the benefit they expect by the breach of their covenant . . . and such power there is none before the erection of a commonwealth" (Hobbes 1958: 120). In other words, it would be reasonable for people to keep their agreements only if the penalty for breach of contract nullified the potential rewards; and ensuring that such penalties will be imposed requires the establishment of government. "The only way to erect such a common power," Hobbes writes, "is, to confer all their power and strength upon one man, or upon one assembly of men, that may reduce all their wills, by plurality of voices, unto one will" (Hobbes 1958: 142). Hobbes refers this person or assembly of persons as the "sovereign."

Hobbes's position is that to escape the state of nature, people must agree, not only to erect a government, but to confer upon it absolute power. It is "as if every man should say to every man, *I authorize and give up my right to governing myself to this man, or to this assembly of men, on this condition, that thou give up thy right to him, and authorize all his actions in like manner*" (Hobbes 1958: 142). To keep people in awe, the government must be granted powers to do *whatever is necessary* to enforce the laws. "[I]t belongeth of right, to whatsoever man or assembly that hath the sovereignty . . . to do whatsoever he shall think necessary . . . for the preservation of peace and security" (Hobbes 1958: 147). The only alternative to totalitarian rule, Hobbes insists, is anarchy.

If Hobbes is right, then given the choice, reasonable people will agree to surrender control of their lives to an absolute sovereign. And even if people do not explicitly agree to this, reasonable people *would* make such an agreement if they fully explored the consequences of living without government. The reasoning:

(1) People must choose between an absolute sovereign (knowing that such immense power may be abused) and anarchy (which is a "perpetual war of every man against his neighbor").
(2) Life may be bad under an absolute sovereign, but it would be much worse without it.

Therefore:

(3) Reasonable people will choose an absolute sovereign.

Hobbes lived during an age of absolute monarchs and experienced firsthand the ravages of civil war (when forces led by Oliver Cromwell battled supporters of the British crown.) This historical context explains certain aspects of Hobbes's political philosophy and his sympathy for authoritarian rule. But given the prevalence of liberal democracies in the world today, we know that Hobbes's argument is a false dilemma: the choice is not between an absolute sovereign—that is, totalitarianism—and anarchy, but between *some* form of government and anarchy. With this in mind, we can direct our attention to the second premise of Hobbes's argument. Would life in the state of nature be as bad as Hobbes imagined? Is government necessary to maintain social order? Is it desirable?

7.3. Is Government Necessary?

Throughout most of human history, people lived, and in some remote areas continue to live, in stable, anarchist communities—in small, roaming bands of hunter-gatherers and in larger social units without centralized government. Commenting on one group of modern hunter-gathers—the Bushmen of the central Kalahari Desert in Botswana—anthropologist George Silberbauer writes:

> Until the last decade they were hunters and gatherers, living in bands of 40 to 80 men, women and children. These were autonomous, making their own social, political and economic order. . . . Plainly they did not value the acquisition of power and material wealth as we do. . . . [Rather] there was another value being pursued, namely the establishing and maintaining of harmonious relationships. . . . G/wi [the oblique stroke "/" denotes a click consonant] bands were egalitarian: that is, there were as many valued social positions as there were those who sought them. Statuses were not ranked (with the exception of the culturally limited authority which parents had over their children). . . . Politics, the conduct of the affairs of public policy, were similarly nonexclusive in the distribution of power and advantage. Political process was a series of consensus decisions in which all adults and near-adults could, and usually did participate. Consensus is neither unanimity nor majority will; it is consent to the judgment of those who make it. (Silberbauer 1993: 19-20)

Hobbes, while probably unaware of Kalahari Bushmen, was well aware of Native Americans, though evidently not of how they actually lived. For he says that "the savage people in many places of America . . . have no government at all; and live at this day in that brutish manner" (Hobbes 1958: 108). Hobbes was right in saying that Indian tribes, such as the Iroquois, lived without "government" in the sense in which he understood the term—as authoritarian rule. But if by living in a "brutish manner" Hobbes meant that Native Americans lived in a condition of war, "and such a war, as is of every man, against every man," he was quite mistaken. In fact, Iroquois society, like that of the Kalahari Bushmen, at least approximated the anarchist ideal of consensus democracy. According to one source:

> Although chieftainships often were inherited, personal ability was the basis for the influence that was exercised by a chief. . . . Particularly important to a chief was his ability to persuade. . . . Typically, the councils of the Indians involved the making of speeches, although the intent of this oratory was not to impress others with mere rhetoric but to find a solution to the issue at hand that all could agree to. If unanimity was not achieved, no action could be taken. The dissidents would either continue to express their opposition or withdraw; in either case, the effectiveness of the group would be weakened. Speech making, then, served as a means of ascertaining the diversity of opinion within the group and the manner in which consensus could be reached, for commonly each speaker summarized the opinions previously expressed before offering his own.

The most elaborate and powerful political organization developed in this area was that of the Iroquois Confederacy, but even this league rested on the political principles to be found elsewhere. The five Iroquois tribes were the Mohawk, Oneida, Onondaga, Cayuga, and Seneca. Unanimity was required.[1]

It is an open empirical question as to whether and how social order can be maintained without centralized government in modern, technologically advanced, multicultural societies, but the anthropological evidence shows that centralized government is not necessary to maintain order in *all* societies. The fact that the anarchist community was the dominant model of social organization until the past few thousand years proves, contrary to Hobbes, that there are dimensions of human nature that permit systems of social cooperation to operate without governmental coercion.

The explanation for this may be rooted in our evolutionary history. Hobbes believed that people are always and only motivated by self-interest, which invariably leads to competition and conflict. But unrestricted competition, as Hobbes's analysis of the state of nature shows, is a poor survival strategy. A more successful strategy is cooperation. This has led some sociobiologists to speculate that human beings have evolved an innate moral sense which motivates them to cooperate with one another for their mutual benefit. According to one philosopher of biology, Michael Ruse, "Our moral sense, our altruistic nature, is an adaptation—a feature helping us in the struggle for existence and reproduction—no less than hands and eyes, teeth and feet" (Ruse 1995: 230). The moral sense, Ruse argues, is the product of the same evolutionary forces that have shaped human physiology. Morality is simply an adaptation, like an opposable thumb, which human beings have evolved because of its advantages in the contest for survival and reproduction. "To make us cooperate with one another for our biological ends, evolution has filled us full of thoughts about right and wrong, the need to help our fellows, and so forth" (Ruse 1995: 230).[2] Anarchists have always maintained that people can behave morally and cooperatively for reasons other than the fear of punishment, and this contention is supported by research in sociobiology and moral psychology (cf. Hauser 2006). The threat of punishment, it seems, is one way of maintaining social order, but not the only way.

7.4. Is Government Desirable?

In *Death by Government*, political scientist R. J. Rummel coined the term "democide" to describe "the intentional government killing of an unarmed person or people" (Rummel 2004: 36). According to Rummel:

> [T]here is the common and fundamental justification of government that it exists to protect citizens against the anarchic jungle that would otherwise threaten their lives and property. Such archaic or sterile views show no appreciation of democide's existence and all its related horrors and suffering. They are incon-

sistent with a regime that stands astride society like a gang of thugs over hikers they have captured in the woods, robbing all, raping some, torturing others for fun, murdering those they don't like, and terrorizing the rest into servile obedience. This exact characterization of many past and present governments, such as Idi Amin's Uganda, hardly squares with conventional political science. (Rummel 2004: 26)

Libertarian John Hospers makes a similar observation:

Government is the most dangerous institution known to man. Throughout history it has violated the rights of men more than any individual or group of individuals could do: it has killed people, enslaved them, sent them to forced labor and concentration camps, and regularly robbed and pillaged them of the fruits of their expended labor. Unlike individual criminals, government has the power to arrest and try; unlike individual criminals, it can surround and encompass a person totally, dominating every aspect of one's life, so that one has no recourse from it but to leave the country (and in totalitarian nations even that is prohibited). Government throughout history has a much sorrier record than any individual, even that of a ruthless mass murderer. (Hospers 2002: 432)

The problem for the Hobbesian is obvious. If governments are established to protect citizens from criminals, then who protects citizens from governments? A mass murderer, acting alone, might kill dozens, but a government can slaughter millions. A common thief might steal a portion of someone's wealth, but a government can seize it all. A lone kidnapper might hold several people hostage, but a government can enslave an entire nation. Is it reasonable to grant absolute power to some criminals in order to receive protection from other, less dangerous criminals? According to Hobbes, people create governments for safety and security. Yet, the more powerful governments are, the more dangerous they are, which means that people may actually be less safe under governments than they would be in the state of nature.

R. J. Rummel has estimated that between the years 1900 and 1988 governments murdered about 170 million people, not including armed combatants killed in wars. "In total," he writes,

during the first eighty-eight years of this century, almost 170 million men, women, and children have been shot, beaten, tortured, knifed, burned, starved, frozen, crushed, or worked to death; buried alive, drowned, hung, bombed, or killed in any other of the myriad ways governments have inflicted death on unarmed, helpless citizens and foreigners. The dead could conceivably be nearly 360 million people. (Rummel 2004: 9)

Of the nearly 170 million people murdered by governments in the twentieth century, Joseph Stalin killed 42,672,000, Mao Tse-tung killed 37,828,000, and Adolf Hitler killed 20,946,000. "Putting the human cost of war and democide together," he says, "Power has killed over 203 million people in this century" (Rummel 2004: 13). Referring to the Second World War, he points out that "the

60 million figure for the number of war dead . . . is way above the calculated estimate of 15 million killed in battle and military action" (Rummel 2004: 25). According to Rummel, then, the civilian-soldier death ratio in World War II was 3-1. This is not unusual. "If we . . . accept the calculations that have been made of those killed in all international wars since 30 B.C.," he points out, we arrive at the figure of "40,457,000 dead" (Rummel 2004: 71). This is less than a third of the democide calculations for the same period:

> Of all this pre-twentieth-century killing—massacres, infanticide, executions, genocides, sacrifices, burnings, deaths by mistreatment, and the like—that to which we can put numbers adds up to a grand total of from nearly 89 million to slightly over 260 million men, women, and children. An appropriate mid-democide estimate might be around 133 million killed. (Rummel 2004: 69)

A conservative estimate, therefore, of the total number of people killed by governments since shortly before the dawn of the Common Era is a staggering 376,457,000, most of these deaths having occurred in the twentieth century. Rummel notes:

> Whatever the true statistics, there is no need to know the actual number killed to see that government has been truly a cold-blooded mass murderer, a global plague of man's own making. While diseases may have killed more people in a shorter time (perhaps 25 million died form the Black Plague in Europe form 1348 to 1349), government-committed, encouraged, or permitted murder has been a continuing year-by-year scourge up to and through the twentieth century. (Rummel 2004: 69)

The institution of government is desirable only if people, in the long run, are better off under government than they would have been without it. Yet, the anarchist can argue, with the ever-increasing sophistication of military technology and the proliferation of weapons of mass destruction, governments, far from ensuring people's safety and security, threaten human survival.

Notes

1. From "Eastern Woodland Indians," *Encyclopedia of Britannica*, <www.britannica.com/eb/article?eu=127689>.
2. Interestingly, Ruse's thesis calls into question the objectivity of ethics. As we saw in the second chapter, a solid case can be made for moral realism on the basis of commonly shared ideas about the nature of morality. But, Ruse argues, we have these ideas because we have been engineered by evolution to believe in the objectivity of ethics. If we thought that morality was entirely conventional, we would not be strongly motivated to behave morally, which would make it impossible for us to establish and maintain the systems of social cooperation necessary for our survival. The evolutionary hypothesis, he contends, completely explains why we believe in the objectivity of ethics, and so undermines the case for moral realism.

8. The Ethics of Wealth and Poverty

In Cambodia, where more than half of young children have stunted physical and intellectual development from chronic malnutrition, scavengers comb through garbage for scraps of food or salvageable items. Nicholas Kristof (2004) describes the scene at one dump:

> Nhep Chanda is a 17-year-old girl who is one of hundreds of Cambodians who toil all day, every day, picking through the dump for plastic bags, metal cans and bits of food. The stench clogs the nostrils, and parts of the dump are burning, producing acrid smoke that blinds the eyes.

> The scavengers are chased by swarms of flies and biting insects, their hands are caked with filth, and those who are barefoot cut their feet on glass. Some are small children.

> Nhep Chanda averages 75 cents a day for her efforts. For her, the idea of being exploited in a garment factory—working only six days a week, inside instead of in the broiling sun, for up to $2 a day—is a dream.

Nhep Chanda, and about 1.2 billion other people in the developing world, live in what is described as "absolute" or "extreme" poverty, getting by on $1.25 or less a day. Life at this level is characterized by chronic hunger and malnutrition (more than 800 million people do not get enough to eat); substandard housing (a billion people live in slums); no electricity (1.6 billion people live without electricity); little or no education (more than three-quarters of a billion adults are illiterate); inadequate sanitation (2.4 billion people have no sanitation facilities); no clean water (three-quarters of a billion people have no access to clean drinking water); and inadequate healthcare (about two million children die each year from preventable illnesses).[1]

A disproportionate amount of the world's resources, which might be used to provide food, housing, clean water, basic healthcare, and other necessities to the world's poor are instead used to sustain the living standards of affluent consumers. It has been estimated that if all people consumed as much as the average American, it would require four planet earths to sustain them.[2] Why is this? Why should a small percentage of the world's population live in abundance while fully one-sixth of humanity languishes in poverty? Who has the right to decide how the world's resources are used, what goods and services are produced, and how wealth is distributed? Should all people participate in making these decisions? Or only a few? These are the questions we will examine in this chapter by taking a look at the debate between capitalists and socialists on the ethics of wealth and poverty.

8.1. Capitalism versus Socialism

The cornerstone of capitalism is private ownership of the "means of production"—farmland, mines, factories, manufacturing plants, business offices, and whatever else is used by workers in producing goods and services. By concentrating ownership of the means of production in one group, capitalism creates a "class system" in which one class—the propertied class or "bourgeoisie"—generates its wealth through the labor of another class—the working class or "proletariat." For example, suppose you own farmland. You hire workers who plant and harvest crops. The produce is sold. The costs of production are subtracted, and what remains is your profit. The income you receive as a landowner is not the result of your own labor but the labor of your workers. Or suppose you own stock in an oil company. If the company is profitable, you receive an income from stock dividends. Again, the income you receive is not the result of your own work, but the work of others—the employees of the oil company. True, you may work as hard as anyone else in managing your financial affairs and researching investment opportunities. But the capitalist system does not require this. There are stockbrokers, accountants, bankers, and other professionals whose occupation is to make and manage investments for the propertied class. To accumulate wealth, all that capitalism requires is ownership of wealth-generating property.

Those who defend capitalism defend the capitalist class-system and the institution of private ownership on which the system is based. Those who oppose it—"socialists"—advocate a classless society in which capitalist ownership is abolished and the proletariat control the means of production. Under socialism, workers themselves decide how the world's resources are to be used, what goods and services are to be produced, and how these products are to be distributed. The guiding principle is: "From each according to his ability; to each according to his needs."[3] One socialist, Alan Maass, describes such a society in this way:

A socialist society would not only take away the exiting wealth of the ruling class, but also its economic control over the world. The means of production—the factories and offices and mines and so on—would be owned by all of society. Rather than leaving important economic decisions to the chaos of the free market and the blind competition of capitalists scrambling to make a profit, under socialism, the majority would plan what to do democratically. (Maass 2004: 69)

It is sometimes said that capitalism is an "economic democracy" in which consumers "vote" for products by purchasing them. One defender of the capitalist system, John Hospers, writes:

Every time a housewife goes to the supermarket and buys, let us say, twenty products from the shelves, she is casting a vote for these products. The plebiscite is going on every day in every store in the land. The products that receive the most votes are the ones whose producers reap the most profits with the result that more of these products get produced in order to meet the demand. (Hospers 1971: 104-5)

But as Alan Maass points out:

In order for the free market to produce what's needed for everyone in society, there would have to be a roughly equal distribution of dollars to "vote" with. But in the real world, the rich have far more "votes" than anyone else. So the system is bound to put a priority on making products to meet their needs rather than the needs of society. (Maass 2004: 55)

Because of inequalities in income, some people cast more votes than others, and many people are barred from voting altogether. As a result, the capitalist system reflects the values and priorities of an affluent consumer class. Rather than providing decent living standards for all people, the system churns out an endless stream of trivial commodities—video games, jewelry, movies, sports magazines, plasma-screen televisions, designer clothes, cosmetics. Annually, Americans spend $6.8 billion on music, $8 billion on women's two-piece bathing suits, $10.7 billion on movie tickets, $11 billion on Disney theme parks, $13.1 billion on video games, $17.8 billion on sports tickets, $40 billion on pizza, $48 billion on coffee, $70.15 billion on lottery tickets, and $210 billion on alcohol.[4] Yet, according to the United Nations, it would cost as little as $30 billion a year to eradicate world hunger.[5]

Socialism can be seen as an extension of the democratic principle of "one person, one vote" to economic planning. Under what is commonly called "democratic socialism," guaranteed employment, housing, food, education, medical care, and other social programs are administered by a democratically elected government and funded through redistributive taxation and the nationalization of major industries. Scandinavian countries, such as Sweden and Norway, at least approximate the socialist model and provide for their citizens some of the highest standards of living in the world. Even the United States has implemented some socialist programs, such as public education, Social Security, and unemployment benefits. If people have the democratic right to participate in making decisions of social importance, shouldn't the democratic system encompass economic planning?

8.2. The Case for Capitalism

There are two arguments for capitalism that are often woven together as one. Capitalism, it is argued, has the potential to create abundance for all, but this potential has been only partially realized, resulting in extreme disparities in the distribution of wealth. According to a study by Oxfam in 2015, the richest twenty percent of the total population owns 94 percent of the world's wealth, leaving only six percent of global assets for the remaining 80 percent of the population.[6] This is not necessarily unjust, defenders argue, because such disparities can arise without violating anyone's rights. While the situation of the world's poor is unfortunate, it would be wrong to attempt to solve this problem through the redistribution of wealth. People have a right to the unlimited accumulation of wealth, and the rights of the propertied class outweigh considerations of social utility. So long as the wealthy have amassed their riches without violating the rights of the poor, the poor have no rights against the wealthy. The problem of poverty, it is argued, is due to governmental interference in the operations of the free market. The solution is to eliminate such interference, privatize the operations of government, expand private property, open new markets, create jobs, and otherwise allow capitalism to flourish.

One thread of this argument is utilitarian:

(1) The ideal economic system is one that produces the greatest amount of prosperity for the greatest number of people.
(2) This system is capitalism.

Therefore:

(3) Capitalism is the ideal economic system.

The other thread of this argument is essentially libertarian:

(1) Individuals have the right to own the means of production and the right to own whatever wealth is generated through such ownership.
(2) Capitalism is the only economic system that respects people's property rights.
(3) An economic system that respects people's property rights is morally superior to one that does not.

Therefore:

(4) Capitalism is morally superior to all other economic systems.

Both arguments are valid, but they rest on questionable assumptions. Does capitalism create the greatest amount of prosperity for the greatest number of people? Do individuals have the right to own land and other resources as private property? In the remainder of this chapter, we will explore both arguments, beginning with the utilitarian argument.

8.3. The Utilitarian Argument for Capitalism

"To produce for profit, and trade one's product or service non-coercively on a free market," writes John Hospers, "is the means to greater wealth than any other system ever designed by man—this is a lesson that history teaches beyond any shadow of a doubt" (Hospers 1971: 112). How can this bold statement be supported? Hospers argues:

> In a free economy—one in which wages, costs, and prices are left to the competitive market—profits have a very important function: they help to decide what products shall be made, of what kinds, and in what amounts. . . . The hope of profits also makes for an enormous increase in the efficiency of production, for, other things being equal, the most efficient producer—the one who can cut out waste and motivate his workers to produce the most and best products—will earn the highest profits. (Hospers 1971: 216)

By contrast, governments are inherently wasteful and inefficient:

> The intervention of the government in economic affairs . . . is almost always wasteful and inefficient. Owners of private businesses and corporations who have put their own money into the enterprise will be careful as to how it is spent; but the government bureaucrat who administers public funds (taken from the taxpayer) is not spending what he himself has earned—he is spending money that the taxpayer has earned; and one is seldom if ever so careful of other people's money as of one's own—particularly when no matter how badly it is spent, and how great the losses are, one never faces personal bankruptcy because of it: one simply passes the loss on to the taxpayer, who is forced to absorb it. (Hospers 1971: 128)

The reasoning is simple. Businesses compete with one another for profits. But when the government monopolizes some area of the economy, it is not subject to the same pressures; the government can afford to be wasteful and inefficient, because it has no competitors.

Part of Hospers' argument concerns the motivation of workers. The most efficient producer is "the one who can cut out waste and motivate his workers to produce the most and best products." But why should workers be more highly motivated under capitalism than under democratic socialism? Imagine two companies, A and B. Both companies operate for a profit, but whereas the profits of company A are collected by private investors, the profits of company B are collected as tax revenue to fund social programs. Why should the workers of company A be more highly motivated than the workers of company B? Hospers speaks of the role that producers play in motivating workers, but the "producers" that Hospers has in mind are not outside investors—the bourgeoisie of the capitalist class-system—but workers who run their own businesses. Because of their financial stake in the businesses they own and operate, producers have an incentive to cut costs and motivate their employees. This is true, but what role does a *nonproductive* propertied class play in explaining the efficiency of the capitalist system? This is the crucial question and one which Hospers does not address. For this reason, his argument does not support the capitalist class-system.

Hospers claims that governmental interference in economic affairs is "almost always wasteful and inefficient" because governments lack the incentive to operate efficiently. Is this true? Suppose a country undergoes a socialist revolution and nationalizes its oil industry. All that this entails is that the profits of the industry, previously reaped by private investors, become public funds. (Even with declining gas prices, in 2013 the five leading oil companies generated $93 billion in profits for their investors.[7]) By itself, this redirection of profits would have no affect upon the internal organization of the oil industry. It could continue to employ the same workers, manage the same oil fields, operate the same refineries, maintain the same contracts, meet the same production quotas. Why, then, should the industry operate less efficiently? If it did, this would be the result of poor management, not the absence of competitive pressures. Under democratic socialism, the managers of nationalized industries would be responsible to the public rather than to private investors; and the public would have an incentive to ensure that their industries were properly managed: the profits generated by these industries would be used to fund housing, healthcare, education, and other social programs.

These considerations cast doubt on the utilitarian argument for capitalism. Does utilitarianism support socialism? Many philosophers think so, for the following simple reason. Small additions in income can dramatically improve the lives of poor people but make little or no difference in the lives of affluent people. In distributing wealth, therefore, the needs of the poor should be given priority over the interests of affluent consumers. Distributing wealth "in accordance with people's needs" would do the most good for the most people.

Yet, the debate between capitalists and socialists cannot be settled by theoretical considerations alone. According to Hospers, "Everywhere that the free market has been permitted to flourish, prosperity for the masses of people has followed" (Hospers 1971: 131). Is this borne out by history?

8.4. Wage Slavery

For centuries, Africans destined for slavery in the Americas were transported across the Atlantic Ocean in what became known as the "Middle Passage." Somewhere between nine and sixteen million people survived the journey. Perhaps a million more did not. The importation of slaves into the United States was not officially banned until 1808, but the practice of slavery persisted for decades. A census taken in 1860, just prior to the Civil War, reported that 3,953,696 human beings had the legal status of property. Although slavery is now officially abolished throughout the world, the practice has never been completely eradicated. Indeed, according to an article in *The Washington Post*, more people exist in slavery today than at any other time in human history—fully 30 million, including 60,000 in the United States. These are not "slaves" in a diluted sense of the term; they are people living "as forced laborers, forced prostitutes, child soldiers, child brides in forced marriages and, in all ways that matter, as pieces of property, chattel in the servitude of absolute ownership."[8]

During the colonial period (the seventeenth and eighteenth centuries), the majority of immigrants, fully two-thirds, who settled in North America, mostly from England, Ireland, and Germany, were brought to American shores as indentured servants. To pay for the cost of travel, these immigrants were sold into bondage for a period of between five and seven years. It is estimated that 10,000 people were sold into bondage each year in England alone. Sometimes there was no choice in the matter, and sometimes the period of enslavement was much longer. A bill passed in 1618 permitted children eight-years of age and older to be abducted and sent to America where the boys would be owned by the Virginia Company for as long as sixteen years, and the girls for as long as fourteen years. (In fact, so common was this practice that a new term, "kidnapping," entered the English language to describe such abductions.) On over-packed, undersupplied ships, disease and starvation were commonplace. On one ship, sailing from Belfast to Boston, 46 of the 106 passengers died of starvation, "six of them eaten by the survivors" (Zinn 1999: 43), according to one historian's account. People were treated like disposable cargo. One passenger, on a ship sailing from Germany, reported, "On board our ship, on a day on which we had a great storm, a woman about to give birth and unable to deliver under the circumstances, was pushed through one of the portholes into the sea" (Zinn 1999: 44). Indentured servants, arriving on American shores, were sold like commodities. "Just arrived at Leedstown," reads one announcement in 1771, "the Ship Justitia, with about one Hundred Servants, Men Women & Boys. . . . The Sale will commence on Tuesday the 2nd of April" (Zinn 1999: 44). Predictably, indentured servants were beaten, whipped, and otherwise abused. Female servants were raped. "In some colonies," writes Derrick Jensen, "one third to one-half of even the most healthy indentured servants—those in their late teens—did not live to see their freedom. In others, 80 percent of the indentured servants died their first year" (Jensen 2002: 79).

Few people today would openly defend the institution of slavery. But when workers depend upon the propertied class for their livelihoods, and have no alternative but to accept subsistence wages and deplorable working conditions, how different are their circumstances from those of slaves? During the nineteenth century, only a small minority in the agricultural South comprised the plantation elite—a few thousand families. Two-thirds, or even three-fourths, of white southerners did not own slaves. According to historian Howard Zinn, "Millions of southern whites were poor farmers, living in shacks or abandoned outhouses, cultivating land so bad the plantation owners had abandoned it" (Zinn 1999: 236). What were conditions like for workers in the industrial North? "In New York City," writes Zinn, "girls sewed umbrellas from six in the morning to midnight, earning $3 a week, from which employers deducted the cost of needles and thread. Girls who made cotton shirts received twenty-four cents for a twelve-hour day." "A traffic in immigrant child laborers developed, either by contract with desperate parents in the home country or by kidnapping." "As the twentieth century opened, 284,000 children between the ages of ten and fifteen worked in mines, mills, factories." "In New York, 100,000 people lived in the cellars of the slums; 12,000 women worked in houses of prostitution to keep from starving; the garbage, lying 2 feet deep in the streets, was alive with rats" (Zinn 1999: 234, 240, 266, 346).

In "Slaves of the State," Paul Wright makes the following important observation concerning the demise of slavery:

> While some think that slavery—i.e., unpaid, forced labor—offers enormous profit potential for the slave owner, there are historical reasons slavery is no longer the dominant mode of economic production. First, the slave owner has a capital investment in his slave: regardless of whether the slave is working or producing profit he must be fed, housed, and so on, in minimal conditions to ensure the slave's value as a labor producer remains. With the rise of industrial capitalism in the 18th and 19th century capitalists discovered that capitalism has its boom and bust cycles characterized by over-production. Thus idle slaves would become a drain on the owner's finance because they would still require feeding, housing, etc., regardless of whether they were working. However, if the slave were "free" he could be employed at low wages and then laid off when not producing profit for the employer, the wage slave was free to starve, free to be homeless, and so on, with no consequences for the owner.[9]

Slaves were not paid for their labor by plantation owners. They did, however, receive food, clothing, and shelter. Workers in the mines, mills, and factories of America were paid for their labor, but this money was used to buy food, clothing, and shelter. Slaves were not free to choose their masters. Workers were free to change employers (if alternative employment opportunities existed), but they were still enslaved by a system that afforded them nothing more than a subsistence level of existence. Indeed, the argument has been made that slaves were actually treated *better* than workers (at least when there was a pool of excess labor), because workers, unlike slaves, could be replaced at no cost to capitalists.

According to Derrick Jensen, "In 1850, an average field laborer cost between $1,000 and $1,800, three to six times the annual wage of an American worker, the equivalent of $50,000 to $100,000 today" (Jensen 2001: 88). To purchase a field laborer required a substantial investment. To hire a field laborer required no investment at all. It is predictable, then, that hired laborers would be subjected to more grueling, more dangerous working conditions than those to which slaves were subjected. Jensen quotes John Henry Hammond, a pre-Civil War politician and defender of slavery, who, in a letter to a British abolitionist, comments that in Great Britain "the poor and laboring classes of your own race and color . . . are more miserable and degraded, morally and physically, than our slaves" (Jensen 2001: 144). Hammond referred to reports that "British women and children worked twelve to sixteen hours per day, with men sometimes being worked twenty hours per day. Children often commenced work at five or six years of age, and in some fields, such as lace-making, they began work at two" (Jensen 2001: 145). Hammond's point, of course, is that "no rational slave owner would work his slaves so hard, so young" (Jensen 2001: 145). In America, conditions were equally brutal. Children as young as five worked in cotton mills. "The average life of the children after they go into the mills is four years," commented an article in *The Washington Post*. "It would be less brutal for a state to have children painlessly put to death than it is to permit them to be ground to death by this awful process" (Jensen 2001: 145). Conditions for industrial workers only gradually improved. "In 1900," writes political scientist Michael Parenti,

> the United States and most other capitalist nations were part of the "Third World" well before the term had been invented. Within the industrialized nations could be found widespread poverty, high unemployment rates, low wages, child labor, 12-hour workdays, six- and seven-day work weeks, malnutrition, and the diseases of poverty such as tuberculosis and typhoid. In addition, there were no public services, occupational safety regulations, consumer protections, or environmental safeguards to speak of. Only after decades of struggle, mostly in the 1930s and again in the aftermath of World War II, did we see dramatic advances in the conditions of those who had to work for a living. (Parenti 2002)

For reasons that are now apparent, capitalism has been castigated by its critics as a system of "wage slavery"—an expression coined during the Industrial Revolution to describe the oppressive conditions of factory workers. Although defenders argue that unregulated capitalism creates prosperity for the working class, the historical record counts against this. Socialists point out that improvements in the status of American workers over the past several decades—an eight-hour workday, a forty-hour work week, minimum wage laws, unemployment benefits, the abolition of child labor—have occurred only *because* of governmental intervention in the capitalist system. Actual experiments in unregulated, *lassie-faire* capitalism—which roughly describes the period of the Industrial Revolution—hardly support such robust claims as that of John Hospers: "Everywhere that the free market has been permitted to flourish, prosperity for the masses of people has followed."

8.5. The Libertarian Argument for Capitalism

Libertarianism is a political philosophy concerned with the limits of the state's power over the individual. Its roots can be traced back as far as the seventeenth-century British philosopher John Locke, who maintained that governments are instituted for the purpose of protecting people's natural rights to life, liberty, and property. One contemporary philosopher, Jan Narveson, defines libertarianism as

> the doctrine that the only relevant consideration in political matters is individual liberty: that there is a delimitable sphere of action for each person, the person's "rightful liberty," such that one may be forced to do or refrain from what one wants to do only if what one would do or not do would violate, or at least infringe, the rightful liberty of some other person(s). No other reasons for compelling people are allowable: other actions touching on the life of that individual require his or her consent. (Narveson 2001: 7)

For libertarians, the only legitimate function of government is to protect people's rights; the exercise of political power for any other reason—to regulate workplace conditions or the terms of employment, to insure product safety for consumers, to provide public education, housing, or healthcare benefits for the poor—is a violation of people's rights and strictly forbidden (cf. Murray 1997: 37-40). Indeed, some libertarians, such as Murray Rothbard, maintain that the state is by nature a criminal institution and ought to be abolished. "In a truly free society," he writes,

> [the state] would necessarily cease to exist. Its myriad of invasive and aggressive activities, its vast depredations on the rights of person and property, would then disappear. At the same time, those genuine services which it does manage badly to perform would be thrown open to free competition, and to voluntarily chosen payments by individual consumers. (Rothbard 2002: 173)

> All of the services commonly thought to require the State—from the coining of money to police protection to the development of law in defense of the rights of person and property—can be and have been supplied far more efficiently, and certainly more morally, by private persons. The State is in no sense required by the nature of man; quite the contrary. (Rothbard 2002: 188)

All libertarians believe that government should play an extremely limited role in the organization of society, or no role at all. The fundamental difference between anarchist thinkers on the libertarian left and conservative thinkers on the libertarian right concerns economics rather than politics. Anarchists are "social libertarians" who believe that capitalism should be abolished and replaced by an economic system democratically organized by workers. Conservatives—at least those on the fringe of the libertarian right, such as Rothbard—are "anarcho-capitalists" who believe that all functions of government should be privatized and operated by businesses for profit.

Libertarianism—that is, the conservative brand of libertarianism in the Lockean tradition—is a political philosophy based upon "natural" rights. ("Natural" rights, unlike legal rights, do not depend upon the institution of government. They are rights possessed by individuals in the state of nature.) The libertarian conception of rights can be captured by four claims.

Only rights are enforceable. In the third chapter, we saw that rights license the legitimate use of force. In part, this means that all rights are enforceable. The libertarian takes this a step further in maintaining that *only* rights are enforceable. For this reason, the only legitimate use of governmental power is to protect people's rights.

Rights are negative. "Libertarianism has generally been identified with the thesis that our fundamental moral rights are exclusively negative," writes Jan Narveson. "The fundamental general right, according to it, is the right to do whatever we wish, unhindered, as nearly as possible, by others—subject, of course, to the restrictions inherent in the similar right of others" (2001: 59). For libertarians, rights represent moral boundaries on our behavior toward others; respecting these boundaries does not require that we assist others, but only that we refrain from interfering in their lives. John Hospers puts it well:

> Each individual's right is his "no trespassing" sign in relation to me and others. I may not encroach upon his domain any more than he upon mine, without my consent. Every right entails a duty, true—but the duty is only that of *forbearance*—that is, of *refraining* from violating the other person's right. If you have a right to life, I have no right to take your life; if you have a right to the products of your labor (property), I have no right to take it from you without your consent. (Hospers 2002: 429)

Ayn Rand explains how the rights to life, property, and free speech are interpreted as negative rights by the libertarian:

> The right to life means that a man has the right to support his life by his own work (on any economic level, as high as his ability well carry him; it does *not* mean that others must provide him with the necessities of life.
>
> The right to property means that a man has the right to take the economic actions necessary to earn property, to use it and to dispose of it; it does *not* mean that others must provide him with property.
>
> The right of free speech means that a man has the right to express his ideas without danger of suppression, interference or punitive action by the government. It does *not* mean that others must provide him with a lecture hall, a radio station or a printing press through which to express his ideas. (Rand 1964: 97)

Rights are absolute. To say that rights are "absolute" means that rights outweigh all other moral considerations and, consequently, that it is *always* wrong to violate people's rights. According to Narveson, "The libertarian would like to say that her proffered fundamental right to liberty outweighs all else: no incursion of liberty can be justified by anything—except where the alternative is a still greater incursion on liberty" (Narveson 2001: 53). Libertarians would "like" to say this, and some do, such as Rothbard (cf. Rothbard 2002: 77, 151). Other libertarians are a bit more circumspect. In his now classic defense of libertarianism, *Anarchy, State, and Utopia*, Robert Nozick remarks: "The question of whether [rights] are absolute or whether they may be violated in order to avoid catastrophic moral horror . . . is one I hope largely to avoid" (1974: 30). The fact that Nozick would mention "catastrophic moral horror" as only a *possible* reason for violating someone's rights is striking.

Property rights are fundamental. According to Jan Narveson, "the libertarian thesis is really the thesis that *a right to our persons as our property is the sole fundamental right there is.*" He explains:

> If we think that the right to liberty is the most fundamental right there is, then what, after all, do we thereby think? Surely that we may *do* as we want. But doing as we want is doing as we want *with* (various parts of) ourselves; and it is not doing as we want with anything else unless we have in some way acquired the right so to do.

For this reason, he suggests, libertarianism can be summed up by the bold thesis that "Liberty is Property" (Narveson 2001: 66-67). John Hospers writes:

> The political philosophy that is called libertarianism (from the Latin *Libertas*, liberty) is the doctrine that every person is the owner of his own life, and that no one is the owner of anyone else's life, and that consequently every human being has the right to act in accordance with his own choices unless those actions infringe on the equal liberty of other human beings to act in accordance with their choices. (Hospers 2002: 427)

And Murray Rothbard:

> The key to the theory of liberty is the establishment of the rights of private property, for each individual's justified sphere of free action can only be set forth if his rights of property are analyzed and established. "Crime" can then be defined and properly analyzed as a violent invasion or aggression against the just property of another individual (including his property in his own person). (Rothbard 2002: xlviii)

With this in mind, we can understand why libertarians regard property rights as absolute. "Few socialists," writes Jan Narveson, "accept that if you are blind and I have two good eyes, then in the interests of equality I am morally bound to part with one of them and turn it over to you, should it be medically possible to do that; or that what should be done with my left arm is properly a matter for majority decision" (Narveson 2001: 67). If my external property is, in a sense, an extension of my body, then it is difficult to imagine what would constitute a legitimate infringement on my property rights. To confiscate some of my wealth for the purpose of helping the poor would be comparable to taking one of my eyes for the purpose of restoring sight to the blind.

Libertarians insist that, while we can rightfully be forced not to harm others, we cannot rightfully be forced to help or assist them. This follows from the claim that property rights are both negative and absolute. John Hospers asks, "Should government have a role in assisting the needy, in providing social security, in legislating minimum wages, in fixing prices and putting a ceiling on rents, in curbing monopolies, in erecting tariffs, in guaranteeing jobs, in managing the money supply?" To these and similar questions, Hospers' answer is "an unequivocal no" (Hospers 2002: 437). Jan Narveson writes: "If someone is starving, we may pity him or we may be indifferent, but the question so far as our *obligations* are concerned is only this: how did he *get* that way? If it was not the result of my previous activities, then I have no obligation to him, and may help him out or not, as I choose" (Narveson 2003: 167). No one, according to Narveson, has a right to our assistance, but only a right not to be harmed; and we are never obligated to assist anyone unless we are morally responsible for that person's misfortune. We might choose to feed the starving, Narveson argues, but "enforced feeding of the starving [crosses] the line, invading the farmer or the merchant, forcing him to part with some of his hard-earned produce and give it without compensation to others. That, says the advocate of liberty, is theft, not charity." (Narveson 2003: 167)

In fairness, it should be pointed out that libertarians are not saying that there is nothing wrong with failing to assist others, but merely that it is wrong to *force* people to assist others. It may be true (as Peter Singer has persuasively argued) that affluent people have an obligation to assist the poor by making substantial donations to humanitarian organizations, such as UNICEF. But does anyone or any government, however well-intentioned, have the right to *take* money from affluent people and donate it to UNICEF? For some, the violation of people's property rights might be outweighed by a reduction in poverty, but for libertarians, property rights can never be overridden by utilitarian considerations.

On this score, libertarianism has important implications concerning the legitimacy of taxation. There is a difference between what might be called "service" taxation (payment for services that governments provide all citizens, such as police protection) and what is called "redistributive" taxation (payment for public education, public housing, healthcare programs, and other forms of assistance for the poor and working class). While the first form of taxation is essentially no different than payment for any service, such as electric or cable-television service, redistributive taxation is simply theft, so far as the libertarian is concerned.[10] You can, if you choose, donate money to your electric company to subsidize electricity for the poor, but suppose your electric company simply added a certain amount to your monthly bill and threatened to cut off your service unless you paid the extra cost. Would this be right? Or suppose you stole thousands of dollars from a corporation to pay for your college education, or your rent, or your medical expenses. If you would not be justified in doing this, how could the government be justified in taxing corporations for the purpose of providing people with public schools, or college grants, or housing, or healthcare? According to libertarians, while service taxation may be justified, redistributive taxation is a violation of people's property rights and is inherently criminal.

We are now in position to understand the libertarian's argument for the moral superiority of capitalism. If rights are absolute, as libertarians maintain, then respect for people's rights takes precedence over *all* other moral considerations. If, in addition, capitalism is the only economic system that respects people's rights, then capitalism is morally superior to all other economic systems. And this is true even if socialism produces more prosperity for more people. In an interesting twist, libertarians argue that it is socialism, rather than capitalism, that is inherently exploitative, because the positive rights claimed by socialists— for employment, for food, for housing, for medical care, for education—cannot be respected except through systematic theft. As Ayn Rand argues:

> Jobs, food . . . , homes, medical care, education, etc., do not grow in nature. These are man-made values—goods and services produced by men. *Who* is to provide them?
>
> If some men are entitled *by right* to the products of the work of others, it means that those others are deprived of rights and condemned to slave labor.
>
> Any alleged "right" of one man, which necessitates the violation of the rights of another, is not and cannot be a right.
>
> No man can have a right to impose an unchosen obligation, an unrewarded duty or an involuntary servitude on another man. There can be no such thing as *"the right to enslave."* (Rand 1964: 96)

Does capitalism (by reducing workers to wage slaves) exploit the working class, as socialists maintain? Or does socialism (through redistributive taxation) exploit the propertied class, as libertarians argue? We cannot answer these questions without examining the concept of property rights.

8.6. The Libertarian Theory of Property Rights

As we have seen, libertarians maintain that property rights are fundamental; the right to life, the right to free speech, and other familiar rights are reducible to the fundamental right to property. Your right to life, for example, is your right to self-ownership. For the libertarian, your body and mind are your property in the same sense in which your books and clothes are your property. Your right to free speech is simply a special case of your right to self-ownership, which permits you to use your faculty of speech to express your opinions. Of course, people ordinarily claim to own much more than their bodies and minds, and the validity of such claims is essential to the libertarian defense of the capitalist system. What is the moral basis for such claims?

Libertarians build upon the theory of property rights adumbrated by John Locke. In the *Second Treatise of Government* (Chapter V, Paragraph 27), Locke writes:

> Though the earth, and all inferior creatures be common to all men, yet every man has a property in his own person. This nobody has any right to but himself. The labor of his body and the work of his hands, we may say, are properly his. Whatsoever then he removes out of the state that nature has provided, and left it in, he has mixed his labor with, and joined to it something that is his own, and thereby makes it his property. It being by him removed from the common state nature placed it in, has by this labor something annexed to it that excludes the common right of other men. For his labor being the unquestionable property of the laborer, no man but he can have a right to what that is once joined to, at least where there is enough, and as good left in common for others.

Locke's claim is that a man has the right to the products of his own labor (subject to the important restriction that "there is enough, and as good left in common for others"). His argument for this, however, is rather perplexing. Because "every man has a property in his own person," whatsoever he takes from the state of nature and "mixes with his labor," he joins to it something that is his own, and it becomes his rightful property. But why should it be that something becomes my rightful property simply because I have joined with it something that is my own? If I am the first to arrive on an island (or on an entire continent), can I make the land my rightful property simply by joining to it something that is my own, such as a flag? If I cut timber and construct a log cabin, it seems plausible to say that the cabin is my rightful property because of the amount of labor I invested in it. But suppose I simply dust off something I find on the ground. Does this minimal investment of labor transform the object into my property?

Locke's account captures the intuition that workers have a right to the products of their labor. But, as it stands, it does not explain how people can rightfully possess the products of other people's labor; nor does it explain how people can acquire the right to land and other resources used in production. As to the first issue, libertarians contend that people can acquire property through voluntary transactions and gifts. In such cases, the original property owner transfers ownership rights to someone else. If I sell you a book for $10.00, then we exchange ownership rights: you acquire the ownership right to my book, and it becomes your book; I acquire the ownership right to your $10.00, and it becomes my money. In the case of a gift, there is a transfer of property rights, but no exchange. For libertarians, such transfers are the only other way—that is, other than by original acquisition—that property is acquired.

There remains the important question of how people can rightfully possess land and other resources. One explanation is offered by John Hospers:

Tilling the soil and growing crops may give someone title to the crops, but does that entitle him or her to the land on which they grow? True, without the land the crops can't be grown; but how does clearing the land and growing the crops entitle someone to *own* land? The most obvious answer is a negative one: How does it entitle anyone else to the land? The *farmer* has done the work; if others (or a government) come in and claim the land, they are expropriating the fruits of another's labor. What have the expropriators done to earn it? If the one who worked the land doesn't deserve it, who does? (Hospers 1982: 256)

Perhaps the answer is "no one." The problem with Hospers' explanation is that he takes for granted what remains to be shown: that land and other resources can rightfully be owned as private property. Assuming that this is true, Hospers' explanation is plausible enough. But why should we assume that it *is* true? This question is especially important since the main criticism leveled by socialists against the capitalist system is that the bourgeoisie do *not* have the right to private ownership of land and other means of production.

Rothbard offers a more plausible explanation of land acquisition:

[T]he justification for the ownership of ground land is the same for that of any other property. For no man actually ever "creates" matter: what he does is to take nature-given matter and transform it by means of his ideas and labor energy. But this is precisely what the pioneer—the homesteader—does when he clears and uses previously unused virgin land and brings it into his private ownership. The homesteader—just as the sculptor, or miner—has transformed the nature-given soil by his labor and his personality. The homesteader is just as much a "producer" as the others, and therefore just as legitimately the owner of his property. (Rothbard 2002: 49)

Whatever its merits, Rothbard's explanation is simply an extension of Locke's account of original acquisition and subject to the same shortcomings. If I walk over the ground, I have "mixed my labor" (the labor of walking) with the soil. But why should this activity transform the ground underneath my feet into my rightful property? Surely someone else might have a more meaningful claim to the land. Suppose a land baron is the first to arrive and take possession of a piece of land which he then uses to grow daffodils. Suppose further that he "owns" (in Rothbard's sense) all other farmable land within a radius of a thousand miles. Sometime later landless peasants arrive who need the land to grow food. Does the land baron have the right to squander the land on daffodils while the peasants starve? Don't the peasants have a more compelling claim to the land? Locke himself qualified the right to original acquisition with the requirement that homesteaders leave "enough and as good" in common for others.[11] This qualification would seem to apply here, since the peasants are certainly made worse off by the land baron's acquisition. Other libertarians, however, recognize no such restriction.

Suppose you are adrift at sea in a lifeboat. There are several other people in the water who will drown unless they climb aboard. Rothbard imagines a case like this and argues that "the *right* to allocate spaces in the lifeboat belongs to the owner of the boat." If the lifeboat is yours, then you have the right to refuse anyone access to the boat; and this is true even if the boat could accommodate everyone. According to Rothbard, "any forcible interference with such owner's allocation . . . is at the very least an act of invasion of property right for which the aggressor may be repelled on the spot, and for which the aggressor would later be liable for prosecution" (Rothbard 2002: 151). If property rights are absolute, as libertarians maintain, then it would be wrong for anyone to board the boat without your consent. Your property right, in this situation, gives you the power of life and death over anyone stranded in the water.

Although this is an imaginary situation, how different is it from the actual situation in which the propertied class controls the resources upon which all people depend for their survival? One consequence of libertarianism is that the propertied class literally has the right to decide who lives and who dies—a right which it exercises by determining how the world's resources are utilized, and for whose benefit. For Rothbard, no country has the right to nationalize its base industries or even to tax companies to fund social programs for its citizens. The natural resources of a country belong, not to the citizens of that country, but to those companies that are the first to extract and make productive use of those resources (cf. Rothbard 2002: 72).

If Rothbard is right, then an oligarchy of land barons and corporations could rightfully own an entire country. Indeed, a logical implication of libertarianism is that an oligarchy (or even one person) could rightfully own and rule the entire world![12] For the libertarian, if someone acquires territory through homesteading (or the transfer of property rights), then that person has the right to restrict how that territory is used and to impose rules upon anyone who might subsequently occupy the land. If I am a guest in your home, while you do not have the right to attack me, you do have the right to greatly restrict my freedom. I would not be free to eat your food, or to spread a mat on your floor and worship Allah, or to organize a political demonstration in your living room, or to practice a lifestyle that offended you, or to engage in any other behavior that you disapproved of. As a guest in your home, I am subject to your rules. In the same way, land barons have the right to control the lives of their tenants. The tenants have no right to make use of the land to grow food, or to practice their religion, or to organize for some political purpose, or to engage in any other behavior that the land barons do not permit. Libertarianism, paradoxically, far from a philosophy of individual liberty, provides theoretical support for the despotism of absolute monarchs.

8.7. The Socialist Theory of Property Rights

This would seem to be a *reductio ad absurdum* ("reduction to absurdity") against the libertarian theory of property rights. Wherein does the problem lie? Socialists will point to the institution of capitalist ownership. If resources cannot be owned as private property, then the propertied class has no legitimate claim to its position of power over the working class. "[T]rue liberty is based on economic opportunity," wrote anarchist revolutionary Alexander Berkman. "Without it all liberty is a sham and a lie, a mask for exploitation and oppression. In the profoundest sense liberty is the daughter of economic opportunity" (Berkman 1972: 265). The socialist alternative to private ownership for personal profit is collective ownership for the public good.

We saw earlier that the key premise of the libertarian argument for private property is that workers have a right to the products of their labor. This is a reasonable assumption, but it may not lead to the conclusion that libertarians reach. Alexander Berkman explains:

> Everybody agrees that a person has a right to own the thing that he himself has made.
>
> But *no one* person has made or can make anything all by himself. It takes many men, of different trades and professions, to create something. The carpenter, for instance, cannot make a simple chair or bench all by himself; not even if he should cut down a tree and prepare the lumber himself. He needs a saw and a hammer, nails and tools, which he cannot make himself. And even if he should make these himself, he would first have to have the raw materials—steel and iron—which other men would have to supply.
>
> Or take another example—let us say a civil engineer. He could do nothing without paper and pencil and measuring tools, and these things other people have to make for him. Not to mention that first he has to learn his profession and spend many years in study, while others enable him to live in the meantime. This applies to every human being in the world to-day.
>
> You can see then that no person can by his own efforts alone make the things he needs to exist. . . . That is to say: *all labor and the products of labor are social*, made by society as a whole.
>
> But if all the wealth we have is social, then it stands to reason that it should belong to society, to the people as a whole. (Berkman 1972: 6-7)

Berkman's argument:

(1) People rightfully own the products of their labor.
(2) Every product is the creation, not of a single individual, but of society as a whole.

Therefore:

(3) Every product is rightfully owned, not by any single individual, but by society as a whole.

To illustrate Berkman's argument, we might randomly select a common product, such as a cotton shirt, and trace the history of its production. The production of a cotton shirt involves almost unimaginably many steps. To name a few: extracting raw materials used to manufacture industrial equipment; manufacturing farming equipment; manufacturing the equipment and chemicals used to spin, weave, and dye cotton; manufacturing sewing equipment; clearing farmland; planting, harvesting, and processing cotton; sewing the garment; transporting the garment to a clothing store. Also, the workers involved in each of these steps of production must be fed, clothed, housed, and trained; and so must the workers involved in the production of these goods and services. It's not much of an exaggeration to say that the production of a cotton shirt is directly or indirectly linked to all other productive activities.

There are objections that can be raised against Berkman's argument, but it captures an important truth: that an economic system is a complex system of social cooperation in which all members of society depend upon one another for the satisfaction of their needs. If this characterization is essentially correct, then no single member of society can claim full ownership of any product, since no product is the creation of one individual acting alone. Peter Singer, who has written for decades on the problem of poverty, makes essentially the same point in the following passage:

> The Nobel Prize-winning economist and social scientist Herbert Simon estimated that "social capital" is responsible for at least 90 percent of what people earn in wealthy societies like those of the United States or northwestern Europe. By social capital Simon meant not only natural resources but, more important, the technology and organizational skills in the community, and the presence of good government. These are the foundation on which the rich can begin their work. "On moral grounds," Simon added, "we could argue for a flat income tax of 90 percent." Simon was not, of course, advocating so steep a rate of tax, for he was well aware of disincentive effects. But his estimate does undermine the argument that the rich are entitled to keep their wealth because it is all a result of their hard work. If Simon is right, that is true of at most 10 percent of it. (Singer 2006)

Although libertarians claim that resources can be privately owned, it is far from clear how this claim can be established; moreover, it leads to the paradoxical conclusion that the propertied class can reduce the remainder of humanity to servitude or starvation. If this conclusion is unacceptable, then so is the theory of property rights on which it is based. Of course, questions also arise concerning the socialist theory of public ownership. If resources cannot be privately owned, how can they be publicly owned? This is a legitimate question, but it may rest on a misunderstanding of the meaning of "public" ownership. To say that the world's resources are rightfully public property means that no elite group has the exclusive right to make decisions concerning how these resources are used; this right belongs to the people affected by those decisions. In the absence of a compelling justification for the dominant position of the propertied class, the socialist would seem to be standing on solid ground in insisting that the public has such a right.

Notes

1. See "11 Facts about Global Poverty," < https://www.dosomething.org/us/facts/11-facts-about-global-poverty>.

2. "How many Earths do we need?" *BBC News*, < http://www.bbc.com/news/magazine-33133712>.

3. This principle was originally set forth by the French socialist Louis Blanc and later adopted as a motto by Karl Marx and other socialists.

4. According to statistics from 2014 and 2015 reported in <www./money.cnn.com/2015/02/11/news/companies/lottery-spending/> and <www.researchamerica.org/advocacy-action/research/research-takes-cents>.

5. See <www.borgenproject.org/the-cost-to-end-world-hunger/>.

6. "Richest one percent will own more than all the rest by 2016," <www.oxfam.org/en/pressroom/pressreleases/2015-01-19/richest-1-will-own-more-all-rest-2016>.

7. Center for American Progress, "With Only $93 Billion in Profits, the Big Five Oil Companies demand to Keep Tax Breaks," <www.americanprogress.org/issues/green/news/2014/02/10/83879/with-only-93-billion-in-profits-the-big-five-oil-companies-demand-to-keep-tax-breaks/>.

8. "This map shows where the world's 30 million slaves live. There are 60,000 in the U.S.," <www.washingtonpost.com/news/worldviews/wp/2013/10/17/this-map-shows-where-the-worlds-30-million-slaves-live-there-are-60000-in-the-u-s/>.

9. Article available online at <www.thirdworldtraveler.com/Prison_System/Slaves_State.html>.

10. This statement should be qualified. Libertarians will point out that there *is* an essential difference between being billed for electric service and being taxed for police protection. The difference is that taxation is compulsory. You can choose to live without electricity and never pay another electric bill, but you cannot choose to live without police protection and never pay taxes. This provides an argument against government which resonates with anarcho-capitalists, such as Rothbard. Other libertarians accept some forms of taxation as legitimate.

11. An additional requirement was that nothing be allowed to spoil. In the state of nature, anyone is permitted to take as much as he can make use of before it spoils. But "whatever is beyond this is more than his share, and belongs to others" (*Second Treatise of Government*, Chapter V, Paragraph 31). Nonetheless, Locke believed that both restrictions were overcome with the introduction of money. Money does not spoil, and if the land acquired by the homesteader is used to produce goods that are offered for sale, then others are not made worse off by the homesteader's original acquisition. (Presumably, the starving peasants in our imaginary example have no grounds for complaint if the land baron offers them daffodils for sale.)

12. To see how this might happen, suppose homesteaders divide the earth into small plots which they use for various productive purposes. Some of these homesteaders sell their plots to others, setting in motion the process whereby landownership becomes increasingly concentrated. Eventually, the entire landmass of the earth is owned by a few individuals, or even by one individual. These land barons would be in a position of absolute power over the remainder of humanity.

9. The Ethics of Punishment

For the crime of treason, the punishment in seventeenth-century England was to be hanged, drawn, and quartered. Such was the fate of Major General Thomas Harrison and his fellow regicides. "That you be led to the place from whence you came," the sentence read,

> and from thence be drawn upon a hurdle to the place of execution, and then you shall be hanged by the neck and, being alive, shall be cut down, and your privy members [genitals] to be cut off, and your entrails be taken out of your body and, you living, the same to be burnt before your eyes, and your head to be cut off, your body to be divided into four quarters, and head and quarters to be disposed of at the pleasure of the King's majesty. And the Lord have mercy on your soul. (Abbott 1994: 225-26)

Although this is an extreme example, corporal punishment has been the norm throughout most of human history. For capital crimes, offenders have been boiled alive, impaled on stakes, even sawn in half. For minor offenses, they have been whipped, mutilated, or branded. Even today corporal punishment is still practiced in some countries. In Malaysia, illegal immigrants are whipped. In Singapore, drug offenders are caned. In Saudi Arabia, thieves are mutilated (by having their right hands severed). In Iran, homosexuals are hanged (in Afghanistan, under the Taliban, they were buried alive). In Pakistan, people can be put to death for blasphemy; in Southeast Asia, for drug trafficking; and in China, for bribery.

Although the United States has abandoned other forms of corporal punishment, it is the only Western nation that still practices capital punishment. In fact, it consistently ranks fifth with respect to the number of executions occurring annually. In 2015, the United States, with 28 executions, followed Saudi Arabia with 158 reported executions, Pakistan with 326, Iran with 977, and number-one ranking China with well over a thousand.[1] For serious crimes, imprisonment—which, as Michel Foucault observes, tortures the soul rather than the body—is now the standard punishment. Shockingly, the United States, with only five percent of the world's population, houses the greatest number of prison inmates: 2,217,000 in 2012. China, with four times the population, ranks second with 1,649,804 prisoners.[2] Even more shockingly, the United States remains the only country that sentences children—or people who were under eighteen when their crimes were committed—to life imprisonment with no possibility of parole.[3]

A defining characteristic of punishment is that it involves *intentionally* harming people, sometimes quite seriously, in response to their criminal conduct. To harm people is to make them worse off—in body or mind—than they were before, at least in the short run. It typically involves making them suffer. For many people, punishment is the appropriate response to crime. But critics of the penal system argue that some combination of the following practices can replace punishment:

(1) *Incapacitation.* Offenders are "incapacitated" when they are prevented from repeating their criminal offences. This is one justification for imprisonment, but there are other methods of incapacitation depending upon the nature of the offense. Drunk drivers can be incapacitated by having their automobiles impounded. Sex offenders can be incapacitated through the use of anti-androgen drugs. Electronic surveillance, such as ankle monitoring, is an alternative to incarceration for a wide range of offenses. Regardless of the method employed, incapacitation is not a form of punishment because, even if offenders suffer from the restrictions imposed upon them, the aim in imposing these restrictions is not to make them suffer but rather to protect the public. The harm done, if any, is an unintended side effect. (For comparison, patients with infectious diseases are sometimes quarantined. But to quarantine patients is not to punish them, because the aim is not to make them suffer but to protect the public. Institutionalizing the criminally insane does not count as punishment for the same reason.)

(2) *Restitution.* Unlike fines, enforced restitution—forcing offenders to make amends for their crimes by compensating their victims—is not intended to make offenders suffer but rather to repair or "make whole" the victims of crime. Offenders may suffer from the financial burdens imposed upon them, but this is not the point. For this reason, restitution, like incapacitation, is not a form of punishment.

(3) *Rehabilitation.* Rehabilitation differs from punishment because the aim of rehabilitation is not to harm offenders but rather to correct their criminal tendencies and reduce recidivism. Far from harming them, rehabilitation, if successful, benefits offenders by improving their character.[4]

It is ordinarily considered wrong to harm people, especially to do so intentionally. How, then, is it permissible to punish them? In what follows, we will critically examine three possible answers to this question corresponding to three different models of punishment: the deterrence model; the retribution model; and the so-called "mixed" model of punishment.

9.1. The Deterrence Model of Punishment

States maintain social order by deterring crime, and states deter crime by punishing criminals. According to the deterrence model of punishment, this justification is sufficient. The evils associated with criminal deterrence are outweighed by its social benefits.

As a rationale for punishment, deterrence has been challenged on both practical and moral grounds. Abolitionists point out that the threat of punishment deters crime only insofar as it renders it irrational to commit crime. It has no effect on the behavior of irrational people, who are arguably the most "dangerous" members of society, or on the commission of "crimes of passion," which statistically include the bulk of murders and a large portion of other violent crimes. Moreover, given the extremely low rate at which offenders are apprehended, tried, convicted and eventually punished for their crimes—around three percent, for most offenses—it is debatable whether even rational people are deterred by the threat of punishment. But even if the threat of punishment does exert some downward pressure on crime rates, it is offenders who pay the price for this social benefit, and this raises a serious moral problem. Common morality prohibits harming some people for the purpose of preventing harm to others, but this is precisely how offenders are treated when they are punished for the purpose of deterring crime.

To appreciate the problem, imagine that you are a judge presiding over a criminal trial. The case has received a great deal of biased media attention and the public is convinced that the defendant—call him Bruno—is guilty. Yet, having carefully reviewed all the evidence, you know that Bruno is innocent. Should you nevertheless send him to prison? To deter crime in the general population it is essential to create the public perception that the guilty are punished, but this does not preclude punishing the innocent so long as it supports this perception. Still, it seems terribly wrong to punish an innocent person just to create the public perception that criminals are punished for their crimes. If so, then deterrence by itself does not justify punishment; something more, or different, is needed.

A similar problem arises in connection with the severity of punishment. For a punishment to be just, it must be proportionate to the crime, neither too lenient nor too harsh. But there is no connection between the severity of a crime and the severity of the punishment necessary to deter it. It is not the case, for example, that because murder is a more serious crime than shoplifting, a more serious punishment is necessary to deter it; in fact, the reverse is probably true (since there is often little to gain by murdering someone). If deterrence alone justifies punishment, we might well be justified in fining murderers while boiling shoplifters in oil.

9.2. The Retribution Model of Punishment

The traditional alternative to the deterrence model of punishment is the retribution model. For the retributivist, criminals should be punished, not to deter crime or to achieve other social benefits, but simply because criminals *deserve* to be punished. According to Immanuel Kant—perhaps the most influential advocate of the retribution model—what morality fundamentally requires is that we treat every person as an end and never merely as a means. To punish a criminal as part of a social policy designed to deter crime is to treat that person merely as a means to an end, and this is inherently wrong. Punishment, Kant says, "must be imposed only because the individual on whom it is inflicted *has committed a crime*. For one man ought never to be dealt with merely as a means subservient to the purpose of another" (Kant 2000: 368). If, for example, the justification for capital punishment is that it effectively deters murder, then murderers are put to death for the purpose of discouraging other people from committing murder. To do this is to treat murderers as mere things, as instruments for achieving social goals, rather than as persons. On the other hand, to punish murderers simply because they deserve it is to treat them as persons who are morally responsible for their actions.

Kant's reasoning is simple and appealing. Because criminals are persons and not mere things, they are morally responsible for their actions. If we are to treat criminals *as* persons, then, we must hold them responsible for their actions, and this requires that we punish them for their crimes. Therefore, regardless of the social benefits of punishment, morality requires that criminals be punished as an end in itself. Kant illustrates his position with the following famous example:

> Even if society resolved to dissolve itself with the consent of all its members—as might be supposed in the case of a people inhabiting an island resolving to separate and scatter themselves throughout the whole world—the last murderer lying in the prison ought to be executed before the resolution was carried out. This ought to be done in order that every one may realize the desert of his deeds, and that bloodguiltiness may not remain upon the people; for otherwise they might all be regarded as participators in the murder as a public violation of justice. (Kant 2000: 369-70)

Strictly speaking, it is not retributivism that supports Kant's position on capital punishment, but retributivism combined with the principle of proportionality (also known as *lex talionis*, or "law of the talons," commonly referred to as "eye for an eye" retributivism). Kant writes:

> [T]he undeserved evil which anyone commits on another is to be regarded as perpetrated on himself. Hence it may be said: "If you sander another, you slander yourself; if you steal from another, you steal from yourself; if you strike another, you strike yourself; if you kill another, you kill yourself." This is the right of retaliation. (Kant 2000: 369)

In short, justice requires that the punishment match the crime; that the evil inflicted upon criminals as punishment be the same or equal in severity to the evil that criminals have inflicted upon their victims. Thus, murderers should be put to death, rather than sentenced to life imprisonment or punished in some other way, because the death penalty is the only punishment that matches the crime of murder.

Should we accept the principle of proportionality? Two objections are commonly raised against it. One is that "eye for an eye" retributivism sometimes requires excessively brutal or inhumane punishments. "It is unclear," David Lyons argues, "that we would always be justified in treating wrongdoers as they have treated others, since this would mean torturing those who have tortured others and raping those who are guilty of rape" (Lyons 1995: 318). The following story illustrates the objection:

> In Iran, a 27-year-old man who was rejected by a woman attacked and threw acid on her, causing her to be blind and disfigured. The Supreme Court has upheld his sentence, which is chemical blinding in both eyes. He will be strapped down and have drops of hydrochloric acid placed in each of his eyes.[5]

A second objection is that the principle of proportionality cannot always be applied because sometimes there is no punishment that matches the crime. "How can we follow the formula," Lyons asks, "to determine punishments for those who lie, cheat, defraud, blackmail, or bribe others?" (Lyons 1995: 318) Even when the principle can be applied, the result is sometimes comical, as illustrated by the following story:

> In Memphis, Tennessee, a judge ordered that it was permissible for a victim to enter a burglar's house, unannounced, and take something of comparable value. A Florida judge ordered a young teenager to wear an eye patch because he had thrown a brick and blinded the victim in one eye. (Hauser 2006: 106-7)

These are important objections, but the retributivist need not say that the punishment should match the crime. What defines retributivism is not the notion of proportional punishment but the belief that offenders should be punished simply because they deserve it.

The retribution model of punishment does not encounter the same difficulties as the deterrence model, because rights can be forfeited, and criminals do forfeit certain rights in committing crimes. If I steal from you, I have no right to complain if you steal from me. If I strike you, you have the right to strike back in retaliation (or at least in self-defense). The retribution model, unlike the deterrence model, provides a plausible explanation of how governments can punish law breakers without violating their rights. But just as deterrence by itself does not justify the practice of punishment, neither does retribution. If it did, the state would be justified in punishing criminals irrespective of the goal of protecting citizens from crime and even if the practice made society less safe, as some criminological evidence suggests.[6] But surely this conflicts with the *point* of punishing criminals, which is to reduce crime and preserve social order. If so, then essential to the justification for punishment is that it does, in fact, lead to this outcome.

9.3. The Mixed Model of Punishment

Considerations such as these have led some philosophers to adopt a "mixed" model of punishment that combines elements of both the deterrence and retribution models. According to the mixed model, there is a point to punishing criminals, and this is to deter crime; at the same time, there are deontological restrictions on the practice: governments must respect the rights of offenders.

The principle of proportionality provides a useful guide in determining what rights offenders forfeit and what rights they do not. (People unjustly convicted of crimes, of course, forfeit none of their rights.) If by unjustifiably inflicting an evil upon another person I forfeit only the right not to have the same evil (or one comparable in severity) inflicted upon me, then, for example, by stealing ten dollars from someone, I forfeit only the right not to have ten dollars taken from me, which means that (independently of the costs of restitution) any fine imposed upon me in excess of ten dollars would violate my rights. (This is assuming, of course, that my loss of ten dollars would be an evil equivalent to your loss of ten dollars, which would not be the case if you were rich and I was poor. This may be an important consideration in assessing how severely the poor may be punished for crimes of theft.) In the case of more extreme crimes, the state would be justified in imposing harsher penalties. For the crime of murder, the state would be justified in imposing the death penalty, assuming that this was an effective deterrent.

If people can forfeit rights only by violating other people's rights, then one important consequence of the mixed model of punishment is that the state can rightfully exercise its power over citizens only for the purpose of protecting people's rights. (This, it will be recalled, is the libertarian conception of government.) According to the mixed model, the reason why the state can punish criminals without violating their rights is that criminals forfeit rights by violating the rights of others. If the state can execute murderers, for example, without violating their right to life, this is only because murderers forfeit this right by violating the right to life of their victims. In the case of "victimless" crimes, however, no one's rights have been forfeited because no one's rights have been violated, and so the state could not punish people for such crimes without violating their rights.

The mixed model of punishment overcomes the problems raised earlier concerning the ethics of deterrence, but a serious problem remains. Is it possible to devise a system of deterrence that is *both* effective and just—effective in the sense that it renders crime irrational, and just in the sense that it respects people's rights? As we shall see, while this may be theoretically possible—just as it is theoretically possible to wage war without innocent causalities—it may not be practically possible.[7]

9.4. The Rights of the Innocent

Because no criminal justice system is infallible, it is unavoidable that some people will be accused, tried, convicted, and eventually punished for crimes they did not commit. According to James McCloskey, who worked for many years on behalf of the innocent in prison, "An innocent person in prison . . . is about as rare as a pigeon in the park" (McCloskey 1995: 304). The explanation is complex. Police perjure themselves. Witnesses lie for the prosecution. Exculpatory evidence is suppressed. Public defenders are overworked, underpaid, and often incompetent. (About 90 percent of the people currently on death row could not afford to hire their own attorneys.) The result, according to McCloskey, is "that at least 10 percent of those convicted of serious and violent crimes are completely innocent" (McCloskey 1995: 304).

This number may or may not be accurate, and McCloskey's estimate only concerns "serious and violent crimes," but we may reasonably assume that the number of innocent people behind bars is significant. (There is an additional reason for saying this. If people can forfeit rights only by violating the rights of others, then anyone imprisoned for a victimless crime is an innocent person. Approximately half of all people in U.S. federal prisons are there for drug violations.) According to the mixed model of punishment, the point of punishing criminals is to create safety and security for the public, but in pursuing this goal, the state must respect everyone's rights. To punish a criminal is not necessarily to violate that person's rights, as we have seen, because criminals forfeit certain rights in committing crimes. However, to punish someone unjustly convicted of a crime is itself a criminal act because innocent people do not forfeit any of their rights. Thus, the state commits robbery whenever it fines an innocent person; it commits kidnapping whenever it imprisons an innocent person; and it commits murder whenever it executes an innocent person. If it is not practically possible to devise a deterrence system that does not punish innocent people, then it is not practically possible for the state to fulfill its basic social function (of protecting people from crime) without stealing, kidnapping, murdering, or committing other serious crimes.

To appreciate the moral gravity of this problem, return to the "Bruno" example discussed earlier. Clearly it would be wrong to send Bruno to prison knowing that he was innocent, even if it was occasionally necessary to send innocent people to prison in order to effectively deter crime. Does it matter whether the identity of the innocent person is known? Suppose ten people are accused of crimes, and you know that one of them is completely innocent, but you don't know which one. If you nonetheless send the entire group to prison, knowing that one person is innocent, is this less seriously wrong than sending Bruno to prison for a crime you know he did not commit? Suppose you don't know the exact number of innocent people in the group, but you know that one, two, maybe more are completely innocent. Does this matter? Due to flaws in the criminal justice system, we can know with statistical certainty that a percentage of people punished for crimes are completely innocent. If it is wrong to punish innocent people in order to deter crime, then it is wrong to do so even if the identities of the innocent people, or their exact numbers, are unknown.

This problem is particularly vexing in the case of capital punishment; for once someone has been executed, there is no possibility of correcting the system's mistake. "Unlike all other criminal punishments," one critic of the death penalty, Hugo Bedau, rightly points out, "the death penalty is irrevocable" (Bedau 2000: 242). The problem is more pervasive than we might imagine. According to Bedau:

> Since 1900, in this country, there have been on average more than four cases each year in which an entirely innocent person was convicted of murder. Scores of these individuals were sentenced to death. In many cases, a reprieve or commutation arrived just hours, or even minutes, before the scheduled execution. (Bedau 2000: 242)

Not everyone falsely convicted of murder, of course, escapes execution. Here is one such case, recounted by Bedau:

> In 1990, Jesse Tafero was executed in Florida. He had been convicted in 1976 along with his wife, Sonia Jacobs, for murdering a state trooper. In 1981 Jacobs' death sentence was reduced on appeal to life imprisonment, and 11 years later her conviction was vacated by a federal appeal court. The evidence on which Tafero and Jacobs had been convicted and sentenced was identical; it consisted mainly of the perjured testimony of an ex-convict who turned state's witness in order to avoid a death sentence. Had Tafero been alive in 1992, he no doubt would have been released along with Jacobs. (Bedau 2000: 244)

Over the past several years, well over a hundred people falsely convicted of murder have been freed from prison because of exculpatory DNA evidence. According to one story from 2002:

> Eddie Joe Lloyd has served 17 years of a life sentence for the rape and murder of a Detroit teenager, a crime he confessed to. At his sentencing, the judge said he regretted that Michigan had no death penalty. But yesterday the same judge freed Mr. Lloyd after prosecutors and defense lawyers submitted DNA evidence exonerating him. Mr. Lloyd is the 110th person nationwide to be freed based on DNA testing. . . .
>
> Every DNA reversal is a lesson in the problems with one prosecutorial tool or another. Witnesses are unreliable. Criminals will lie in exchange for lenient treatment. Mr. Lloyd's case shows that even a signed confession is not always what it seems. And it provides further proof that the American justice system is imperfect at best, and frequently far too flawed to rely on capital punishment.

In 1985 Mr. Lloyd's judge decried Michigan's lack of a death penalty, but its absence now appears to be all that prevented him from sentencing an innocent man to die.[8]

The following story from 2016—concerning Keith Allen Harward, who served 33 years in prison for crimes he did not commit—is eerily similar:

> Harward was released from the Nottoway Correctional Center on Friday after the Virginia Supreme Court agreed that DNA evidence proves he's innocent of the 1982 killing of Jesse Perron and the rape of his wife. . . .
>
> The Innocence Project got involved in Harward's case about two years ago and pushed for DNA tests, which failed to identify Harward's genetic profile in sperm left at the crime scene. The DNA matched that of one of Harward's former shipmate's, Jerry L. Crotty, who died in an Ohio prison in June 2006, where he was serving a sentence for abduction. . . .
>
> Harward initially faced the death penalty, but a loophole in the law caused his capital murder conviction to be overturned in 1985.[9]

The problem of fallibility, as illustrated by these two cases, is damning evidence against the practice of capital punishment. But the problem is not confined to the death penalty. Consider the case of Bruce Godschalk, who served fifteen years in prison before DNA testing proved his innocence:

> In 1986, when he was 26, Mr. Godschalk was convicted of raping two women, who lived in the same housing complex and sent to prison for 10 to 20 years. For seven years the Montgomery County district attorney's office fought his efforts to obtain DNA testing. Last month, two laboratories, one retained by the prosecution, the other by the defense, found the same results: Both rapes were committed by the same man, and that man was not Bruce Godschalk. . . .
>
> Six months after the two rapes, after studying Mr. Godschalk's picture in a mug shot array for more than an hour, one victim identified him as her rapist. The second victim could not make an identification. After several hours of interrogation, Mr. Godschalk made a confession that he later recanted. His motion to throw out the confession was denied in the trial. . . .
>
> While Mr. Godschalk was in prison, his sister, his only sibling; his father; and his mother all died. His mother left money in her will to pay for DNA testing. The tests cost about $10,000.[10]

It is wrong to punish innocent people, whether by execution or by imprisonment, because doing so violates their rights. Some rights violations are more serious than others, but all rights violations must be weighed in the moral balance. If social utility does not outweigh the rights violations associated with capital punishment, does it outweigh the rights violations associated with imprisonment, or even with fines?

9.5. The Rights of the Guilty

Criminals, I have suggested, forfeit some of their rights in committing crimes, but not *all* of their rights. If you inflict an evil upon me, you lose the right not to have the same evil (or one of comparable severity) inflicted upon you, but you retain whatever other rights you had before your evil deed. Thus, if you steal ten dollars from me, you lose the right not to have ten dollars taken from you, and this explains how the state can fine you as punishment for theft without violating your property rights. You do not, however, forfeit whatever other rights you had before your thievery, and these rights impose moral limits on how you may be punished. Having one of your hands severed, for example, would be a serious violation of your rights, even if this were, as it is in some countries, the socially sanctioned punishment for theft. As Alan Goldman correctly points out:

> My warning you that I will assault you if you say anything I believe to be false does nothing to justify my assaulting you, even if you could avoid it by saying nothing. A society's giving warning that it will cut off the hands of thieves does not justify its doing so. . . . The harm imposed must be independently justified. (Goldman 1995: 347)

This is an important point and it is worth emphasizing: the mere fact that the state threatens some form of punishment—such as the loss of a hand for theft, or a life sentence for a third felony conviction—does nothing to justify that punishment.

Our sympathies, of course, are for the victims of crime, not for criminals. But victims *are* victims precisely because their rights have been violated, which means that criminals are also victims when their rights are violated. There is no rational basis, then, for defending the rights of the innocent but disregarding the rights of the guilty. We have seen that, because of flaws in the criminal justice system, it is predicable that some people will be punished for crimes they did not commit. Some systems are more flawed than others, but it is unrealistic to suppose that this problem can ever be completely resolved. We turn now to a more pervasive problem: Can the state effectively deter crime without systematically violating the rights of criminals?

To understand the logic of deterrence, it is helpful to think of criminal behavior as a type of gambling behavior. Suppose you are contemplating whether or not to steal ten dollars. Let us suppose that the penalty for theft is an equivalent fine (paid, of course, after the stolen item is returned). How likely must it be that you will be punished in order for it to be irrational for you to take the money? The answer is that it must be more likely than not that you will be punished. (In precise terms, your mathematical expectation of loss—calculated by multiplying the amount to be lost by the probability of losing—must be greater than your mathematical expectation of gain—calculated by multiplying the amount to be won by the probability of winning.) Therefore, if the penalty for stealing a certain amount of money is an equivalent fine, it will be irrational for you to steal the money only if it is more probable than not that you will be punished.

This simple analysis reveals a serious problem with criminal deterrence. If the state is restrained by the principle of proportionality—which entails that the punishment cannot surpass in severity the crime—then, for the state to effectively deter theft, the rate at which it apprehends and punishes thieves must be above 50 percent. If this rate is unrealistically high, then the state can effectively deter theft only by inflicting excessive punishments on criminals (and in so doing violating their rights). In the case of violent crimes, such as murder, rape, and assault, we can make a similar but less precise observation, because there may be little or nothing that criminals hope to gain by committing such crimes. Whether or not the state can effectively deter crime largely depends upon the rate at which it punishes offenders. The less efficient the state is in apprehending criminals, the more severe its punishments must be in order to deter crime. If, in actual practice, no government is especially efficient in apprehending criminals, then in order to effectively deter crime, governments must resort to excessive punishments.

How successful are governments in punishing criminals? By far the largest category of crime in the United States, comprising about 85 percent of the total, is nonviolent property crime, which the F.B.I. defines as burglary, larceny-theft, and motor vehicle theft. In 2014, there were 8,277,829 such crimes reported nationwide, including 1,729,806 burglaries, 5,858,496 larceny-thefts, and 689,527 motor vehicle thefts.[11] According to a study prepared by the National Center for Policy Analysis,[12] the probability of serving a prison sentence for a property crime in the United States is only three percent, and this is *if* the crime is reported. It is estimated that only 50 out of every 100 burglaries are reported to police. Of the 50 burglaries reported, there are on average only 6.9 arrests. Of these 6.9 arrests, there are 6.2 prosecutions. Of these 6.2 prosecutions, there are 4.2 felony convictions. Of these 4.2 felony convictions, there are 1.9 prison sentences. This means that the actual probability of serving a prison sentence for burglary is only 1.9 percent. With such a slim chance of serving prison time, writes one critic of the penal system, "a rational odds-taker would gamble on crime every time" (Morris 1995: 27).

It would be unreasonable to expect a dramatic improvement in the rate at which criminals are arrested, tried, convicted, and eventually punished for their crimes, which means that, realistically speaking, the state cannot effectively deter crime without committing widespread rights violations.[13] The moral problem, which we must leave unresolved, is this: Does the goal of criminal deterrence outweigh the rights violations of a flawed penal system? If not, then we must give serious thought to the development of alternative methods for maintaining social order.

Notes

1. According to a report issued by Amnesty International, <www.amnesty.org/en/ documents/act50/3487/2016/en/>.
2. According to the Institute for Policy Research, <www.prisonstudies.org/highest-to-lowest/prison-population-total?field_region_taxonomy_tid=All&=Apply>.
3. According to the Huffington Post, <www.huffingtonpost.com/2013/09/20/juvenile-life-without-parole_n_3962983.html>.
4. It might be pointed out, though, that punishment is sometimes seen as a method of rehabilitation. When parents punish their children, for example, their usual intention is to help their children to become better people in the long run by making them suffer in the short run. The notion that suffering—whether imposed from the outside as a form of punishment or self-inflicted as a form of penance—leads to moral improvement is by no means an uncommon one. Thus, rehabilitation is not always an alternative to punishment. Sometimes it is a justification for it.
5. "The 13 Most Brutal and Inhumane Judicial Punishments Still Used Today," <http://brainz.org/13-most-brutal-and-inhumane-judicial-punishments-still-used-today/>.
6. According to a study prepared by the Bureau of Justice Statistics, about two-thirds (67.8 percent) of released prisoners are rearrested within three years. See <http://www.nij.gov/ topics/corrections/recidivism/pages/welcome.aspx >. The evidence suggests that people who pass through the prison system tend not emerge on the other side as better people. "Jails are, to a proverb, seminaries of vice," William Godwin wrote long ago, "and he must be an uncommon proficient in the passion and practice of injustice, or a man of sublime virtue, who does not come out of them a much worse man than when he entered" (Ward 1973: 120).
7. My discussion of this issue draws on Alan Goldman's "The Paradox of Punishment." It was Goldman who originally made the point I argue for in what follows: that because governments are not efficient in apprehending criminals, they must resort to excessive punishments in order to effectively deter crime.
8. "110 Wrongful Convictions, and Counting," *The New York Times*, August 27, 2002.
9. "Exonerated man released from Virginia prison after 33 years," <www.seattlepi.com /news/crime/article/Exonerated-man-released-from-Virginia-prison-7237069.php >.
10. "DNA Testing in Rape Case Frees Prisoner After 15 Years," *The New York Times*, February 15, 2002.
11. According to an F.B.I. report, "2014, Crime in the United States," <www.fbi.gov/ about-us/cjis/ucr/crime-in-the-u.s/2014/crime-in-the-u.s.-2014/offenses-known-to-law-enforcement/property-crime>.
12. "Crime and Punishment in America, 1999," <www.ncpa.org/pub/st229 >.
13. This, it will be noticed, bolsters the anarchist's claim that governments are illegitimate—indeed, criminal. The role of government is to provide safety and security for people. This it does, in part, by preventing crime. But if the state cannot prevent crime without committing it, then it is itself a criminal institution. A related argument for anarchism hinges on the morality of war. Governments provide safety and security for their citizens, not only by punishing criminals, but by waging war. But if the state cannot wage war without violating people's rights, then, again, the state cannot fulfill its basic social function without resorting to crime. We will discuss the morality of war in the following chapter.

10. The Ethics of War

The American invasion of Afghanistan, in the wake of the 9-11 terrorist attacks, left thousands of civilians dead or wounded. "A woman named Rose lay on a bed in the corner of the room," reads one story in *The New York Times* (December 12, 2001). "Early on Sunday morning, shrapnel from an American bomb tore through the woman's abdomen, broke her 4-year-old son's leg and ripped into her 6-year-old daughter's head, doctors here said. A second 6-year old girl in the room was paralyzed from the waist down." Another *Times* article (July 21, 2002) reads: "[A]n American AC-130 gunship attacked four villages around the hamlet of Kakrak. American soldiers later found villagers gathering up the limbs of their neighbors. Local officials counted 54 dead, most of them women and children, and at least 120 wounded." According to the same article: "Field workers with Global Exchange, an American organization that has sent survey teams into Afghan villages, say they have compiled a list of 812 Afghan civilians who were killed by American airstrikes." Marc Herold, an economics professor at the University of New Hampshire, analyzed press reports from international sources and reached the conclusion that "at least 3,767 civilians were killed [in Afghanistan] by US bombs between October 7 and December 10 [2001] . . . an average of 62 innocent deaths a day" (Arnove 2002). To put this figure into perspective, about 3,000 innocent civilians were killed in the 9-11 terrorist attacks.

Civilian causalities quickly mounted in the Iraq War. On March 21, 2003, two days after the war began with a tactical bombing raid over Baghdad, *The New York Times* reported: "On Friday officials took reporters to El Yarmouk Hospital with wards filled with many of the 215 Iraqi civilians said to have suffered injuries in the attacks. . . . Many of those injured were women and children. Some victims appeared to have suffered severe burn and blast injuries, while a majority had more minor wounds, mostly from shards of glass and shrapnel." On March 23, the *Times* reported: "Iraq said 77 civilians were killed

Saturday in Basra . . . and 503 were wounded by coalition air strikes across the country. German public television ARD said a cruise missile hit a residential area in Baghdad on Sunday morning, destroying five houses and injuring at least two people."

During the first week of the war, a U.S. warplane bombed a passenger bus carrying Syrian civilians fleeing the hostilities, killing five people and wounding ten others. In another incident, an errant missile struck a working-class district of Baghdad, killing seventeen civilians and wounding 45 others. On March 27, 2003 the *Times* reported that "a whole family—father, mother, three children— had burned to death in one of the cars." According to coverage by *NPR News* (March 26, 2003), "A teenager thrust a can at reporters. He said it contained the brains of one of the victims. Others showed off a severed hand. 'Is this what you call human rights?' scoffed one young man. 'Is this what you call liberation?' asked another."

During the second week of the war, an errant bomb struck a marketplace in an impoverished district of Baghdad, killing at least 35 civilians, and possibly as many as 55, most of them young children, elderly or women. At a military checkpoint, soldiers killed an unarmed man who drove his pickup truck through a barbed wire roadblock. This occurred only hours after another incident in which soldiers fired at a van carrying thirteen women and children, killing seven of the occupants, mostly children, and injuring two others. "You just killed a family because you didn't fire a warning shot soon enough!" one officer is quoted as saying (*The New York Times*, April 1, 2003).

The Iraq Body Count Project—a group of professors and peace activists from the United States and Great Britain—kept a daily tally of civilian deaths during the war. Based upon credible media reports from international sources, the Project concluded that somewhere between 554 and 710 Iraqi civilians were killed during just the first two weeks of the conflict. Thirteen years later, the same group estimates that between 156,887 and 175,538 civilians have been killed.[1]

These figures do not take into account the number of civilians wounded in the Iraq War—a number somewhere between three and five times as great as the number of civilians killed. There is the story of a bewildered boy, "perhaps 10 or 11, separated from his parents, lying on a hospital gurney. . . . Once on the operating table, quickly anesthetized, he knew nothing. His wounded arm was un-bandaged and amputated rapidly by the surgeon just below the elbow." There is the story of Hussein Ali Hussein, lying "on a bed, the stump of one leg covered in a bloody bandage, a mass of flies settling on the gauze. He said that he had been in a car that was hit by an American tank shell." And there is the story of Bassan Hoki, who was riding on a bus when it was struck by a bomb. "Surgeons had amputated his right arm above the elbow, and seeping bandages covered deep wounds on both his legs" (*The New York Times*, April 3, 2003). British journalist Robert Fisk (2003) described some of the video footage shot by the *Al Jazeera* cable network. "A middle-aged man is carried into the hospital in pajamas," he wrote, "soaked head to foot in blood. A little girl of perhaps 4 is brought into the operating room on a trolley, staring at a heap of her own intestines protruding from the left side of her stomach." An article carried in the *Star* (April 26, 2003) reported that during the first month of the war one hospital had already amputated more than a hundred arms and legs from children.

The moral presumption against war is obvious. War is the most violent and destructive of all organized human activities, and the principal victims of war are innocent people—"innocent" in the sense that they have done nothing to forfeit their rights. If it is presumptively wrong to violate people's rights, and if wars cannot be waged without widespread rights violations—90 percent of the people killed in war are innocent people—then war is presumptively wrong. If war is sometimes justified, this presumption must be outweighed by the importance of achieving the goals for which wars are fought: national security, the overthrow of a brutal dictatorship, the spread of democracy, the prevention of terrorism. In the moral balance, how much weight should be assigned to the rights of innocent people? What goals, if any, are worth the price of war? These are the difficult questions addressed in this chapter.

10.1. The Problem of Collateral Damage

The phrase that is commonly used to describe civilian casualties in war is "collateral damage." This is a flexible notion, referring to both the direct and indirect effects of war and to accidental as well as predictable casualties. Here are five notorious examples from recent U.S. history:

1. In retaliation for a terrorist bombing of a Berlin discotheque, Ronald Reagan ordered a military strike against Libya and its leader, Muammar Khadafi. Bombs fell on Tripoli, killing perhaps a hundred people, mostly civilians, including Khadafi's adopted infant daughter. Khadafi himself was unharmed.

2. In 1989, George H. W. Bush ordered an invasion of Panama to arrest its head of state, Manuel Noriega. The bombing raids on Panama City ignited a firestorm in a poor neighborhood, killing thousands of people. In total, somewhere between 2,500—according to the United Nations—and 4,000— according to the Association of the Dead of December 20—Panamanians were killed in the conflict. Twenty thousand people lost their homes.

3. During the Persian Gulf War, 177 million pounds of explosives, roughly the equivalent of five Hiroshima bombs, were dropped on Iraq, killing hundreds of thousands of people and destroying much the country's civilian infrastructure, resulting in a protracted humanitarian crisis. Water and sanitation systems, destroyed during the war, could not be repaired because of an embargo on spare parts, resulting in increased incidences of water-borne diseases, such as typhoid, cholera, and acute diarrhea. Eventually, well over a

million people died, mostly children, from the combined effects of war and economic sanctions.

4. "In February 1991, during the Persian Gulf War, a U.S. bomb punched a hole through the roof of the Al-Amiriya bomb shelter; seconds later a missile plowed through the opening. By Iraqi count, the blasts killed 408 civilians, mostly women and children. Many were killed by the concussion, the rest by a fire so intense it left flash-burned outlines of women and infants on the walls that are still visible today. The United States has said it believed it was targeting a military command center." (Johnson 2002)

5. In 1998, Bill Clinton ordered bombing raids on targets in Africa and Afghanistan in retaliation for terrorist attacks on American embassies in Tanzania and Kenya in which hundreds of people, including twelve Americans, were killed. One target was the Al Shifa pharmaceutical plant in Sudan. The Al Shifa plant, destroyed in the raids, was responsible for manufacturing over 50 percent of Sudan's medicine, including 90 percent of its most critical drugs. According to one article (Flounders and Parker 1999), "The bombing will inexorably cause the suffering and death of tens of thousands of innocent people all over Africa, many of them children, by depriving them of basic medicines against malaria, tuberculosis, and other easily curable diseases."

Referring to examples of such as these, one critic of U.S. foreign policy, Howard Zinn (2001), writes:

> The absurdity of claiming innocence in such cases becomes apparent when the death tolls from "collateral damage" reach figures far greater than the lists of the dead from even the most awful act of terrorism. Thus, the "collateral damage" in the Gulf War caused more people to die—hundreds of thousands, if you include the victims of our sanctions policy—than the very deliberate terrorist attack of September 11. The total of those who have died in Israel from Palestinian terrorist bombs is somewhere under 1,000. The number of dead from "collateral damage" in the bombing of Beirut during Israel's invasion of Lebanon in 1982 was roughly 6,000.

This suggests one way of framing the problem of collateral damage: Can we consistently condone government-sponsored military action and yet condemn terrorism? Approximately 3,000 innocent people were killed in the terrorist attacks of September 11, 2001. But a far greater number of innocent people were killed by U.S. forces during just the first two months of the war in Afghanistan. How can it be wrong, inexcusably wrong, for Islamic terrorists to kill innocent Americans and yet an acceptable "cost of war" for American soldiers to kill innocent Muslims? Opponents of war, such as Howard Zinn, seem to reason as follows:

(1) Terrorism is wrong because innocent people are killed in terrorist attacks.
(2) If this explains why terrorism is wrong, and if innocent people are killed in war, then war must also be wrong.
(3) Innocent people are killed in war.

Therefore:

(4) War is wrong.

We cannot assume that terrorists do not fight for important goals.[2] But if terrorism is wrong regardless of its goals, don't we have to conclude that war is wrong regardless of its goals?

10.2. The Doctrine of Double Effect

In military ethics, the solution to this problem rests upon a distinction between the *intentional* and the merely *predictable* killing of innocent people. This is known as the doctrine of double effect. According to this, while it is wrong to intentionally kill innocent people, it is sometimes permissible to kill innocent people as an unintended effect of an action aimed at a different effect (hence the doctrine of "double effect"). Acts of terrorism are wrong, so the doctrine says, because they target innocent people; conventional military operations, though they may involve as many or even more civilian causalities, are permissible insofar as they do not target the innocent.

To illustrate the doctrine, consider the following pair of examples (first brought up in Chapter 3):

The Journalist Case: A terrorist group threatens to detonate a bomb, killing dozens of people, unless the authorities meet their demand. Their demand is that a journalist, who has written articles ridiculing the Prophet, be publicly executed. If the authorities execute the journalist, one innocent person will die; but if they don't, dozens of innocent people will die. Should the authorities meet this demand?

The Hijack Case: An airplane has been hijacked by a terrorist group. Their intention is to fly the airplane into a large office building. If they are successful, not only will everyone on the airplane be killed, but so will everyone in the office building. The authorities can prevent the terrorist attack, but only by blowing up the airplane, in which case *they* (not the terrorists) will murder the passengers. What should be done?

Many people feel that it would be wrong for the authorities to execute the journalist in the first case but permissible for them to blow up the airplane in the second. This is supported by the doctrine of double effect. One side of the doctrine says that it is wrong to harm innocent people as an end in itself or as a means to an end. This would explain our feelings about the Journalist Case, because here the authorities would be killing an innocent person as a means to preventing the terrorist attack. The other side of the doctrine says that it is sometimes permissible to harm innocent people as an unintended side-effect of an otherwise permissible action. This would explain our intuitions about the Hijack Case, because here the authorities would not be killing the airplane passengers as a means to preventing the terrorist attack but as an unintended side-effect.

It is important to understand what the doctrine of double effect says and what it doesn't say. It does say that it is wrong to inflict harm upon an innocent person as an end in itself or as a means to an end. It also says that it is *sometimes* permissible to unintentionally harm innocent people, but it does not say that it is *always* permissible to do so. Carefully stated, the doctrine identifies four conditions that must be met to justify an action that has both good and bad effects. First, considered independently of the bad effect, the action must be morally permissible. Second, the bad effect must not be intended. Third, the bad effect must not be the means by which the good effect is achieved. And fourth, the good effect must be "proportionate" to the bad effect (in the sense that the good effect is at least as great as the bad effect). The Journalist Case fails to meet the third condition, since in this instance the bad effect (the death of the journalist) would be the means by which the good effect (the prevention of the terrorist attack) would be achieved. The Hijack Case, however, satisfies all four conditions. First, considered independently of the bad effect (the death of the airplane passengers) the action would be morally permissible. Second, the bad effect would not be intended. Third, the bad effect would not be the means by which the good effect (the prevention of the terrorist attack) would be achieved. And fourth, the good effect would be proportionate to the bad effect, because more lives would be saved than would be lost. According to the doctrine of double effect, then, it would be permissible to blow up the plane.

The most common justification for war is national defense. Does the doctrine of double effect excuse the collateral damage that occurs when a country defends itself against unjustified aggression? Consider the following example:

The Missile Case: You are the president of the United States. You have just learned that an enemy government plans to launch an unprovoked missile strike against a major American city. The information you have received is completely reliable and the attack is imminent. The only way you can prevent the attack is by ordering a preemptive missile strike, destroying the enemy's missile system, which happens to be located in a densely populated city. If you order the strike, thousands of people will be killed as collateral damage. If you don't, thousands of Americans will be killed. What should you do?

Intuitively, it would be permissible for you to order the missile strike, even though thousands of innocent people would be killed. This is consistent with the doctrine of double effect and suggests that a nation is justified in inflicting collateral damage upon an enemy when fending off an attack. Since this is the most common justification for war, the doctrine of double effect seems to solve the problem of collateral damage.

The Missile Case may be a bit misleading, however. Generally speaking, when a country defends "itself" against aggression, it is not defending its civilian population but its system of government. One authority, Brain Orend, goes so far as to define war as an "intentional and widespread armed conflict between political communities wherein the ultimate objective is to force the other side to accept one's will regarding governance" (Orend 2006: 50). Most of the European colonial wars from 1500 to 1950, he notes, had regime change as their objective. "The Europeans found 'new' territories governed by locals (i.e., natives or aboriginals) and left them as lands ruled by European appointees, with European-style state structures" (Orend 2006: 190). The United States was established as the result of a violent regime change (the American Revolutionary War) and throughout its history has been engaged in such struggles against other governments. Orend gives a cursory overview:

> There was the bitter Civil War experience in 1861-65, which ultimately revolved around liquidating the Confederate regime and forcibly reconstructing it. The United States had many military entanglements in Latin America (especially Cuba and Mexico) as well as in Indonesia in the transition period from the 1800s to the 1900s, and several of those entanglements were attempts at forcing regime change. Some were successful, others not. . . . The reconstruction of Germany and Japan, from 1945 to 1955, probably count as the most successful and praiseworthy regime transformations in recent world history. On the other hand, the Bay of Pigs invasion of Cuba in 1961—trying to oust Castro's communists by force—was a complete and embarrassing flop. Somewhere in-between reside such other examples as the Dominican Republic (1965), Grenada (1983), Panama (1989), Haiti (1994), Bosnia (1995) and Afghanistan (2001). There are also controversial cases—where US involvement in forcing regime changes was real but indirect—such as Guatemala (1954) and Serbia (1999). And of course there is the current case of Iraq. (Orend 2006: 192)

When the goal of military aggression is to impose a new system of government on a civilian population, the citizens of the defending nation must ask themselves whether their own system of government is worth killing or dying for, or whether the new system would be so deplorable that resisting it with violence is justified, even if this entails inflicting collateral damage on the aggressor. This, obviously, is a very different issue from the one raised by the Missile Case.

Regardless of the goals for which they are fought, wars are won by destroying the enemy's capacity to wage war—by killing enemy combatants, by demolishing munitions factories, missile systems, airfields, and other military assets—

and this can involve extensive collateral damage. In the Missile Case, it seems permissible to destroy an enemy's offensive capacity, even if thousands of innocent people will be killed. But consider:

> The Gun Store Case: You have received completely reliable information that a terrorist intends to attack a shopping mall, but he must first obtain ammunition for his assault rifle. There is only one gun store in town, and you can prevent the terrorist from obtaining the ammunition he needs by demolishing the store with a missile. Unfortunately, the store is crowded with shoppers, which means that a number of people will be killed as an unintended side-effect, but fewer, we imagine, than would be killed by the terrorist. Assuming that you cannot otherwise prevent the terrorist attack, would it be permissible for you to bomb the store?

Even granting the bold assumptions made in this case, it seems wrong to bomb the store knowing that innocent people will be killed. But if it would be wrong to bomb the store, how could it be right to destroy a munitions factory (or a missile system, or an airfield, or other military assets) in a populated area knowing that civilians will be killed?

While there are examples that support the doctrine of double effect, other examples show that the doctrine does not solve the problem of collateral damage. The Gun Store Case is one such example. Here's another, very different example:

> The Burning Building Case: A building is on fire. Six people are trapped on a fourth-floor balcony, clamoring for help. There is a long beam which you could lean against the side of the building. If you did this, the people trapped on the balcony could slide down the beam to safety. However, the beam supports a platform on which five people are standing. If you remove the beam, they will fall to their deaths. Would it be permissible to remove the beam?

Intuitively, it would be wrong to remove the beam, but according to the doctrine of double effect, it would be permissible. First, considered independently of the bad effect (killing five people), the action would be morally permissible. Second, the bad effect would not be intended. Third, the bad effect would not be the means by which the good effect (rescuing six people) would be achieved. And fourth, the good effect would be proportionate to the bad effect, since a greater number of people would be rescued than would be killed.

We may conclude that the doctrine of double effect does not capture the relevant features of those situations in which collateral damage is justified. What features are missing? Here's an example imagined by Tom Regan:

The Tank Case: "A terrorist has taken possession of a tank and has commenced to kill, one by one, the twenty-six innocent hostages he has bound to a wall. All attempts to negotiate release of the hostages are flatly rejected, and there is every reason to believe that the terrorist will kill all the hostages if nothing is done. Under the circumstances the only reasonable way to save these hostages is to blow up the tank. Suppose the means to blow it up are at hand. Only suppose the terrorist has taken the precaution of strapping another innocent hostage to the tank. Any means used to blow up the tank will kill that hostage. What ought we to do?" (Regan 1983: 291-92)

It seems plausible to say that we ought to blow up the tank, or at least that it would be permissible to do so. This has important implications concerning the problem of collateral damage. Regan's example is analogous to a case in which an enemy government uses its own civilian population to shield itself from attack. It is also analogous to a case in which enemy fighters hide among civilians, as occurs in guerilla warfare. In such cases, it is impossible to effectively engage the enemy without civilian casualties. Regan's example suggests that collateral damage is acceptable when civilians are used as "innocent shields."

How closely does Regan's imaginary example resemble an actual case in which enemy forces use civilians as innocent shields? Consider the following example from the war in Afghanistan:

The toll of civilians killed in bombing by coalition forces on Tuesday night was much higher than the official figure of 21, and may be as high as 50 or even 80, residents reached by telephone said Thursday.

The tally differed from that given by a government administrator of the Sangin region, Ezatullah, who uses only one name. He said he had spent four to five hours in the village of Sarwan Qala on Thursday and said the civilian death toll remained 21. . . .

A resident of the bombed village, Abdul Nasir, who was away from the village on Tuesday night, said more than 60 people had been killed and many more wounded.

"It was around 4 p.m. when the foreign vehicles came through on the main road," he said. "The Taliban shot at them and they turned back. Then airplanes came and bombed the village at 10 p.m.," he said. The Taliban were in the village during the day but left later and were not in the village at the time of the bombing," he said. . . .

Ezatullah blamed the Taliban for drawing fire on the village. "This is the fault of the Taliban, and they are using civilian houses to fight from," he said. (Gall 2007)

Even if the Taliban was at fault for drawing fire on the village, does this excuse the collateral damage that resulted from the coalition air strike? Or consider another actual example, this time from the Israeli-Palestinian conflict:

> On the night of July 22, [2002] an Israeli F-16 dropped a one-ton bomb in a densely populated area of Gaza City, killing Hamas military wing leader Salah Shehadeh and 16 others, of whom 15 were civilians and 9 were children, including Shehadeh's wife and child. Over one hundred others were injured in the attack.[3]

Al Jazeera (April 10, 2004) quoted one spokesperson for the Israeli Foreign Ministry as saying, "If we hadn't killed those Palestinian children, then the terrorist would have killed three or four times as many Israelis." When a one-ton bomb is dropped on a densely populated neighborhood, we can know in advance that innocent people will be killed. What we cannot know is that more innocent lives will be saved than will be lost. Would Salah Shehadeh have killed three or four times as many innocent people if the Israelis had not carried out this attack, as alleged by the Israeli spokesperson? How would Hamas respond to the bombing? Would it retaliate with deadly terrorist attacks, claiming even more innocent lives? That such questions are unanswered and perhaps unanswerable strongly suggests that while it is important to save lives, it is more important to respect people's rights.

All things considered, then, it is at least unclear whether conventional war is morally more defensible than terrorism. Certainly, there is no difference from the standpoint of the victims of violence. According to an interview with Osama bin Laden, the terrorists who staged the 9-11 attacks "did not intend to kill babies; they intended to destroy the strongest military power in the world." Bin Laden was adamant that "the Prophet Mohammed forbade the killing of babies and women," which presumably meant the *intentional* killing of babies and women. The Twin Towers, he argued, "are an economic power and not a children's school. Those that were there are men that supported the biggest economic power in the world" (Singer 2004: 60-61). Bin Laden was aware that innocent people were killed in the terrorist attacks, but excused such deaths as "collateral damage."

10.3. The "Good War" Myth

American socialist and war critic Eugene Debs once wrote: "Wars throughout history have been waged for conquest and plunder. . . . And that is war in a nutshell. The master class has always declared the wars; the subject class has always fought the battles" (Zinn 1991: 189). Debs was not alone in making this observation. According to General Smedley D. Butler, writing in *The New York Times* (August 21, 1938):

> I helped make Mexico safe for American oil interests in 1914. I helped make Haiti and Cuba a decent place for the National City Bank boys to collect revenue in. I helped purify Nicaragua for the international banking house of Brown Brothers. . . . I brought light to the Dominican Republic for sugar interests in 1916. I helped make Honduras "right" for American fruit companies in 1903. Looking back on it, I might have given Al Capone a few hints.

Americans will not enthusiastically rally behind the corporations, military contractors, and other special interests that benefit from war, but they will rally behind a government that defends its citizens and supports democratic ideals abroad—or so they are led to believe. For this reason, some critics argue, Americans have been instilled with a false conception of the nature and purpose of war—the "good war" myth.

According to the Congressional Research Service, from 1798 to 1995 the United States intervened militarily abroad no fewer than 251 times. In the twentieth century alone, the United States engaged in well over a hundred military interventions, beginning in 1901 when troops were deployed in Oklahoma to crush a Creek Indian revolt (the war against Philippine independence, which began in 1898 in the aftermath of the Spanish-American War, continued until 1910) and ending in the 1990s with the Persian Gulf War, the occupation of Somalia, bombing raids in Sudan and Afghanistan, and an air campaign against the former Yugoslavia. How many American wars are "good wars"? The most plausible candidate is World War II,[4] but how representative is this one example? Consider the Vietnam War. Over 60,000 American soldiers, and between three and five million Vietnamese, Cambodians, and Laotians, killed. Were the interests of ordinary Americans at stake in this war? Or take the Philippine War, which lasted for nearly as long as the Vietnam War. Four thousand American soldiers and 200,000 Filipinos (according to some estimates, upwards of one million) killed. Was this war fought to protect the lives, the liberties of ordinary Americans, or to uphold democratic ideals abroad? Was the Mexican War (in which half of Mexico was stolen)? The Indian wars (no fewer than 50 between 1811 and 1890)? World War I (in which nine million people died)? The current wars in Iraq and Afghanistan?

Let us consider two examples of "good wars" from American history: the Revolutionary War and the Civil War. The Revolutionary War is remembered as a war for freedom and democracy, which are important social values, arguably worth the price of war. But who was freed as a result of the war? And who won democratic rights? Upon its founding, the United States was a slave-holding nation (nearly one-half of the signers of the Declaration of Independence owned slaves) and only a small minority of Americans (specifically, wealthy white men, subject to certain religious qualifications) won the right to vote. The American Revolution was by no means a revolution for slaves, American Indians, the poor, Jews, Catholics, or women.[5] In fact, according to one of the Founding Fathers, John Adams, only about one-third of the colonists supported the war, and an equal percentage opposed it. Consistent with Eugene Debs' remark that "The master class has always declared the wars; the subject class has always fought the battles," men in Connecticut could be excused from military service by paying five pounds—a price not affordable by the poor. (This trend continued. During the Civil War, the rich could buy their way out of military service by paying $300. J. P. Morgan escaped military service in this way, and so did John D. Rockefeller, Andrew Carnegie, James Mellon, William Vanderbilt, and 73,500 other affluent men.) As Douglas P. Lackey points out, the Revolutionary War is "widely viewed as a war that produced a great moral good; but if the war had not been fought, the history of the United States would be similar to the history of Canada (which remained loyal)—and no one feels that the Canadians have suffered or are suffering great injustices that the American colonies avoided by war" (Lackey 2003: 19).

The Civil War is remembered as the war that ended slavery, and slavery is certainly an abominable institution. It is true that slavery was officially abolished after the war, but was the war fought for this purpose? The facts tell a different story.[6] For one thing, racial attitudes in the North were about as bad as those in the South. Abolitionists constituted a small minority: only about two percent of the Northern adult population belonged to abolitionist societies. Almost all Northern states denied blacks the right to vote, and even the right to serve on juries or to deliver testimony in court against whites. The Fugitive Slave Act, which required runaway slaves to be returned to their owners, was upheld by the U.S. Supreme Court and by all Northern states. Even Abraham Lincoln was an avowed racist. "I have no purpose to introduce political and social equality between the white and black races," he once said. "[I] am in favor of the race to which I belong having the superior position. I have never said anything to the contrary" (Dilorenzo 2002: 11). Furthermore, slavery also existed in the North—specifically, in Delaware, Maryland, Kentucky, and Missouri. Even though slavery was abolished throughout the United States by the Thirteenth Amendment after the Civil War in 1865, the Emancipation Proclamation, issued during the war (on January 1, 1863, to be exact, long after the first major battle of the war in July of 1861), applied *only* to Confederate states. And even within the Confederacy, Lincoln's order did not apply to those areas, such as parts of New Orleans, that were under Union control. Lincoln was clear about his intentions:

> My paramount object in this struggle is to save the Union, and is *not* either to save or to destroy slavery. If I could save the Union without freeing *any* slave I would do it; and if I could save it by freeing some and leaving others alone I would also do that. What I do about slavery and the colored race, I do because I believe it helps to save the Union. (Dilorenzo 2002: 35)

At least initially, the Civil War was not about slavery at all, but about secession—specifically, the right of Southern states to secede from the Union. Was Lincoln justified in waging a protracted and immensely costly war, in which an estimated 750,000 Americans were killed (including 50,000 civilians), for the purpose of maintaining the power of the federal government over Southern states?

If war is ever justified, there must be moral goods that are worth the price of war. Given the high cost, the burden of proof is upon those who favor military action rather than upon those who oppose it. A thorough analysis of American military history may reveal that this burden is rarely, if ever, met.

Notes

1. The Iraq Body Count Project, <www.iraqbodycount.org>.
2. In 1998, more than two years before the 9-11 terrorist attacks, Osama bin Laden and several other militant Islamic leaders issued a statement calling for: (1) a withdrawal of American troops from Saudi Arabia, as promised by the first Bush administration; (2) an end to the embargo against Iraq, which by that time had claimed the lives of over 500,000 Iraqi children; and (3) an end to the Israeli occupation of Palestinian territories. These "crimes," according to the statement, amounted to "a clear declaration of war by the Americans against God, his Prophet, and the Muslims." It is in response to these crimes that Osama bin Laden and the other signatories of the statement issued a *fatwa* or ruling against the United States, calling upon Muslims everywhere "to kill Americans and their allies, both civil and military . . . until their armies, shattered and broken-winged, depart from all the lands of Islam, incapable of threatening any Muslim." ("A Manifesto for War," *The Miami Herald*, September 29, 2001.)
3. Crimes of War Project, "Case Study: The Israeli Strike Against Hamas Leader Salah Shehadeh," September 19, 2002, <www.crimesofwar.org/onnews/news-shehadeh.html>.
4. This can be questioned. It is estimated that during the World War II, Allied forces killed about 5.5 million enemy soldiers, and about one million civilians. Was the Allied victory worth this price? One philosopher, Douglas P. Lackey, has doubts. "No one denies that a Nazi victory in World War II would have had morally frightful results," he writes. "But . . . killing six and one-half million people is also morally frightful, and preventing one moral wrong does not obviously outweigh committing the other" (Lackey 2003: 20).
5. In the 1820s and 1830s, property qualifications, which disenfranchised the poor, and religious qualifications, which excluded Jews and Catholics, were lifted in some states. In 1870, the Fifteenth Amendment held that a person could not be denied the right to vote because of "race, color, or previous condition of servitude," which in theory enfranchised all African American men (though poll taxes, literacy tests, good-character tests, residency requirements, grandfather clauses, the Ku Klux Klan, and lynch mobs effectively disenfranchised the majority of blacks in Southern states by the end of the nineteenth century.) Women did not win the right to vote until 1920. American Indians did not win the right until 1924 when they were officially recognized as United States citizens. Congress overturned nineteenth-century laws denying citizenship, and hence the right to vote, to Asian immigrants as recently as 1952. (Soilfer 2001: Ch. 10)
6. My discussion in this paragraph is based upon Thomas J. Dilorenzo's *The Real Lincoln*.

Appendix: Argument Patterns

Whether an argument is valid or invalid is determined by its structure. For example, consider the following pair of arguments (taken from the second chapter):

Argument 1:

> If subjectivism is true, then people can know whether an action is right or wrong simply by examining their feelings.
> People cannot know whether an action is right or wrong in this way.
> Therefore, subjectivism is false.

Argument 2:

> If there are moral facts, then it should be possible to prove things in ethics.
> It is not possible to prove things in ethics.
> Therefore, there are no moral facts.

These arguments differ from one another in content—the first argument is about moral subjectivism, whereas the second is concerned with moral nihilism—but they are nonetheless alike in form or structure. The form of both arguments may be represented as follows:

> If P then Q
> Not Q
> Not P

Here "P" and "Q" stand for sentences, such as "Subjectivism is true" and "It is possible to prove things in ethics." The underline separates the premises from the conclusion and corresponds to "Therefore." This is argument pattern is valid in the sense that no matter what sentences are substituted for "P" and "Q" the result is valid. The result may not be a sound argument, because it may have one or more false premises (the second argument is an example), but *any* argument that has this form is valid. (Remember, to say that an argument is valid simply means that *if* the premises are true, then, as a matter of logical necessity, the conclusion must be true.) In formal logic, this argument pattern is known as "Modus Tollens."

Consider another pair of examples:

Argument 3:

All Sunnis are Muslims.
All Muslims are monotheists.
Therefore, all Sunnis are monotheists.

Argument 4:

All human fetuses are innocent human beings.
All innocent human beings are beings with a right to life.
Therefore, all human fetuses are beings with a right to life.

These two arguments also have the same structure, which may be represented thus:

All A are B
All B are C
All A are C

Here "A," "B," and "C" do not stand for sentences but for terms or expressions, such as "Sunnis" or "innocent human beings." This argument pattern is also valid: no matter what terms are substituted for "A," "B," and "C" the result is a valid argument. Again, an argument of this form may not be sound—certainly, Argument 4 is a controversial example—but it is nonetheless valid. Logicians in the Middle-Ages named this argument pattern "Barbara."

Now consider the following argument:

Argument 5:

All murderers are people who should be punished.
All criminals are people who should be punished.
Therefore, all murderers are criminals.

This argument may seem plausible, but the reasoning is invalid. For compare the above argument with the one below:

Argument 6:

>   All dogs are animals.
>   All giraffes are animals.
>   Therefore, all dogs are giraffes.

These are quite different arguments, but they nonetheless have exactly the same structure:

>   All A are C
>   <u>All B are C</u>
>   All A are B

We can see, in light of Argument 6, that this is an invalid argument pattern. If it is possible to reason from true premises to a false conclusion, the reasoning cannot be valid. This argument pattern also has a name. It is known as the fallacy of the "undistributed middle term."

The following are valid patterns of reasoning:

Modus Ponens	**Modus Tollens**	**Chain Argument**
If P then Q	If P then Q	If P then Q
<u>P </u>	<u>Not Q </u>	<u>If Q then R</u>
Q	Not P	If P then R

Disjunctive Argument	**Barbara**	**Celarent**
Either P or Q	All A are B	All A are B
<u>Not P (not Q)</u>	<u>All B are C</u>	<u>No B are C</u>
Q (P)	All A are C	No A are C

The following are invalid argument patterns:

Affirming the Consequent	**Denying the Antecedent**	**Undistributed Middle Term**
If P then Q	If P then Q	All A are C
<u>Q </u>	<u>Not P </u>	<u>All B are C</u>
P	Not Q	All A are B

Identify the patterns of reasoning underlying the following arguments.

1. All turkeys are birds.
    All birds are feathered creatures.
    Therefore, all turkeys are feathered creatures.

2. All turkeys are feathered creatures
    All birds are feathered creatures.
    Therefore, all turkeys are birds.

3. If zombies eat brains then they are not vegetarians.
    Zombies eat brains.
    Therefore, zombies are not vegetarians.

4. If Edward is a vampire then he drinks blood.
    Edward drinks blood.
    Therefore, Edward is a vampire.

5. If Andrea drives a Tesla then she drives an electric automobile.
    Andrea drives an electric automobile.
    Therefore, Andrea drives a Tesla.

6. If Key West is in northern Florida then it's a long drive from Miami.
    Key West is a long drive from Miami.
    Therefore, Key West is in northern Florida.

7. If Carlos is a skydiver then he has a dangerous hobby.
    If Carlos has a dangerous hobby then his insurance costs are high.
    Therefore, if Carlos is a skydiver then his insurance costs are high.

8. All dragons are creations of myth.
    No creations of myth are actual creatures.
    Therefore, no dragons are actual creatures.

9. Either life is the product of chance or it is the product of intelligent design.
    Life is not the product of chance.
    Therefore, life is the product of intelligent design.

10. All reptoids are subterranean creatures.
    No subterranean creatures are sunbathers.
    Therefore, no reptoids are sunbathers.

11. All Chihuahuas are animals.
    All dogs are animals.
    Therefore, all Chihuahuas are dogs.

12. All pigs are winged creatures.
    All winged creatures are devil worshippers.
    Therefore, all pigs are devil worshippers.

13. If Madame Marie can read tarot cards or tell fortunes then she is a psychic.
    Madame Marie cannot read tarot cards or tell fortunes.
    Therefore, she is not a psychic.

14. All giraffes are four-legged.
    All tables are four-legged.
    Therefore, all giraffes are tables.

15. All college graduates are successful people.
    All successful people are millionaires.
    Therefore, all college graduates are millionaires.

Glossary

altruism. The consequentialist theory according to which the right thing to do is whatever has the best consequences for others.

anarchism. The word derives from the Greek *an-archos*, which refers to the absence of leadership, authority, or government. Anarchists are committed to two claims: first, that no government has legitimate authority over its citizens; and second, that the institution of government is neither necessary (to maintain social order) nor desirable. By "government" in this context is meant, more precisely, "centralized government," which refers to a hierarchical system of political organization in which power over society is concentrated in a central authority. For anarchists, the ideal form of social organization—indeed, the only form of social organization that fully respects people's rights—is one that is decentralized, free, and democratic.

anti-natalism. The view that it is bad to have children, or that people have a moral obligation not to procreate.

appeal to nature. The fallacy of reasoning that something is moral because it is natural, or that something is immoral because it is contrary to nature.

appeal to religion. The fallacy of reasoning that something is moral because it is condoned by one's chosen religion, or that something is immoral because it is condemned by one's chosen religion.

appeal to the people. The fallacy of reasoning that something is moral because most people approve of it, or that something is immoral because most people disapprove of it.

appeal to tradition. The fallacy of reasoning that something is moral because it has been practiced for a long time, or that something is immoral because it is contrary to an established practice.

applied ethics. A branch of ethics concerned with concrete moral problems, such as the problem of abortion, euthanasia, or capital punishment.

argument. An argument is a set of statements, one of which is the conclusion and the others premises. The "conclusion" of an argument is what is argued for, and the "premises" are the reasons given for believing the conclusion.

argument from a woman's rights. The argument that abortion is permissible because a woman has a right to decide what happens in and to her own body.

argument from autonomy. The argument for active euthanasia based upon a patient's right to choose death.

argument from divine dominion. The argument that active euthanasia is wrong because a person (or a person's body) is rightfully the property of God.

argument from fallibility. The argument against active euthanasia based upon the fallibility of medical science.

argument from gratitude. The argument for the legitimacy of government based upon the "debt" that citizens owe to their government.

argument from inequality. The argument for meritocracy based upon the natural inequality of human beings.

argument from innocence. The argument that abortion (euthanasia) is wrong because it is wrong to kill an innocent human being.

argument from mercy. The argument that active euthanasia is sometimes justified because it ends a patient's suffering.

argument from parental authority. The argument for the legitimacy of government based upon the authority that parents have over their children.

argument from passive euthanasia. The argument for active euthanasia based upon the permissibility of passive euthanasia.

argument from personhood. The argument that abortion is permissible because the fetus fails to be a "person" in the morally important sense.

argument from potentiality. The argument that abortion is wrong because the fetus is potentially a human being.

argument from religion. The argument against abortion based solely upon religious considerations, such as that the Bible condemns abortion.

argument from social utility. The argument for the legitimacy of government based upon the premise that the institution of government is necessary to maintain social order.

argument from tacit agreement. The argument for political authority based upon the tacit agreement that citizens make to obey their government.

argument from the wrongness of killing. The argument that abortion is wrong because it inflicts a great loss upon the fetus.

argumentum ad hominem. The fallacy of directing an argument at a person rather than at the person's views. In the *tu quoque* form, this fallacy occurs whenever someone attempts to deflect moral criticism by pointing out that the person making the accusation is guilty of similar offenses.

bourgeoisie. The (non-productive) propertied class of the capitalist class-system.

capitalism. An economic system characterized by private ownership of the means of production and competition for profits.

categorical imperative. The fundamental principle of morality, according to Immanuel Kant. In one formulation, the principle reads: "Act only according to that maxim by which you can at the same time will that it should become a universal law." In another formulation: "Act so that you treat humanity, whether in your own person or in that of another, only as an end and never as a means only."

class system. A social system in which one socioeconomic group occupies a dominate position.

collateral damage. Civilian causalities that occur as an unintended side-effect of war.

consequentialism. The view that whether and action is right or wrong is determined solely by its consequences. Examples of consequentialism are egoism, altruism, and utilitarianism.

conservative. On the abortion issue, someone who maintains that abortion is permissible, if at all, only when pregnancy threatens the mother's life.

continuity defense. The argument that human life begins at conception because conception is the only non-arbitrary answer to the question "When does human life begin?"

cultural relativism. The skeptical view that morality is culturally dependent. According to this view, moral standards are nothing other than cultural norms. The right thing for a person to do is whatever that person's culture believes is right.

democratic socialism. An economic system in which guaranteed employment, housing, food, education, medical care, and other social programs are administered by a democratically elected government and funded through redistributive taxation and the nationalization of major industries.

deontologism. The view that whether an action is right or wrong is not determined solely by its consequences. (Deontologism is sometimes called "nonconsequentialism.") For the "moderate" deontologist, the consequences of our actions are important in distinguishing between right and wrong, but other considerations are important too. For the "extreme" deontologist, whether an action is right or wrong has nothing to do with its consequences. Examples of deontologism include Kantian ethics, the divine command theory, and the theory of moral rights. Both the Kantian and the divine command theorist are extreme deontologists. Rights theorists are often moderate deontologists who believe that rights impose moral limits on the means by which we can achieve morally desirable ends.

deterrence model. The model of punishment according to which criminals should be punished in order to deter crime. This is a consequentialist justification because it seeks to explain the permissibility of punishment solely in terms of its social consequences.

divine command theory. The deontological theory that bases ethics upon the will of God. According to this theory, what makes an action right is that God commands it, and what makes an action wrong is that God forbids it.

doctrine of double effect. The doctrine designed to explain why it is sometimes permissible to kill innocent people in war. The doctrine identifies four conditions both necessary and sufficient to justify an action that has both good and bad effects. First, considered independently of the bad effect, the action must be morally permissible. Second, the bad effect must not be intended. Third, the bad effect must not be the means by which the good effect is achieved. And fourth, the good effect must be "proportionate" to the bad effect (in the sense that the good effect is at least as great as the bad effect).

egoism. The consequentialist theory according to which the right thing for a person to do is whatever has the best consequences for that person.

ethical holism. A moral outlook based upon the "land ethic" of Aldo Leopold. According to Leopold, "A thing is right when it tends to preserve the integrity, stability, and beauty of the biotic community. It is wrong when it tends otherwise." For Leopold, actions should be judged right or wrong, not on the basis of how they affect individual living beings (not even human beings), but on the basis of how they affect the *whole* community of life. For this reason, the land ethic is described as "holistic."

euthanasia. The act of killing a patient (active euthanasia) or letting a patient die (passive euthanasia) when it is deemed that the patient's life is no longer worth prolonging. The term literally means "good death."

fallacy. A logically defective argument.

genetic defense. The argument that human life begins at conception because the newly formed fetus has a complete human genetic code.

hedonism. The view that happiness (or the ultimate goal of life) is pleasure and freedom from pain.

Kantian ethics. The deontological theory of the eighteenth-century German philosopher Immanuel Kant. For Kant, morality is based upon a set of absolute rules derived from the categorical imperative.

legitimate authority. The right to rule. To say that a government has legitimate authority over its citizens means that (1) citizens have an obligation to obey the government and (2) the government has the right to coerce obedience (by punishing criminals).

liberal. On the abortion issue, someone who maintains that, at least prior to a certain stage in the development of the fetus, a woman is justified in having an abortion simply because she chooses not to be pregnant. The "classic" liberal believes that there is a definite cut-off point after which abortion is wrong, whereas the "non-classic" liberal denies this.

libertarianism. A political philosophy according to which the only legitimate function of government is to protect people's rights.

meritocracy. A system of government in which only the most qualified people have political power.

meta-ethics. A branch of ethics concerned with the meaning of moral language, the status of moral principles, and the justification for moral belief. Examples of meta-ethical questions are: What does it mean to say that something is right or wrong? Do moral principles have an objective status, or are they merely conventional? Is moral knowledge possible?

mixed model. The model of punishment which combines elements of both the deterrence and the retribution models. According to this, the goal of punishment is criminal deterrence, but in pursuing this goal governments must respect people's rights. The theory explains why punishment is permissible in terms of its social consequences, but at the same time it imposes deontological restrictions on the practice.

moderate. On the abortion issue, someone who believes that abortion is permissible, but only if a woman has a good reason.

moral analogy. A moral argument based upon a comparison between cases.

moral dilemma. A situation in which we have conflicting moral obligations.

moral nihilism. The skeptical theory that there are no moral facts.

moral realism. The view that there are objective moral facts. Objective moral facts are facts that hold independently of people's subjective states (beliefs and feelings) and the conventions that people establish.

moral rights. Enforceable claims against others that they behave or refrain from behaving in certain ways. All rights entail corresponding obligations. A "positive" right entails that others perform certain actions, whereas a "negative" right entails that people refrain from performing certain actions. An "active" right is a right to perform certain actions, whereas a "passive" right is a right not to perform certain actions. All rights can be waived, transferred, and forfeited.

moral skepticism. The view that morality has no objective or independent foundation. For the moral skeptic, either (1) there are moral facts, but these facts are subjective or conventional in nature, or (2) there simply are no moral facts. (Moral skepticism is sometimes called "moral anti-realism.")

moral subjectivism. The skeptical theory that moral statements describe people's feelings of approval or disapproval.

moral syllogism. A moral argument based upon a general moral principle.

normative ethics. A branch of ethics concerned with the understanding of morals and values. The fundamental questions of normative ethics are: What

makes an action right or wrong? What is it to be a good person? What is it that makes life good, valuable, or worth living? What beings count as persons (as opposed to mere things), and why?

person. In the morally important sense, a being with a moral status, a rights-holder, or a member of the moral community. Persons, in this sense, are contrasted with "mere things." There are moral limits to how a person can be treated, but we are free to treat a mere thing however we want. Although some philosophers believe that all and only human beings are persons, this should not be taken for granted. Many philosophers believe that other animals are persons too, and that some human beings (fetuses, for example) are not persons.

personal relativism. The skeptical theory that the right thing for a person to do is whatever that person believes is right. (For the personal relativist, the fact that a person believes that something is right *makes* it right for that person to do it.)

potentiality defense. The argument that human life begins at conception because the fetus has the potential to develop into a recognizable human being.

predation argument. The argument against ethical vegetarianism based upon the morality of the predator-prey relationship.

principle of consistency. The requirement that moral judgments be consistent in the following sense: If we make a moral judgment about one case, then, to be consistent, we must make the same judgment about any other case exactly like it in all relevant respects.

principle of equality (or equal treatment). The principle that different individuals should be treated the same unless there are differences between them that justify treating them differently. When this principle is used to counter some form of prejudice, it is argued that an individual's group-membership (race, sex, ethnicity, religion, nationality, or species) is not in itself important in deciding how that individual should be treated.

principle of proportionality. The principle which says that the evil inflicted upon criminals as punishment should be the same or equal in severity to the evil that criminals have inflicted upon their victims. This is commonly referred to as "eye for an eye" retributivism or the principle of *lex talionis*.

principle of respect. The principle that every person should be treated as an autonomous being, which amounts to respecting that person's right to rationally govern his or her own life.

proletariat. The working class of the capitalist class-system.

pro-natalism. The view that it is good to have children, or that people have a moral obligation to procreate.

retribution model. The model of punishment according to which criminals should be punished simply because they deserve it. This is an extreme deontological justification, because according to this, the consequences of punishment are irrelevant to whether and when punishment is justified.

slippery slope argument. In the context of the euthanasia controversy, the argument that active euthanasia should not be condoned because it would lead to morally unacceptable practices.

slippery slope fallacy. To give a slippery slope argument is to argue that, while a certain practice may not be objectionable in itself, it will lead to another practice that is objectionable. The fallacy occurs whenever it is unreasonable to suppose that the first practice will lead to the second.

socialism. An economic system characterized by public ownership (rather than private ownership) of the means of production and cooperation for the common good (rather than competition for personal profit).

sound. A sound argument is one in which (1) the premises are true and (2) the reasoning is valid.

speciesism. The belief that species-membership in itself is important in deciding how an individual should be treated. For the speciesist, it is permissible to treat other animals in ways in which it would be wrong to treat human beings simply because of a difference in species-membership.

utilitarianism. The consequentialist theory according to which the right thing to do is whatever has the best consequences, everyone considered and considered equally. What distinguishes utilitarianism from other consequentialist theories is that it is universal and egalitarian in its moral outlook.

valid. An argument is valid when the conclusion necessarily follows from the premises in the following sense: if the premises are true, then (as a matter of logical necessity) the conclusion has to be true.

vegetarian. Someone who abstains from all flesh-foods (including poultry and fish). An "ethical" vegetarian is someone who abstains from flesh-foods for ethical reasons. A "vegan" is an especially strict vegetarian who consumes no products of animal origin (including milk, cheese, eggs, and even honey).

virtue ethics. The study of virtue. As applied to the theory of moral conduct, the virtue ethicist maintains either that (1) what makes an action right is that it is a virtuous act and what makes an action wrong is that it is a vicious act, or that (2) what makes an action right or wrong is its positive or negative effect upon the agent's character. The first version of the theory is deontological, whereas the second is consequentialist.

Works Cited

Abbott, Geoffrey. 1994. *The Book of Execution: An Encyclopedia of Methods of Judicial Execution*. London: Headline.

Adams, Carol. 1994. *The Sexual Politics of Meat*. New York: Continuum Publishing.

Aquinas, Thomas. 1989. *Summa Contra Gentiles*. Excerpted in Tom Regan and Peter Singer (ed.), *Animal Rights and Human Obligations*, Second Edition (pp. 6-9), Englewood Cliffs, NJ: Prentice-Hall.

Aristotle. 1973. *Nicomachean Ethics*. In Richard McKeon (ed.), *Introduction to Aristotle: Second Edition Enlarged and Revised* (pp. 346-581), Chicago and London: University of Chicago Press.

Arnove, Anthony. 2002 (March). "Cluster Bombs: The Civilian Impact," *Z Magazine*.

Baldner, Kent. 1990. "Realism and Respect," *Between the Species*, vol. 6, no. 1: 1-8.

Bedau, Hugo. 2007. "The Case against the Death Penalty." In James Rachels and Stuart Rachels (eds.), *The Right Thing To Do: Basic Readings in Moral Philosophy*, Fourth Edition (pp. 137-47), New York: McGraw-Hill.

Benatar, David. 2006. *Better Never to Have Been: The Harm of Coming into Existence*. New York: Oxford University Press.

——. 2015. "We Are Creatures That Should Not Exist: The Theory of Anti-Natalism." <http://www.thecritique.com/articles/we-are-creatures-that-should-not-exist-the-theory-of-anti-natalism/>

Bender, David (ed.). 1991. *Abortion: Opposing Viewpoints*. San Diego: Greenhaven Press.

Bentham, Jeremy. 1948. *The Principles of Morals and Legislation*. New York: Hafner.

Brody, Baruch. 1973. "Abortion and the Sanctity of Human Life." In Joel Feinberg (ed.), *The Problem of Abortion* (pp. 104-120). Belmont, CA: Wadsworth.

Berkman, Alexander. 1972. *The ABC of Anarchism*. New York: Dover Publications.

Burton-Rose, Daniel. 1998. *The Celling of America*. Monroe: Common Courage Press.

Callicott, J. Baird. 1992. "Animal Liberation and Environmental Ethics: Back Together Again." In Eugen Hargrove (ed.), *The Animal Rights/Environmental Ethics Debate* (pp.249-261), New York: State University of New York Press.

Cohen, Carl. 1982. *Four Systems*. New York: Random House.

Damer, T. Edward. 2013. *Attacking Faulty Reasoning*. Belmont, CA: Wadsworth.

Dilorenzo, Thomas. 2002. *The Real Lincoln*. Roseville: Forum.

Dunayer, Joan. 2001. *Animal Equality: Language and Liberation*. Derwood, MD: Ryce Publishing.

Eisnitz, Gail. 1997. *Slaughterhouse*. New York: Prometheus Books.

English, Jane. 2002. "Abortion and the Concept of a Person." In Stephen Satris (ed.), *Taking Sides: Moral Issues*, Eighth Edition (pp. 106-113), Guilford, CT: McGraw-Hill/Dushkin.

Feinberg, Joel. 1987. *Offense to Others: The Moral Limits of the Criminal Law*. New York: Oxford University Press.

Fink, Charles. 2005 (August). "The Predation Argument," *Between the Species*, issue V: 1-15.

——. 2006 (August). "Animals and the Ethics of Domination," *Between the Species*, issue VI: 1-9.

——. 2012. "Buddhism, Punishment, and Reconciliation," *Journal of Buddhist Ethics*, vol. 19: 370-395.

Fischer, John Martin and Mark Ravizza (eds.). 1992. *Ethics: Problems and Principles*. Fort Worth, Texas: Harcourt Brace Jovanovich.

Fisk, Robert. 2003 (March 29). "Al-Jazeera's Harrowing Footage: Bitter Truths about Basra," *Counterpunch*.

Flounders, Sara and John Parker. 1999 (Winter). "The Al Shifa Tragedy," *Covert Action Quarterly*.

Foot, Philippa. 1992. "The Problem of Abortion and the Doctrine of the Double Effect." In John Martin Fisher and Mark Ravizza (eds.), *Ethics: Problems and Principles* (pp. 59-67), Fort Worth, Texas: Harcourt Brace Jovanovich.

Gall, Carlotta. 2007 (May 11). "Civilians Say Civilian Toll in Strikes is Much Higher than Reported," *The New York Times*.

Gay-Williams, J. 1996. "The Wrongfulness of Euthanasia." In Jeffrey Olen and Vincent Barry (eds.), *Applying Ethics: A Text with Readings*, Fifth Edition (pp. 231-234), Belmont, CA: Wadsworth.

Goldman, Alan. 1995. "The Paradox of Punishment." In Michael Gorr and Sterling Harwood (eds.), *Crime and Punishment* (pp. 342-348), Boston: Jones and Bartlett.

Guérin, Daniel. *Anarchism*. 1970. New York: Monthly Review Press.

Hamilton, Edith and Huntington Cairns (eds.). 2005. *Plato: The Collected Dialogues*. Princeton: Princeton University Press.

Hargrove, Eugene (ed.). 1992. *The Animal Rights/Environmental Ethics Debate*. New York: State University of New York Press.

Harris, Sam. 2005. *The End of Faith: Religion, Terror, and the Future of Reason*. New York: W. W. Norton.

Hauser, Marc. 2006. *Moral Minds*. New York: HarperCollins.

Hill, John. 1996. *The Case for Vegetarianism: Philosophy for a Small Planet*. Lanham: Rowman and Littlefield.

Hobbes, Thomas. 1958. *Leviathan*. New York: Bobbs-Merrill.

Holmes, Robert. 1989. *On War and Morality*. Princeton: Princeton University Press.

Hospers, John. 1971. *Libertarianism*. Los Angeles: Nash Publishing.

——. 1982. *Human Conduct: Problems of Ethics*, Second Edition. New York: Harcourt Brace Jovanovich.

——. 2002. "The Libertarian Manifesto." In James Sterba (ed.), *Social and Political Philosophy: Classical Western Texts in Feminist and Multicultural Perspectives*, Third Edition, (pp. 427-38), Belmont, CA: Wadsworth.

Howe, Leslie. 2000. *On Goldman*. Belmont, CA: Wadsworth.

Jensen, Derrick. 2001. *The Culture of Make Believe*. New York: Context Books.

Johnson, Larry. 2002 (October 4). "Shrine to Victims of Tragic Error," *The Seattle Post-Intelligencer.*

Kant, Immanuel. 2000. *The Philosophy of Law.* In Louis Pojman (ed.), *Life and Death: A Reader in Moral,* Second Edition (pp. 368-370), Belmont, CA: Wadsworth.

——. 2007. "Foundations of the Metaphysics of Morals." Excerpted in James Rachels and Stuart Rachels (eds.), *The Right Thing To Do: Basic Readings in Moral Philosophy,* Fourth Edition (pp. 82-86), New York: McGraw-Hill.

——. 1963. *Lectures on Ethics.* New York: Harper and Row.

Kristof, Nicholas. 2004 (January 14). "Inviting All Democrats," *The New York Times.*

Lackey, Douglas. 2003. "Pacifism." In James E. White (ed.), *Contemporary Moral Problems: War and Terrorism,* Third Edition (pp. 8-20), Belmont: Wadsworth.

Leopold, Aldo. 1987. *A Sand County Almanac.* New York: Oxford University Press.

Levitt, Steven and Stephen Dubner. 2005. *Freakonomics: A Rogue Economist Explores the Hidden Side of Everything.* New York: HarperCollins.

Liddy, G. Gordon. 1996. *Will.* New York: St. Martin's Press.

Linzey, Andrew. 1995. *Animal Theology.* Chicago: University of Illinois Press.

Locke, John. 1952. *The Second Treatise of Government.* New York: Bobbs-Merrill.

Luper, Steven and Curtis Brown. 1999. *The Moral Life.* Philadelphia: Harcourt Brace College Publishers.

Lyons, David. 1995. "Punishment as Retribution." In Michael Gorr and Sterling Harwood (eds.), *Crime and Punishment* (pp. 317-321), Boston: Jones and Bartlett.

Maass, Alan. 2004. *The Case for Socialism.* Chicago: Haymarket Books.

Machiavelli, Niccolo. 1952. *The Prince.* New York: Oxford University Press.

Marquis, Don. 2007. "Why Abortion Is Immoral." Excerpted in James Rachels and Stuart Rachels (eds.), *The Right Thing To Do: Basic Readings in Moral Philosophy,* Fourth Edition (pp. 89-96), New York: McGraw-Hill.

Mason, Jim and Peter Singer. 1990. *Animal Factories.* New York: Harmony Books.

McCloskey, James. 1995. "Convicting the Innocent." In Michael Gorr and Sterling Harwood (eds.), *Crime and Punishment* (pp. 304-311), Boston: Jones and Bartlett.

McGinn, Colin. 1992. *Moral Literacy: Or How to Do the Right Thing.* Indianapolis: Hackett.

Mill, John Stuart. 1974. *Utilitarianism.* Excerpted in William Frankena and John Granrose (eds.), *Introductory Readings in Ethics* (pp. 297-309). Englewood Cliffs: Prentice-Hall.

Monkerud, Don. 2006 (February). "The Battle Over Execution," *Z Magazine.*

Morgentaler, Henry. 1996. "The Moral Case for Abortion," *Free Inquiry,* vol. 15, no. 3.

Morris, Ruth. 1995. *Penal Abolition: The Practical Choice.* Toronto: Canadian Scholars' Press.

Munson, Ronald. 1979. *Intervention and Reflection: Basic Issues in Medical Ethics.* Belmont, CA: Wadsworth.

Murphy, Jeffrie. 1995. *Punishment and Rehabilitation.* Belmont, CA: Wadsworth.

Murray, Charles. 1997. *What It Means to be a Libertarian.* New York: Broadway Books.

Naess, Arne. 1991. "Should We Try To Relieve Clear Cases of Extreme Suffering in Nature?" *Pan Ecology,* vol. 6, no. 1: 1-5.

Narveson, Jan. 2001. *The Libertarian Idea.* Toronto: Broadview Press.

——. 2003. "Feeding the Hungry." In James Rachels (ed.), *The Right Thing To Do,* Third Edition (pp. 162-73), New York: McGraw-Hill.

Nathanson, Stephen. 2000. *Should We Consent to be Governed?* Second Edition. Belmont, CA: Wadsworth.

Nelson, Soraya Sarhaddi. 2003 (November 14). "Mother Kills Raped Daughter to Restore Honor," *Miami Herald*.

Noonan, John. 1973. In Joel Feinberg (ed.), *The Problem of Abortion* (pp. 10-17), Belmont, CA: Wadsworth.

Nussbaum, Martha. 1995. "Objectification," *Philosophy and Public Affairs*, vol. 24, no. 4: 249-291.

Orend, Brian. 2006. *The Morality of War*. Toronto: Broadview Press.

Parenti, Michael. 2002 (Spring). "Global Rollback," *Covert Action Quarterly*, No. 72.

Plato. 1985. *Crito*. In Edith Hamilton and Huntington Cairns (eds.), *Plato: The Collected Dialogues* (pp. 27-39), Princeton: Princeton University Press.

——. 1991. *Republic*. New York: Vintage Books.

Pojman, Luis (ed.). 1995. *Ethical Theory: Classical and Contemporary Readings*, Second Edition. Belmont, CA: Wadsworth.

——, ed. 2000. *The Moral Life: An Introductory Reader in Ethics and Literature*. New York: Oxford University Press.

——. 2002. *Global Political Philosophy*. New York: McGraw-Hill.

Primoratz, Igor. 1989. *Justifying Legal Punishment*. Atlantic Highlands: Humanities Press.

Rachels, James. 1980. "Euthanasia." In Tom Regan (ed.), *Matters of Life and Death: New Introductory Essays in Moral Philosophy* (pp. 28-66), New York: Random House.

Rachels, James and Stuart Rachels. 2007. *The Elements of Moral Philosophy*, Fifth Edition. New York: McGraw-Hill.

Rand, Ayn. 1964. *The Virtue of Selfishness*. New York: Penguin.

Reaves, Jessica. 2003 (January). "Where's the Beef (In the Teenage Diet)?" *Time Magazine*.

Regan, Tom. 1983. *The Case for Animal Rights*. Berkeley: University of California Press.

Regan, Tom and Peter Singer (eds.). 1989. *Animal Rights and Human Obligations*, Second Edition. Englewood Cliffs: Prentice-Hall.

Ricard, Matthieu. 2006. *Happiness: A Guide to Developing Life's Most Important Skill*. New York: Little, Brown and Company.

Robbins, John. 1987. *Diet for a New America*. Walpole: Stillpoint.

Robinson, Marilynn. 1980. *Housekeeping*. New York: Farrar, Straus and Giroux.

Ross, Kenneth. 2004 (May 13). "Time to Stop 'Stress and Duress'," *The Washington Post*.

Rothbard, Murray. 2002. *The Ethics of Liberty*. New York: New York University Press.

Roy, Arundhati. 2001. *Power Politics*. Boston: South End Press.

Ruggiero, Vincent. 2001. *Thinking Critically about Ethical Issues*, Fifth Edition. Mountain View, CA: Mayfield.

Rummel, R. J. 2004. *Death by Government*. Piscataway: Transaction Publishers.

Ruse, Michael. 1995. "Evolutionary Ethics: A Phoenix Arisen." In Paul Thompson (ed.), *Issues in Evolutionary Ethics*. New York: State University of New York Press.

——. 1998. *Taking Darwin Seriously*. New York: Prometheus Books.

Ryder, Richard. 1975. *Victims of Science*. London: Davis-Poynter.

Sapontzis, Stephen. 1984. "Predation," *Ethics and Animals*, vol. 5, no. 2: 27-38.

Savage, Michael. 2003. *The Enemy Within*. Nashville: WND Books.

Shafer-Landau, Russ. 2004. *Whatever Happened to Good and Evil?* New York: Oxford University Press.

Shantideva. 1997. *The Way of the Bodhisattva*. Boston: Shambhala.

Silberbauer, George. 1993. "Ethics in Small-Scale Societies." In Peter Singer (ed.), *A Companion to Ethics* (pp. 14-28), Boston: Blackwell Publishers.

Singer, Peter. 1972. "Famine, Affluence, and Morality." *Philosophy and Public Affairs*, vol. 1, no. 1: 229-243.

——. 1979. *Practical Ethics*. Cambridge, MA: Cambridge University Press.

——. 1990. *Animal Liberation*, Second Edition. New York: The New York Review of Books.

——, ed. 1993. *A Companion to Ethics*. Boston: Blackwell Publishers.

——. 2002. *One World: The Ethics of Globalization*. New Haven: Yale University Press.

——. 2004. *The President of God and Evil: The Ethics of George W. Bush*. New York: Dutton.

——. 2006 (December 17). "What Should a Billionaire Give—and What Should You?" *The New York Times*.

Soilfer, Paul (et. al.). 2001. *American Government*. New York: Hungry Minds.

Spiegel, Marjorie. 1996. *The Dreaded Comparison: Human and Animal Slavery*. New York: Mirror Books.

Sterba, James. 2002. *Social and Political Philosophy: Classical Western Texts in Feminist and Multicultural Perspectives*, Third Edition. Belmont, CA: Wadsworth.

Sullivan, Joseph. 1989. "The Immorality of Euthanasia." In James Rachels (ed.), *The Right Thing To Do*, First Edition (pp. 196-208), New York: McGraw-Hill.

Tannsjo, Torbjorn. 2015. "You should have kids." <http://leiterreports.typepad.com/files/you-should-have-kids-00000003.pdf>

Taylor, James Stacey. 2005. "Why Not a Kidney Market?" *Free Inquiry*, vol. 25, no. 5.

Thomson, Judith Jarvis. 2007. "A Defense of Abortion." Excerpted in James Rachels and Stuart Rachels (eds.), *The Right Thing To Do*, Fourth Edition (pp. 97-113), New York: McGraw-Hill.

——. 1992. "Killing, Letting Die, and the Trolley Problem." In John Martin Fisher and Mark Ravizza (eds.), *Ethics: Problems and Principles* (pp. 67-77), Fort Worth, Texas: Harcourt Brace Jovanovich.

Tolstoy, Leo. 1984. *The Kingdom of God Is within You*. Lincoln, NE: University of Nebraska Press.

Tooley, Michael. 1973. "A Defense of Abortion and Infanticide." In Joel Feinberg (ed.), *The Problem of Abortion* (pp. 51-91), Belmont, CA: Wadsworth.

Unger, Peter. 1996. *Living High and Letting Die: Our Illusion of Innocence*. New York: Oxford University Press.

van den Haag, Ernest. 2002. "The Death Penalty Once More." In Stephen Satris (ed.), *Taking Sides: Moral Issues*, Eighth Edition (pp. 280-291), Guilford, CT: McGraw-Hill/Dushkin.

Vidal, Gore. 2002. *Perpetual War for Perpetual Peace*. New York: Nation Press.

Ward, Colin. 1973. *Anarchy in Action*. New York: Harper and Row.

Warren, Mary Anne. 2000. "The Personhood Argument in Favor of Abortion." In Louis Pojman (ed.), *Life and Death: A Reader in Moral*, Second Edition (pp. 261-267), Belmont, CA: Wadsworth.

Wenz, Peter. 2007. *Political Philosophies in Moral Conflict*. New York: McGraw Hill.

White, James (ed.). 2003. *Contemporary Moral Problems: War and Terrorism* (Belmont, CA: Wadsworth.

Zinn, Howard. 1991. *Declarations of Independence*. New York: Perennial.

——. 1999. *A People's History of the United States: 1492-Present*. New York: HarperCollins.

——. 2001 (December). "A Just Cause, Not a Just War," *The Progressive*.

Index

Robinson, Marilynn, 60
Ross, Kenneth, 18
Rothbard, Murray, 74-76, 123-25, 129-
   30. *See also* argument
Rummel, R. J., 111-13
Ruse, Michael, 111, 113n2

Salt, Henry, 99n2
Sampedro, Ramon, 77
Sapontzis, Stephen, 94-95
Savage, Michael, 13
Shantideva, 37-38
Shiavo, Terri, 66, 78, 83
Silberbauer, George, 110
Singer, Peter, 1-2, 73, 93-94, 97- 99.
   See also argument
slavery, wage, 120-22
socialism: 115-17, 119, 123-24, 127,
   130-32; democratic, 116
Socrates, 101-3
sound, definition of, 3-4
speciesism, 90-92. *See also* argument
Spiegel, Marjorie, 99n2
Stalin, Joseph, 112
state of nature, 106-113
Sullivan, Joseph, 82-83, 85-86
Swift, Jonathan, 81-82

Tafero, Jesse, 141
Tannsjo, Torbjorn, 59
taxation, 126-27
Taylor, James, 17
Thomson, Judith Jarvis, 7-9, 40, 69, 73-
   74, 76. *See also* argument
Tooley, Michael, 57-58
torture, 6-7, 18, 135, 138
totalitarianism, 109
Truman, Harry, 41-42
Tse-tung, Mao, 112

unforeseeable consequences, problem
   of, 40-42
utilitarianism: 34, 39-42, 59; classical,
   39-40. *See also* argument
vague concepts, 66, 71
validity: definition of, 3-4; exercises
   on, 4-5
van den Haag, Ernest, 17
vegetarianism. *See* meat eating.
virtue ethics, 52-56

Voltaire, 90

war: civilian casualties in, 146-49, 154-
   55; ethics of, 146-58; good war myth,
   155-58. *See also* argument
Warren, Mary Anne, 72-73
Wenz, Peter, 14
Wright, Paul, 121

Zinn, Howard, 120-21, 149, 155, 159

About the Author

Charles K. Fink has taught at Miami Dade College since 1993. He received a Ph.D. in philosophy from the University of Miami, where he specialized in logic. He has published one other book and several articles on ethics, politics, the philosophy of life, and Buddhism.